the
SAILOR'S
handbook

the
SAILOR'S
handbook

THE ESSENTIAL SAILING MANUAL

HALSEY C. HERRESHOFF, CONSULTANT EDITOR

International Marine/McGraw-Hill
Camden, Maine

A Marshall Edition
Conceived, edited, and designed by
Marshall Editions
The Old Brewery
6 Blundell Street
London N7 9BH
www.quarto.com

First published in North America in 2006 by

International Marine/McGraw-Hill
PO Box 220
Camden, ME, 04843

Originated in Hong Kong by Modern Age
Printed in China by Midas Printing International Limited

ISBN 13: 978-0-07-148092-5
ISBN 10: 0-07-148092-7

Library of Congress Catalog Number available on request

Publisher: Richard Green
Commissioning editor: Claudia Martin
Art direction: Ivo Marloh
Project editor: Johanna Geary
Editorial and design: Hart McLeod
Production: Anna Pauletti

10 9 8 7 6 5 4 3 2 1

The Contributors

Halsey Herreshoff, the book's consultant editor, is one of the world's foremost naval architects. The grandson of the great American yacht designer, Nat Herreshoff, he is President of the Herreshoff Naval Museum. He has been the consultant for several books on pilotage and navigation, drawing on his own wide experiences of cruising and racing. He navigated *Courageous* when she won the America's Cup in 1974.

Matthew Sheahan is Technical Editor for *Yachting World* magazine, and has tested and written about hundreds of popular sailing yachts. A yachtsman since childhood, he studied yacht design at Southampton before working for Proctor Masts, where he wrote a bestselling book on rigs and rigging. He has served on the Main Committee of the Royal Ocean Racing Club and its Technical and Special Regulations Committees.

Mike Richey M.B.E. is a past director of London's Royal Institute of Navigation and founder editor of its publication, the *Journal of Navigation*. In 1979 he received the Institute's gold medal for outstanding services to the science of navigation, and in 1986 was awarded the Royal Cruising Club's Seamanship Medal. During the last 40 years he has competed in many of the major ocean races, and has competed regularly in the Single-Handed Transatlantic Race, including the one that took place in 2000.

Ian Dear was in the Royal Marines before pursuing a career in book publishing. He has been a writer of maritime history, particularly yachting, since 1979. His books include *Enterprise to Endeavour: The J-Class Yachts*, *The Royal Yacht Squadron: 1815–1985*, *The Champagne Mumm Book of Ocean Racing*, *The Great Years of Yachting*, and *The Royal Ocean Racing Club: The First 75 Years*.

The following members of the Cruising Association helped with the Cruising Grounds section of this new edition: Mike Howe (Librarian), Carolyn Au, Mike and Rosie Downie, Clive Garner, Ray Glaister, Terrance and Kaye Hennig, Tony Brett-Jones, Keith Livermore, Michael Manton, Patti and James Hunt, David M Stookey; and Don Street.

Further revisions to the 2006 edition were compiled by Mike Senior.

CONTENTS

INTRODUCTION
TO SAILING

THE PIONEERS

The word "yacht" comes from the Dutch *yaght* or *joghte*, meaning a swift, light vessel of war, commerce, or pleasure. The first English yacht was given to King Charles II by the Dutch in 1660. However, sailing as a sport did not progress until yacht clubs began. The world's first was the Water Club of Cork Harbour (now the Royal Cork Yacht Club). Already active in 1720, its members performed only naval maneuvers. Later clubs, such as the Cumberland Sailing Society (now the Royal Thames Yacht Club), formed around 1775, and The Yacht Club (now the Royal Yacht Squadron), founded in 1815, organized racing regattas—a Venetian word imported during the 1770s—on the Thames and in the Solent respectively. In America the New York Yacht Club was founded in 1844, and yacht racing had an enormous boost in popularity when, in 1851, its commodore sailed the schooner *America* to challenge British yachts in their own waters.

Cruising at sea predated organized racing, with founding members of The Yacht Club being among the first to brave sea voyages. In 1815 one visited St. Petersburg in his yacht and another cruised to the Mediterranean. These early pioneers encouraged others to make increasingly adventurous voyages. Thomas Brassey, for example, sailed his three-masted schooner, *Sunbeam*, around the world in 1876–7, the first private yacht to achieve this feat. His wife wrote a bestselling book about the circumnavigation. Other yachtsmen who circled the world in *Sunbeam*'s wake, some of them sailing alone, also wrote about their exploits, and their books inspired later generations, men and women, to perform extraordinary voyages and outstanding feats of seamanship.

Richard McMullen (1830–1891) devoted his life to sailing small yachts off the British coastline. Although sometimes accompanied by his wife, he was an early proponent of single-handed sailing. In writing the classic, *Down Channel*, he became an early chronicler of the precise skills of seamanship; developing the now well-established

Joshua Slocum (1844–c.1910) was an American sea captain whose writings inspired those seeking adventure at sea. In *Voyage of the Liberdade* (1894) he described a 5,000 mile (8,000 km) voyage from Brazil to New York in a 35 ft (10.7 m) canoe he had built from the wreck of his

Claude Worth (1864–1936), an ophthalmic surgeon by profession, was an early enthusiast of cruising offshore in small yachts. With his books, *Yacht Cruising* (1910) and *Yacht Navigation and Voyaging* (1927), he became a leading authority on the subject. He did much to popularize the pastime amongst his contemporaries, one of whom was the American yachting journalist, William Nutting, who founded the Cruising Club of America in 1922.

Bill Tilman (1898–1980) was a British yachtsman-cum-explorer. He made several outstanding voyages in his cutter, *Mischief*, during the 1950s and 1960s, including ones to the Arctic and Antarctic. He wrote several books on his adventures before being lost at sea.

Sir Francis Chichester (1901–1972) won the first single-handed transatlantic race in 1960. Chichester achieved a "first" in 1966 by sailing single-handed non-stop from Plymouth to Sydney in 107 days in *Gypsy Moth IV* (shown right). He then returned non-stop to Plymouth, where he was knighted. These and similar record-breaking attempts, and his writings, sparked off a new kind of ocean racing.

cruising concept of staying offshore in a gale instead of risking being wrecked by running for shelter. He died of a heart attack aboard his lugger, *Perseus* (right), while sailing alone in the English Channel.

ship, which had foundered. In 1898 he became the first person to make a solo circumnavigation. His book, *Sailing Alone Around The World* (1900), about the three-year voyage in the 35 ft (10.7 m) sloop, *Spray*, has become a classic and is still in print. He disappeared after starting another lone voyage in November 1909.

Joshua Slocum

Tern II (left), the 30 ft (9 m) craft in which Claude Worth cruised along the west coast of France in 1912, was one of the most notable of his four cruising boats called *Tern*.

THE EVOLUTION OF YACHTS AND YACHTING

The first vessels to be called yachts were built like their larger naval equivalents. They were few in number and even by 1815, when The Yacht Club was founded, their owners were restricted to a handful of aristocrats. Although organized yacht racing on saltwater did not begin until 1826, large sums were often wagered on two-boat matches, so speed was important to early yacht enthusiatists. One competitor even had a smuggler, renowned for constructing craft that could outsail revenue cutters, freed from prison to build him a winning yacht.

But yacht design was in its infancy and it was not until the schooner *America* beat the cream of the Royal Yacht Squadron's fleet in 1851 that any serious consideration was given to changing the inefficient sails with which British yachts were equipped, or their bluff bows that were thought to prevent a vessel from diving under a sea.

The shape of yachts was also influenced when a consistent method of measuring yachts was introduced as a fairer method of handicapping them when racing. These new measurement systems have dominated yacht design from Victorian times up to the present day, but other factors have also been important. For example the efficiency of rigs has improved dramatically—the change from the four-sided gaff sail to the triangular bermudan sail being the principal one—as have the materials used in the construction of sails, hull, and rig.

For decades wood was the main construction material, flax and cotton were used to make sails, and winches were unknown. Nowadays space-age, hi-tech materials are employed in the never-ending search for greater speed and strength, combined with lightness and durability. Essential for the grueling ocean events that dominate the modern racing calendar, many of these advances eventually percolate down to the humblest production boat for all to enjoy.

1661 The diarist John Evelyn records the first race in England when King Charles II's new yacht, *Catherine*, and *Anne*, built for the King's brother, the Duke of York, sail a match from Greenwich to Gravesend and back.

1844 Nine yachtsmen found the New York Yacht Club aboard J.C. Stevens's schooner *Gimcrack*. They then hold "trials of speed" during a cruise in company to Boston, and their first regatta the following year.

1875 The yawl, *Jullanar*, is designed by E.H. Bentall. She reflects the advances made in marine architecture by embodying the two basic principles of fast yacht design: great length and small wetted surface area.

1893 *Britannia*, the most famous racing yacht ever constructed, is built for the Prince of Wales (later Edward VII) by G.L. Watson to the length and sail area rule. She takes part in 569 races, in 1893–1935, and wins 231 of them.

1720 The first yacht club, the Water Club of the Harbour of Cork, is founded.

1876 American Nat Herreshoff builds *Amaryllis*, the first racing catamaran.

1901 Friendship sloops (above) are built for fishing in Maine and later become pleasure craft.

1775 The first club to organize yacht racing, the Cumberland Sailing Society (now the Royal Thames Yacht Club), is formed. Its members race small boats on the Thames, but later extend their activities to the Thames estuary and then offshore.

1815 Forty-two gentlemen meet in a London tavern to form The Yacht Club for those interested in salt-water yachting. Encouraged by royal patronage it becomes The Royal Yacht Club in 1820—by which time several members have cruised far and wide—and the Royal Yacht Squadron in 1833.

1817 The 191-ton American brigantine, *Cleopatra's Barge*, is the first private yacht to cross the Atlantic. Owned by George Crowninshield Jr., who had the first American yacht built in 1801, she is modeled on one of his trading ships.

1826 The Royal Yacht Club holds the first salt-water race for its members. Seven yachts race for a £100 gold cup. It is a great success and the people of Cowes offer two more cups for prizes in a second race held the same year.

1851 The schooner *America* (left) wins a race around the Isle of Wight and a £100 cup, which later becomes the America's Cup.

1855 The Thames Tonnage Rule is adopted to try to make racing between different sized yachts more equitable. Beneficial at first, it eventually produces extreme types of very narrow, deep-hulled yachts.

1875 The Yacht Racing Association (now the Royal Yachting Association) is founded by Dixon Kemp and others so that yacht clubs have a uniform measurement system and an agreed set of yacht racing rules.

1880 The first organization for cruising yachtsmen, the Cruising Club (now the Royal Cruising Club), is formed.

1881 The cutter *Madge*, a moderate design by Scotsman G.L. Watson to the Thames Tonnage Rule, greatly influences American design when she wins all but one of a series of match races against American yachts.

1882 The American Seawanhaka Yacht Club adopts a version of Dixon Kemp's length and sail area rule, drawn up to replace the Thames Tonnage Rule, but the Yacht Racing Association does not adopt it until 1886.

1891 The famous American designer Nat Herreshoff produces *Gloriana*, a revolutionary cutter with overhanging ends and a cutaway forefoot extending to a very small keel. She outsails every challenging boat.

1906–7 The International Yacht Racing Union (now the International Sailing Federation) and the International Rule are born. The Rule produces yachts from 16½–75½ ft (5–23 m). By the 1920s all have adopted the more efficient bermudan rig of two triangular sails.

1922 The Cruising Club of America is formed by an American journalist, William Nutting, along the lines of the Royal Cruising Club. It has 36 founding members who, in 1923, revived the Bermuda Race.

1925 Seven cruising yachts compete in the first Fastnet Race. Won by E.G. Martin's ex-pilot cutter, *Jolie Brise*, the crews then form the Ocean Racing Club (now the Royal Ocean Racing Club) and Martin is elected its commodore.

1969 Robin Knox-Johnston wins the first single-handed round-the-world race in *Suhaili*. The race, inspired by Francis Chichester's exploits, is the origin of today's global competitions for crewed and single-handed yachts.

KNOW YOUR BOAT

PARTS OF A SAILBOAT

There are a large number of special terms used in sailing. These apply not only to specialized equipment but also to the parts of the boat. One does not talk of the front of the boat, but rather the bow, and the rear is referred to as the stern. Moving towards the bow is described as moving forward (for'ard), and moving towards the stern as moving aft. The normal motion of the boat is described as ahead or forward, and backward motion is called astern. The right-hand side of a boat is known as starboard and the left as port. The widest part of the boat is the beam, and an object to the side is said to be on the starboard (or port) beam. A boat ahead but to one side would be on the port (or starboard) bow, and one behind but to the side is on the port (or starboard) quarter.

Most sailing activity takes place in the cockpit, a low area with seating near the stern of the boat. Some protection from spray and wind is afforded by coamings, low walls surrounding the cockpit, though these are often used as seats to increase visibility or to move the weight further out.

Down below you will find one or more cabins, where there will be bunks (beds), areas for seating and dining (often multi-purpose), navigation, and cooking (the galley). There will usually be a toilet compartment, known as the head. Even the walls and floors have their own nautical names: bulkheads and decks.

The main distinguishing features of a sailing boat underwater are the keel and rudder. The keels of traditional boats are an integral part of the hull, running the length of the boat with the rudder attached at the rear end. This form gives good stability but limits maneuverability.

A tall, thin fin keel below the hull, with separate rudder, lowers the center of gravity. The fin provides the hull with a pivot point so maneuverability is good, but at the expense of stability in a rough sea. A moderate fin with rudder mounted on a separate skeg makes a useful

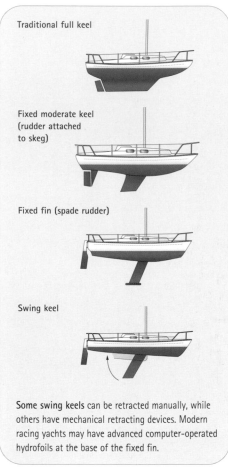

Traditional full keel

Fixed moderate keel (rudder attached to skeg)

Fixed fin (spade rudder)

Swing keel

Some swing keels can be retracted manually, while others have mechanical retracting devices. Modern racing yachts may have advanced computer-operated hydrofoils at the base of the fixed fin.

Sailboat comparisons

The sloop is favored for its performance to windward, especially for racing. Divided rigs, however, can offer more versatility for ocean cruising. Ketches, cutters, and schooners allow a wider variety of sail combinations to meet a range of wind and sea conditions.

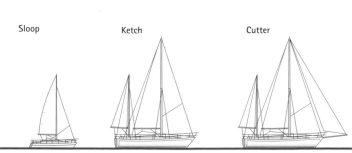

Sloop   Ketch   Cutter

compromise. Some boats have retracting fin keels, enabling them to reach shallow waters. The keel is either raised vertically into a compartment in the hull (lifting keel) or pivoted back (swing keel). If the keel can be fully retracted, the boat can be left at low tide, stable and level.

On a **Bermudan rigged sloop** (shown below) there are two triangular sails: the mainsail and foresail. The mainsail is attached along the whole of its leading edge (luff) to the mast. The foot of the sail is generally attached to a boom, which is pivoted off the mast. On some boats the foot of the sail runs in a track along the boom, but on others it is only attached by the

clew. Occasionally no boom is used (mainly in gaff rigs). Air flowing over the sail causes it to adopt an aerofoil shape, generating lift just as an airplane wing does. A boat normally has only one size of mainsail, but with a means of reducing the area (known as reefing). The mainsail leech (trailing edge) is normally curved to increase the area aloft and a number of battens are fitted along the leech to maintain its shape.

The foresail is attached along the whole of its leading edge to the forestay. Two sheets (ropes) are attached to the free corner (clew) and run down each side of the boat to trim this sail, one for each tack. Various sizes of foresail may be carried. The largest is the genoa, which overlaps the mainsail. The others, in decreasing size, are No. 1 jib, No. 2 jib, and storm jib. Roller reefing genoas, allowing one sail to be easily adjusted for a variety of conditions, are very popular on cruising boats.

A third sail, the spinnaker, can be flown when traveling with the wind. The sail itself is symmetrical and the head is attached to the top of the mast with both sides free. A guy line attached at the tack and threaded through the end of a pole holds out the windward side of the sail. The leeward side is trimmed with a sheet attached to the clew, in a similar manner to the foresail.

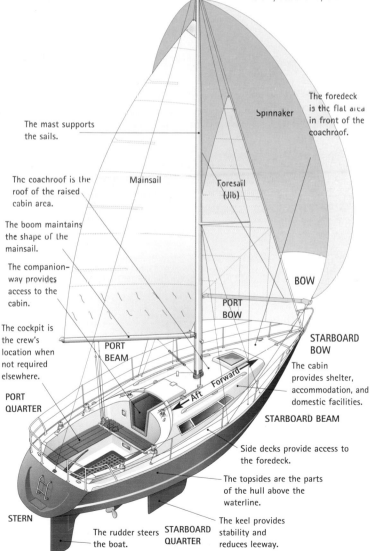

The mast supports the sails.

The coachroof is the roof of the raised cabin area.

The boom maintains the shape of the mainsail.

The companionway provides access to the cabin.

The cockpit is the crew's location when not required elsewhere.

PORT QUARTER

STERN

The rudder steers the boat.

STARBOARD QUARTER

Mainsail

PORT BEAM

Aft — Forward

The keel provides stability and reduces leeway.

Spinnaker

Foresail (Jib)

The foredeck is the flat area in front of the coachroof.

BOW

PORT BOW

STARBOARD BOW

The cabin provides shelter, accommodation, and domestic facilities.

STARBOARD BEAM

Side decks provide access to the foredeck.

The topsides are the parts of the hull above the waterline.

17

ANATOMY OF A BOAT

Of all the vehicles devised by mankind for getting from one place to another, the boat is perhaps the most intriguing. Everyone from youngsters to well-traveled bluewater cruising experts feels a sense of achievement and the satisfying glow that accompanies activity afloat.

Anyone can develop a "boat sense" through practice or study. The modern 30 ft (9 m) cruiser (shown opposite) well illustrates the form and parts of a yacht. From bow to stern, such a vessel requires careful design, meticulous attention in construction, and good owner maintenance to make it fit for the challenge of the sea.

The bow pulpit and lifelines surrounding the working deck contain, moving forward, an anchor well for the ground tackle. Moving aft you find the raised coach/cabin trunk roof with its portholes and handrails for the crew to hold on to when sailing in rough weather. The self-draining cockpit is positioned above the water level so that water taken into it will exit through tubular scuppers or drains. On the coamings around the cockpit are geared winches usually driven by hand with a winch handle, essential to cope with the high loads on genoa and spinnaker sheets.

The single mast of a sloop is secured in place by its standing rigging; usually wire shrouds, forestay, and backstay. Lower shrouds meet the mast at perhaps two-thirds of its height, while the outer or cap shrouds bend around spreaders to transfer their tension at a suitably wide angle to prevent the masthead bending to leeward under the pressure of the wind.

Heeling movement, generated by the action of the wind on the sails, is counteracted by the weight of the keel—in this instance a short and hydro-dynamically-efficient lead-filled or steel fin.

Small cruisers of 18–26 ft (5–8 m) with rectractable weighted keels or light center-boards can be trailed behind a car.

The family cruiser of 25–33 ft (7–10 m) is sometimes designed as much for internal comfort and stability as sailing ability.

The one-design cruiser-racer fulfills racing aspirations and doubles as an efficient, though less comfortable, cruiser.

The motor sailer, although a compromise between sail and power, satisfies the needs of many cruising yachtsmen.

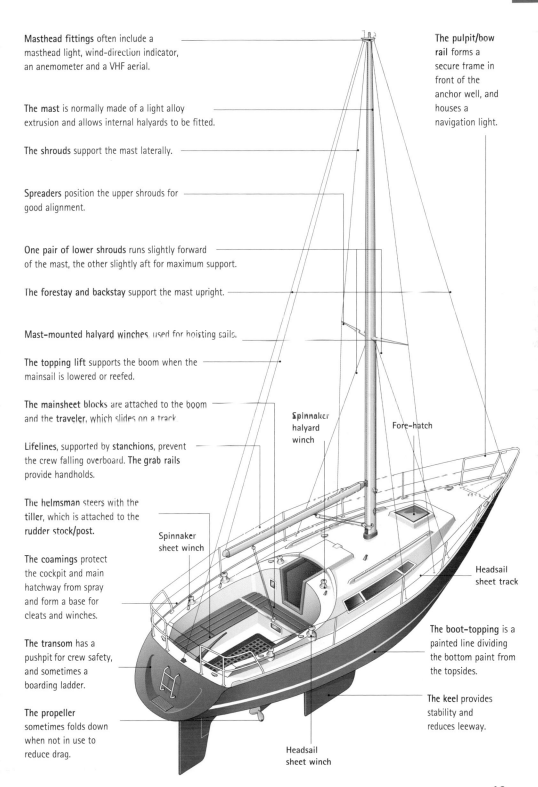

Masthead fittings often include a masthead light, wind-direction indicator, an anemometer and a VHF aerial.

The mast is normally made of a light alloy extrusion and allows internal halyards to be fitted.

The shrouds support the mast laterally.

Spreaders position the upper shrouds for good alignment.

One pair of **lower shrouds** runs slightly forward of the mast, the other slightly aft for maximum support.

The forestay and **backstay** support the mast upright.

Mast-mounted halyard winches, used for hoisting sails.

The topping lift supports the boom when the mainsail is lowered or reefed.

The mainsheet blocks are attached to the boom and the **traveler**, which slides on a track.

Lifelines, supported by **stanchions**, prevent the crew falling overboard. **The grab rails** provide handholds.

The **helmsman** steers with the **tiller**, which is attached to the **rudder stock/post**.

The **coamings** protect the cockpit and main hatchway from spray and form a base for cleats and winches.

The transom has a pushpit for crew safety, and sometimes a boarding ladder.

The propeller sometimes folds down when not in use to reduce drag.

The pulpit/bow rail forms a secure frame in front of the anchor well, and houses a navigation light.

Spinnaker halyard winch

Fore-hatch

Spinnaker sheet winch

Headsail sheet track

The boot-topping is a painted line dividing the bottom paint from the topsides.

The keel provides stability and reduces leeway.

Headsail sheet winch

GRP CONSTRUCTION

Most yachts and boats today are constructed of glass-reinforced plastic (GRP). This strong and resilient material is a combination of a resin (which is made to harden or set chemically) and a strong reinforcement material, usually fibers of glass, which gives the material its common name of fiberglass.

The resin may comprise polyester, solvents, catalysts, and other additives. The reinforcement is either glass fiber cloth (a smooth woven fabric), roving (a coarse, basket-like woven fabric), or mat (a random combination of many short-fiber strands of glass).

Production begins with the formation of a smooth female mold (itself usually made of GRP laminate) over a precisely constructed wooden plug, which establishes the hull shape. The color of the hull is established by gelcoat resin, sprayed against a parting agent, previously applied to the surface of the mold.

Glass and resin are then combined in a hand lay-up process to produce the hull structure. Thickness can be varied by the composition and number of layers and is determined by the correct compromise between the strength and lightness required over different sections of the hull. The deck is produced in the same way.

Thereafter the real skill lies in the fitting out. This includes the construction of bulkheads (athwartships hull-stiffening panels), joinery of the interior and the proper connection of all elements of GRP, wood, and metal. "Sandwich" construction involves laminates of GRP enclosing a core of closed-cell foam or balsa wood. This provides a stiffer structure, weight-for-weight, but has reduced impact resistance. Fittings have to be attached to sandwich hulls and decks carefully, so as not to allow water to seep in and degrade the core.

Increasingly more advanced materials are entering the boat building trade. Epoxy resins and graphite aramid fibers such as Kevlar™, carbon, and other new reinforcements promise remarkable strength, stiffness, and structural weight-efficiency.

Hull and deck are usually made inside a mold in a hand lay-up laminate process.

Bulkheads and interior units are secured by secondary bond laminates before the deck is fitted.

The individual components, such as wooden tables, bunks, lockers, deck fittings, metal winches, and stanchions, are then attached.

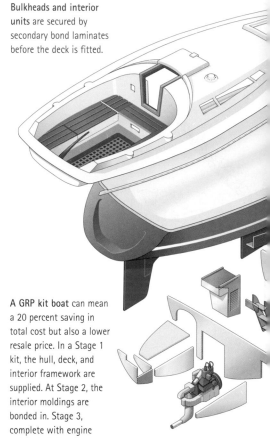

A GRP kit boat can mean a 20 percent saving in total cost but also a lower resale price. In a Stage 1 kit, the hull, deck, and interior framework are supplied. At Stage 2, the interior moldings are bonded in. Stage 3, complete with engine and deck fittings, leaves only the woodwork to be done. Stage 4 is the finished craft.

The laminate consists of woven rovings, 1, and mat, 2, bonded with polyester resin and sealed with gelcoat, 3.

Through-hull bolts and fittings need to be well supported with a backing plate to spread the load.

Completion of the yacht involves trim, painting, varnishing, and check-out of all systems. The head and engine need piping, wiring, and controls and deck fittings must be securely fitted.

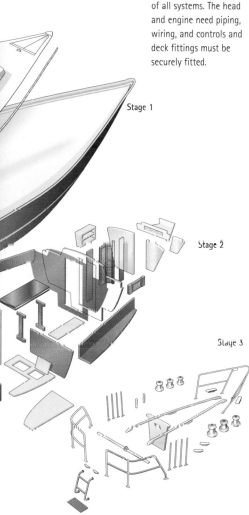

Stage 1

Stage 2

Stage 3

Deck construction

Deck construction normally matches the hull material; however, a traditional wooden deck vastly improves the aesthetic appeal of any hull, particularly of GRP, and produces one of the best non-slip surfaces. Seams between the planks are caulked in the same way as carvel planks, then "payed" with gun-applied mastic or hot marine glue. Wooden or "laid" decks are costly, so plywood is sometimes used. Alternatively, a thin layer of teak planks may be laid on top to create the effect of a traditional laid deck. Since water tends to sit on the deck, a wooden deck needs to be scrubbed regularly.

Construction checklist

1 Edges and corners on GRP hulls should be well rounded for strength, to avoid blow holes, and to reduce the chances of chipping.

2 Hull stiffening should be tapered away at the ends or joined to another member to dissipate the stress. Where a stiffener ends abruptly, look for cracks, tears, or separations.

3 The hull should be smooth, with no bumps or dimples.

4 A coating of deck paint with added grit will reduce slipperiness on a GRP deck.

5 Changes in color tone, such as yellowing or bleaching, indicate ageing and can be painted over.

6 Bubbles, indicating that water is blistering the laminate, are a possible sign of osmosis and must be investigated immediately. Treatment for osmosis, or "boat pox," can be very costly.

Foam in hull cavities improves buoyancy and creates good insulation against temperature, sound, and water.

One way of making a deck-to-hull joint waterproof is by bonding and through-bolting at frequent intervals.

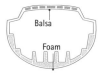

Balsa

Foam

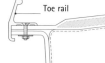

Toe rail

WOODEN CONSTRUCTION

Since the beginning of time, wood has been the traditional boatbuilding material. Ancient ships, and until the nineteenth century, trading and naval vessels, were constructed of wood. Interest in yachting and speed under sail led to lighter but strongly built and carefully designed timber structures. Even 100-year-old yachts, if properly designed, built, and cared for, can still be serviceable.

Carvel has always been the most common form of wooden construction. Generally, a skeleton of steam-bent oak is formed to support planks from stem to stern. These are made of light wood in small boats and harder woods, such as elm, in larger craft. The seams between planks are packed with caulking to make the structure watertight.

Clinker/lapstrake construction, common for small boats in the past, is a method where relatively thin, shaped planks overlap each other at the seam. Mechanical fasteners (often copper rivets) join the plank edges, both to seal against leaks and to secure the shell to internal stiffening pieces.

A smoother finish can be achieved by using a molded wood construction, which involves the fabrication of a single glued-ply unit for the entire hull.

Wooden boatbuilding has had something of a revival in recent years with an increasing number of people rediscovering the joys of more traditional craft. Complete with rigs derived from the working boats of times past, original construction techniques are being enhanced with the use of modern materials, such as epoxy resins, to increase strength and, perhaps most importantly, reduce maintenance while retaining good looks.

The choice of good building materials and a close fit between members are essential to the durability of yachts. Quality construction will go a long way in keeping out water and preventing rot.

The keel forms the backbone of the boat and is connected both to a ballast keel and to a lower keel.

The frames, extending athwartships, make up the skeleton, secure the planking, and provide

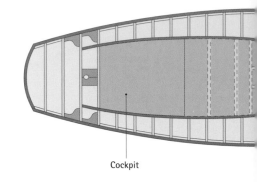

Cockpit

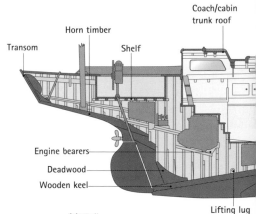

Transom · Horn timber · Shelf · Coach/cabin trunk roof · Engine bearers · Deadwood · Wooden keel · Lifting lug

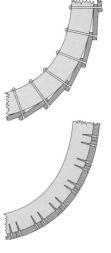

In clinker/lapstrake boats planks are both fastened to the frame and joined to adjacent overlapping planks by rivets. The wood swells in the water to form waterproof seams.

Carvel gives a smooth outer surface. Planks are fastened side-by-side on shaped frames. Caulking is forced into the joints to seal them against leaking.

hull stiffness. Other **stiffening-members** include the bilge stringer, the coaming, and the cabin side. The deck beams are joined to the frames by a longitudinal deck shelf.

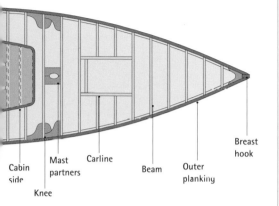

Cabin side • Mast partners • Carline • Beam • Outer planking • Breast hook • Knee

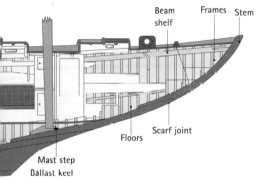

Beam shelf • Frames • Stem • Scarf joint • Floors • Mast step • Ballast keel

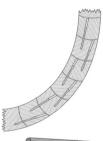

Strip planking comprises narrow, almost square planking, secured with edge-nailed fastenings. They are glued together, not caulked, which produces a smooth, seamless hull.

Plywood construction involves joining sheets of pre-formed plywood, usually over a skeleton. The topsides and the bottom meet at an angle or chine.

Molded wood construction

A molded wood hull is made up of three or more layers of wood veneer glued together over a temporary framework, either a hull plug or a firm temporary grid. The grains of successive thin layers of wood are set at different angles for strength and resistance against splitting in all directions. Molded wood hulls, particularly those with complex, double curvature, can be stiff, durable and weight-efficient. They are smooth both inside and out, and the absence of seams reduces maintenance and the risk of leaks. It was the development of strong, room-temperature curing glues, such as epoxies, that made molded wood construction possible. Sometimes molded wood hulls are covered with a layer or two of GRP to enhance the strength of the hull structure. Modern hulls of all types are frequently coated with sprayed polyurethane paint, which produces a far more attractive and durable finish than traditional paints.

Vacuum bags

A vacuum bag is used in cold molded construction to ensure that the veneers adhere to the mold frames. The cover is taped down to the hull surface to form a bag from which air is extracted via a valved airline. Rope net channels allow air to be sucked evenly from the area.

METAL CONSTRUCTION

The strength and durability of metal construction are appealing, particularly for larger yachts. Except for small craft, the traditional riveted connections for steel or aluminum have given way to welded hulls.

Two types of hull framing are possible. Transverse framing involves curved, angled, or T-section stiffeners inside the hull in the same pattern as the conventional framing of a traditional wooden hull. Longitudinal framing runs fore-and-aft, itself supported by bulkheads.

Welding is used initially to tack shaped and curved hull plates to the framing grid and to position plate edges to each other. Welding passes are then made to fill all butts and seams, for hull strength and water-tightness. Further selective welds are made to ensure satisfactory connection of the hull plating to framing and stiffeners.

During welding, shrinkage of the weld metal as it cools is a critical issue for the ultimate shape. Therefore, a proper welding sequence, from port to starboard and deck to keel, over the plating must be followed to prevent distortion of the yacht's shape from the desired geometry and to prevent the building up of internal stresses, which may limit the external load-carrying ability of the hull structure.

Skillful lofting—the full-sized drawing-out of hull-shape lines, accurate forming of frames, and set-up—plus a proper welding sequence, can achieve an accurate, reasonably smooth hull surface. Nevertheless, for a proper yacht-quality hull surface, a layer of fairing compound is required over the metal plating. After a priming coat to inhibit corrosion and ensure proper bonding, the filler material is troweled on and finally hand-sanded to the desired accuracy and smoothness using long, flexible sanding planks. Conventional or sprayed polyurethane paint coating finishes the job.

Transverse frames are formed to the desired curved shape from angle- or T-shaped sections. Hand-spiling marks the cut-lines for the accurate trimming of plates. Long plates give a better finish, but are difficult to handle; wide plates make chine construction quicker, but are only suitable for the flatter parts of a round chine hull. A patchwork of different-sized plates speeds up work. Plating is

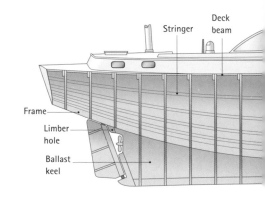

The simple single chine, 1, allows the use of mainly flat plates. The multi-chine hull, **2,** uses smaller plates, so is stronger and more shapely. Round bar or tube welded into the chine will soften the angle of the rolled chine hull, **3.**

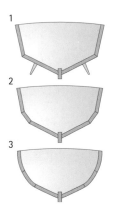
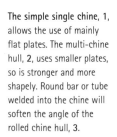

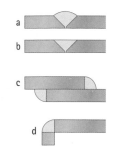

Butt welds, a, are often used in boatbuilding. In thick plate, edges must be chamfered first; on topsides and decks, welds are usually ground flat, **b.** Lap joints are strong, and double bead lap welds, **c,** help to prevent corrosion between mild steel plates. Open corner welds, **d,** produce a smooth curve for coach/cabin trunk roof joins.

curved on rollers or by cramping to frames, or is shaped on hydraulic presses. Plates are joined to each other and to the framing by arc-welding. Deck-edge connections, hatch coamings, and bases for highly stressed fittings are also welded in place. The hull backbone, bilge stiffeners, and other main strength members are built up and made secure by successive welding passes.

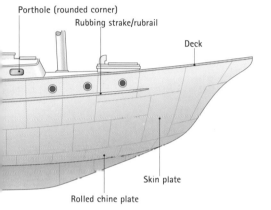

Porthole (rounded corner)
Rubbing strake/rubrail
Deck
Skin plate
Rolled chine plate

Aluminum construction

The main advantage of aluminum construction is its light weight. When it was first applied to boatbuilding it was extremely expensive and vulnerable to electrolytic corrosion. However, the introduction of aluminum-magnesium alloy in the 1930s reduced the problem of electrolysis, and today small, mass-produced aluminum boats are often comparable in price to GRP ones. It is an ideal material for fast racing boats, and aluminum boats have claimed many of the top racing trophies.

Choosing a construction material

1 Fiberglass, or GRP, is resilient, demanding less maintenance than wood in the first few years, although it needs annual cleaning, waxing, and anti-fouling. The smooth, seamless hull should be waterproof, although the deck-to-hull joints can be trouble spots. In older boats, however, osmosis—water gradually getting under the surface—can be an expensive problem. Fiberglass construction often requires fewer man-hours and, therefore, cuts the purchase price. All mass-produced sailboats are fiberglass. These advantages accrue only to long production runs, however; custom-built and home-build boats are more likely to be constructed of wood or metal.

2 Wood is the most aesthetically pleasing and the only natural hull material. It is, however, vulnerable to rot and organic growth. Although they have a long working life, traditional wooden boats require a lot of maintenance. Since the cost of seasoned timber and labor is high, marine plywood became the most popular material. More recently, modern epoxy construction has produced low-maintenance boats at economical prices.

3 Steel is stronger for its weight than any other material, although denting causes problems and repairs can be difficult. Steel will not split like wood, nor is it subject to wear and tear like GRP. It is economical for boats from 40–70 ft (12–21 m) and good for one-offs. Steel boats also tend to be heavy and noisy and limited in hull shape, unless machinery is available to roll the steel plate. Corrosion is the greatest hazard for both steel and aluminum and all fittings of different metal must be bedded on plastic washers.

4 Ferroconcrete is a less common alternative material which is strong and continues strengthening for 10 years after construction. Durable and virtually maintenance-free, it is also heavy, so best suited to boats over 30 ft (9 m) long. It is time consuming and difficult to achieve accurate dimensions and a good smooth finish.

STANDING RIGGING

Masts are held up, or made to stand up, by standing rigging—the forestay, backstay, and shrouds. The mast and standing rigging together comprise what is commonly known as "the rig." There are two main types: masthead and fractional.

Masthead rigs have the forestay running all the way to the top of the mast together with the backstay and the outer shrouds. This arrangement provides a strong, evenly supported structure that, once set up, needs little adjustment. Compression loads on a masthead rig are high, so the mast section will tend to be larger.

Foresails will be large and overlap the mainsail. Their size can make them difficult to handle with large forces being exerted on sheets. The spreaders are most likely to be in-line, that is, extending from the mast at 90° to the centerline of the boat. The illustration on the opposite page shows a typical arrangement with two sets of lower shrouds angled fore and aft to support the lower part of the mast.

Fractional rigs have the forestay meeting the mast at some point below the masthead and is the standard rig for dinghies and keelboats. In recent years they have become increasingly popular on larger boats as their smaller foresails are easier to handle. However, forestay tension is less easy to achieve and as a result upwind performance can suffer.

Aft-swept spreaders are one solution to this problem and, on racing boats, running backstays. One of these run on each side of the boat, from the side of the mast at forestay height to the stern. They have to be tensioned or released as the boat tacks or gybes.

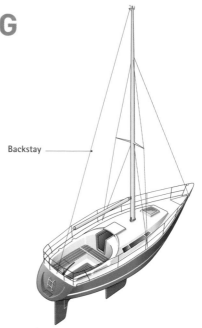

Backstay

The high degree of control in a **fractional rig** is affected by mast bend. The backstay exerts forces on the tapered topmast section, while the shrouds and forestay meet at $3/4$ or $7/8$ the height of the mast.

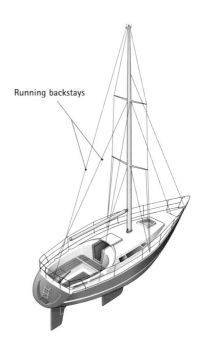

Running backstays

The shorter spreaders on a **double spreader rig** allow the headsails to be sheeted in closer for better upwind performance. The thinner mast is supported by a number of shrouds and stays.

The single-spreader **masthead rig** is common on most production family cruisers. The mast is usually stepped on the coach/cabin trunk roof. It is anchored in place by the forestay, backstay, cap shrouds and two—or better, four—lower shrouds below the spreaders.

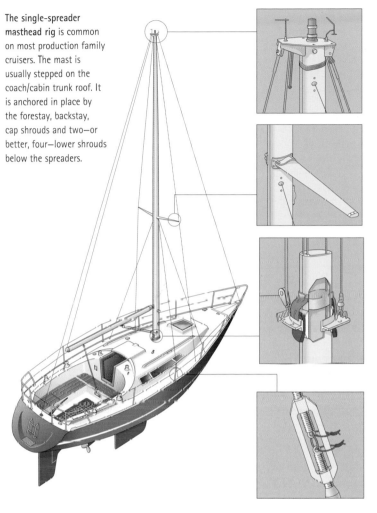

To prevent the masthead becoming too cluttered, it is extended with "cranes" to house halyard sheaves and stay attachments.

The **aerofoil-shaped spreaders** transmit the forces of the cap shrouds to the mast. They are angled upward to bisect the shroud angle.

Keel-stepped masts, found on more sophisticated production boats, are held firmly at the coachroof by wedges. A gaiter will form a waterproof seal.

Shroud lengths are adjusted by means of rigging screws/turnbuckles. Always secure them with monel wire and tape to safeguard clothes and sails.

1

There is a wide variety of aluminum **mast sections** available to suit different types of sailing boat.

2

3

The top section, **1**, would typically be found on a dinghy, whereas the oval, **2**, and bullet, **3**, sections are more typical of modern cruisers.

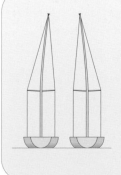

To check that the **masthead is angled correctly**, take a masthead halyard to one cap shroud chain plate, then to the other. Adjust the rigging screws until the lengths are identical. The backstay adjusts forestay tension, which determines fore-and-aft rake.

RUNNING RIGGING

It used to be said that the only rope on a boat was the one in the ship's bell! All the other "ropes" have names according to the task they perform. They can be divided into three main types: halyards, sheets, and control lines.

Halyards are used to hoist sails and will usually run inside the mast, emerging just above head height where they are either led onto a mast-mounted winch, or down to the deck and aft to the cockpit, probably through a rope clutch and then to a winch.

Once a halyard has been adjusted to the correct tension, you don't want it to stretch. So wire (with a rope tail for ease of handling) or increasingly a modern low stretch rope such as Kevlar™ or Dyneema™ core will be used.

Sheets are used to control the angle of sails to the wind. When compared to the lengths of halyards, the short span of most sheets means that cheaper conventional braided polyester ropes can be used with little obvious difference in the total stretch.

Control lines provide the fine adjustment. The kicking strap/vang may comprise a multi-ratio purchase made up of a thin, low-stretch line.

The spinnaker boom uphaul and downhaul, and mainsail outhaul and reefing lines will also be found lined up, neatly labeled if you're lucky, on top of the coachroof.

Inspect ropes regularly for signs of wear, particularly where they are held in cleats or rope clutches. Pay particular attention to rope-to-wire splices on halyards.

Swing rigs, such as Carbospars Aerorig®, are now becoming more popular and incorporate carbon fiber spars, minimal running rigging, and no standing rigging.

The junk rig has so far had only limited success on cruising boats. The fully battened sail is completely controlled by the sheet and halyard. To reef, the foot of the sail is simply lowered by the halyard into the lazyjacks controlled aft by the sheet.

The large sail areas on the traditional **Dutch boat** feature a curved gaff and a loose-footed mainsail. In light airs, watersails, attached to spars around the sides of the boat, add to the area.

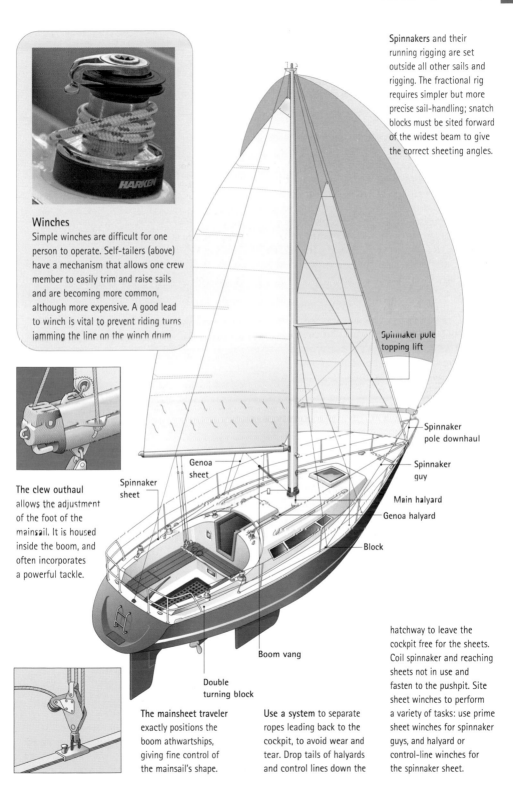

Spinnakers and their running rigging are set outside all other sails and rigging. The fractional rig requires simpler but more precise sail-handling; snatch blocks must be sited forward of the widest beam to give the correct sheeting angles.

Winches

Simple winches are difficult for one person to operate. Self-tailers (above) have a mechanism that allows one crew member to easily trim and raise sails and are becoming more common, although more expensive. A good lead to winch is vital to prevent riding turns jamming the line on the winch drum.

Spinnaker pole topping lift

Spinnaker pole downhaul

Genoa sheet

Spinnaker guy

The clew outhaul allows the adjustment of the foot of the mainsail. It is housed inside the boom, and often incorporates a powerful tackle.

Spinnaker sheet

Main halyard

Genoa halyard

Block

Boom vang

Double turning block

hatchway to leave the cockpit free for the sheets. Coil spinnaker and reaching sheets not in use and fasten to the pushpit. Site sheet winches to perform a variety of tasks: use prime sheet winches for spinnaker guys, and halyard or control-line winches for the spinnaker sheet.

The mainsheet traveler exactly positions the boom athwartships, giving fine control of the mainsail's shape.

Use a system to separate ropes leading back to the cockpit, to avoid wear and tear. Drop tails of halyards and control lines down the

THE RANGE OF ROPES

Establishing what the rope will be used for is the key to selecting the right rope. For example, sheets do not have to have extreme stretch resistance as the spans over which they operate are relatively short. Therefore a conventional polyester (Dacron) double-braid rope (a braided core inside a braided outer cover) will be fine.

However, for an all-rope halyard, or a spinnaker guy, where stretch must be kept to a minimum, a more advanced material is needed for the core of the rope. Two main types are available: aramid fiber, such as Kevlar™, or high modulus polyethylene, such as Dyneema™ or Spectra™. These are more expensive but also have significant strength-to-weight advantages over conventional types—an important consideration for racing boats. These "exotic" materials are also well suited for thinner control lines, such as kicking straps/vangs or outhauls and Cunninghams, as their strength-to-thickness advantage means that weight can be saved all round.

Kevlar™, Spectra™, and other high-tech cores are commonly covered with a braided polyester sheath to protect them from chafe and ultra-violet radiation.

Avoid tying knots in aramid fiber ropes as they are particularly prone to being weakened in this way.

The arch-enemies of synthetic rope are grit and sunshine. Grit squeezes between the strands and finds its way to the interior of the rope where it saws away at the inner fibers. Ultraviolet light accelerates the decay of synthetics, so wash them occasionally in fresh water and stow them in a dark locker after use. Abrasion is a frequent problem with halyards and control lines that constantly wear in the same place.

Three-stranded or laid rope makes good mooring warp. The lightest synthetic, polypropylene, is suitable for a dinghy painter, as it floats.

Dyneema™ rope is produced from high modulus polyethylene material. This fiber does not suffer as badly as the aramid fibers from exposure to chafe and sunlight.

Kevlar™ rope is produced from an aramid fiber and has low stretch properties. However, its fibers lose much of their strength if made to deflect sharply, such as in a knot.

Nylon rope stretches, but is twice as strong as manila and easy to handle, wet or dry. 16-plait nylon rope will bear heavy loads and is used for anchor warps.

Double braid (sometimes called braid-on-braid or braidline) consists of a plaited core of extra-strong inner fibers within a friction-resistant flexible plaited sheath that is easy to handle and grip. Strong, high-stretch and shock-absorbent, nylon double braid makes excellent anchor cable. It is soft, flexible, and does not kink or harden.

Braided (sometimes called plaited) rope, such as polyester 16-plait, gives the combined strength of 24 components and stretches 3.6 percent. It is ideal for control lines and halyards.

Bosun's bag

Every cruiser must carry the basic rope-repairing and improving equipment. Plastic tape is useful for sealing the ends of strands, to prevent unraveling and to guard against chafe. A gas lighter or blow torch can be used to heat seal the ends. Whipping and seizing tools include some spools of waxed and unwaxed whipping twine, two sailmaker's needles and a well-fitting sailmaker's palm, used as a thimble. The Swedish fid, an alternative version of the marlin spike, is useful for splicing synthetic rope. Sail-repair tape must also be included, and spare pieces of sailcloth for each weight of sail that can double as anti-chafe protection for warps and running rigging. A knife with a wooden handle is useful: heat the blade on the cooker to cut and seal a rope in one move.

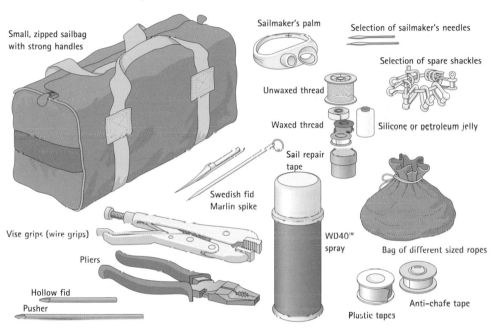

Small, zipped sailbag with strong handles

Sailmaker's palm

Selection of sailmaker's needles

Selection of spare shackles

Unwaxed thread

Waxed thread

Silicone or petroleum jelly

Sail repair tape

Swedish fid
Marlin spike

Vise grips (wire grips)

Pliers

WD40™ spray

Bag of different sized ropes

Hollow fid

Pusher

Anti-chafe tape

Plastic tapes

For easy recognition, many modern boats are equipped with color-coded ropes. The system below is a good example.

Halyards
1 Genoa/jib (port/starboard)—blue
2 Spinnaker (port/starboard)—orange
3 Mainsail—black

Sheets
4 Genoa/jib (port/starboard)—gold
5 Reaching/change sheet—yellow
6 Spinnaker sheets (port/starboard)—red
7 Spinnaker guys (port/starboard)—blue

Control lines
8 Spinnaker pole downhaul—red
9 Baby stay tensioner—black
10 Clew outhaul—gold
11 Cunningham—blue

Mainsail
12 1st reef—red   13 2nd reef—blue
14 3rd reef—yellow

Running backstays
15 Port—red   16 Starboard—blue

Rope clutches are a popular method of fastening control lines.

THE IMPORTANT KNOTS

Strictly speaking a knot is found at the end of a rope, but the word has come to include a "bend," used to tie two ropes together, or a "hitch," used to secure a rope to another object. The simplest way to learn to tie the appropriate knot for the purpose is to volunteer for the deckhand's job when mooring or rigging the boat.

The best multi-purpose knot is the bowline. It can be used to secure a line to a bollard, ring, or crossbeam; to fasten a safety line around your chest; to haul someone out of the water; or to make a bosun's chair or an improvised ladder. It is easily undone and imposes less strain on the rope than other knots. (All rope is weakened when bent sharply under tension as in a knot.)

A bosun's chair can be made from a doubled bowline (see far right illustration). A crew member can sit in the two loops formed and be hoisted aloft on the halyard. This can, however, be extremely uncomfortable as the lower part of the body is compressed. You can make a permanent bosun's chair by incorporating a wooden seat, particularly important if the crew member intends to work aloft. Thread the ends of two rope strops through a hole in each corner of the seat and splice them underneath it; then seize the strops together to form an eye.

In no circumstances should a snap shackle be used to attach the chair to the halyard. Instead, use a large D-shackle and tighten the pin with a wrench or pliers. Two halyards should be used: one for hoisting and one as a safety line, which should be secured around the chest of the person hoisted.

Once the halyard is fixed to the seat, lead it back to the largest sheet winch or mast halyard winch and, when the crew member is seated, smoothly winch it in, taking care to avoid riding turns. Another crew member should maintain a steady hand-over-hand pull and carefully watch the chair and its passenger aloft.

A **bosun's chair** in use. Although it is possible to construct one from rope alone, most modern chairs have plastic seats or strapping (as above).

The simplest knot is the **overhand or thumb knot**, used to stop the end of a rope running through a block or up the mast.

Also made by the thumb or over the hand, the **double overhand knot** can be used on the end of genoa sheets, halyards, and reefing lines, but not on spinnaker sheets or guys, which may need to run free if the sail gets out of control.

The **figure-of-eight knot** is also used to prevent ropes escaping, but if left for a period of time it can prove difficult to untie. For extra bulk, the end can be passed through the loop a second time.

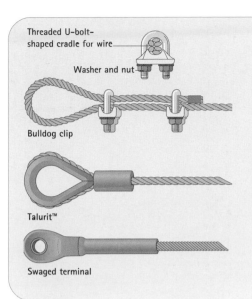

Threaded U-bolt-shaped cradle for wire

Washer and nut

Bulldog clip

Talurit™

Swaged terminal

Wire-to-rope connections

Where wire standing rigging connects to the mast or adjustable rigging screws, it must be bent to form an eye or opened into a self-locking device. In an emergency, such as dismasting, a good temporary eye can be made by bending the end into a loop with a vise grip and securing it with the correct-sized bulldog clips. A Talurit™ eye, suitable for small craft, consists of a soft nickel sleeve that is crimped over the doubled-over wire and secured under great pressure. The wire is bent around a metal thimble for reinforcement. In the swaged terminal the wire is inserted into the terminal, which is then compressed using a lever or hydraulic press, securing it in place.

To make a bowline, hold the rope about 6 in (15 cm) from the end with your "working" hand. Lay the end over the rope, palm down, supporting the rope with the other hand.

Twist the working hand away from you so that the rope end points up towards you through the loop that is produced.

Grasp the crossover between your finger and thumb. Take the end up and behind the rope then feed it down through the loop.

Tighten the knot slowly so that the loop and the turn are in equal tension. The end should be 2–3 in (5–8 cm) long.

For a doubled bowline (on the bight), start to tie a large loop in the end of a rope with a single bowline.

Make the first stage of the bowline with a loop instead of an end. Pass the loop around and down over the lower part of the main loop, to form a second loop.

Work the single loop slowly up and put it over the doubled rope close to the original single knot.

Spread the two bottom loops to form the seat of a bosun's chair. One loop can go around each thigh, or one loop can go around the chest and the other around both thighs.

Handling and coiling ropes

Always coil ropes or the ends of ropes not in use, as kinks will reduce their strength and may jam in a block when the coil comes free. Use both hands to coil a rope, supporting it in, say, the left hand and feeding it with the right. Swing the arms apart, gathering a length across the body, then swing together to collect the coil.

A coiling rhythm produces even lengths of rope. Coil right-handed rope clockwise and left-handed rope anticlockwise; braided rope should be snaked into a figure-of-eight. Hang up ropes that are not in use. When breaking open a new coil, lead off an end anticlockwise, or the rope will kink.

Coil rope clockwise and twist to flatten.

When only 4 ft (1.22 m) of rope remains, take three turns around the coil.

Pass the looped end through the top of the coil.

Take the loop over the top of the coil and pull the free end to fasten.

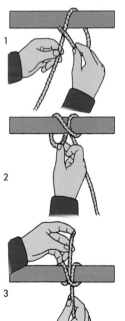

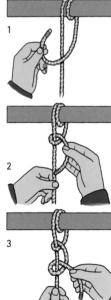
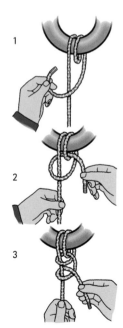

A **clove hitch** can be used to attach a fender to the grab rails. Pass the rope-end forward over the rail, **1**, bring it up to the right, behind the standing part, **2**. Loop over the rail and tuck in to the crossover, **3**.

A **round turn and two half hitches** is a more secure alternative to the clove hitch. Wrap the rope once around the rail, **1**, and then tie two half hitches on the standing part, **2**. It is used to tie a rope to a spar, rail or shroud.

A **fisherman's bend** will secure a rope to a ring or an anchor, and thick rope to a thin shroud or lifeline. Pass the rope through the ring twice, **1**; pass the end around, **2**, and back through the turns, **3**.

To make a **"Trucker's hitch,"** form an eye, **1**, take a loop of rope through it, **2**, and pass the free end through a hook and back through the loop, **3**.

34

Heaving a line

When heaving a line, always re-coil the rope and check (by eye) that it is long enough to reach the quay or another boat before throwing it. Hold a few coils in one hand and throw the rest of the rope in tighter coils by swinging the arm back and leaning the opposite shoulder towards the target. Aim well above the target and allow the rope to fly free.

Cleating rope

A rope may jam or slip if it is incorrectly cleated. Always take the rope to the back of the cleat first and take a round turn around the base, **1**. Then take several figure-of-eight turns around both horns, **2**. For extra security, take a final full turn around the base of the cleat, **3**.

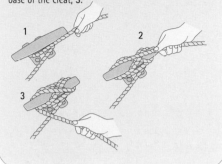

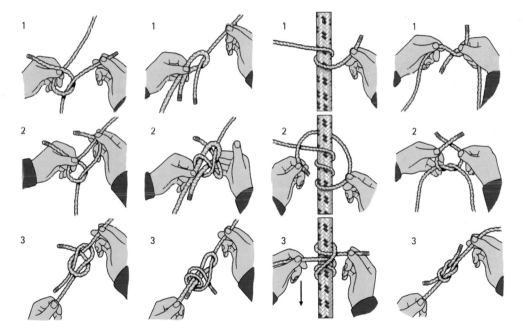

Use a **sheet bend** to join two ropes. Make a loop with the thicker rope, **1**, and pass the other up through it, around the back, **2**, then across under itself, **3**. Both short ends must lie the same side or it will slip.

A **double sheet bend** is used when one rope is much thinner. Make a loop in the thicker rope, **1**, continue as for a single sheet bend, **2**, but making two turns or more, **3**.

A **rolling hitch** can be used to free a sheet or halyard from a riding turn on the winch. Wrap the end twice around the sheet, **1**, take it back, make a half hitch, **2**, and tighten, **3**. Wind the end on a free winch.

When tying **reefing points**, use the reef knot; it holds well under pressure, but is easily freed. Tied correctly, **1** and **2**, the reef knot appears as two symmetrically linked loops, **3**.

SPLICES AND EYES

Splicing

Splicing is the joining of two ropes in an attempt to preserve their strength. After a few basic starting sequences, it consists mainly of tucking the strands over and under each other. The simplest and quickest way of forming an eye in a rope or joining two ropes together is the tuck splice. The tucked join, **1**, is made by twisting the ends of two ropes together. The tucked eye, **2**, is formed by laying the end of the rope under a strand in several places. Whip or tape the ends.

Preparing rope for splicing

Preparation is essential on all synthetic ropes because they unravel easily. All splices are started by untwisting the rope to the desired length. At the point where the unlaying ends, tape or whip the limit of the strands and the end of each strand, to prevent further unraveling. Join two ropes together with a short splice to get the feel of the sequence of tucking in the ends. Always make the tucks against the lay of the other rope, and at right angles to it.

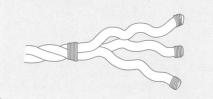

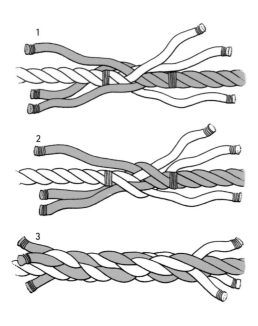

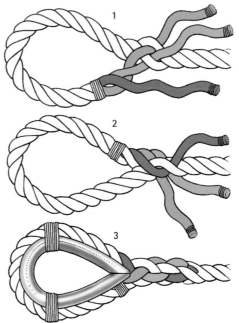

To make a short splice, unlay the ends of both ropes for three turns, **1**. Mesh the strands together so that each passes between two strands of the other rope, **2**. Splice in one end at a time, passing each over its neighbor and under the next strand, against the lay of the rope. Repeat twice. Pull the ends tight, turn the work over and splice in the other three strands, **3**. Tighten and roll between the hands; and trim and seal the ends.

To make a permanent eye, unlay four turns, form a loop and tuck the center, and then the left-hand strand, against the lay, **1**. Turn the splice over to tuck in the third strand, **2**. Take two extra tucks. Cut the ends and heat-seal. To reinforce a "soft" eye, incorporate a metal or nylon thimble, **3**, and secure with whipping.

Splicing rope to wire

To splice rope to wire, when making or repairing a halyard, for example, first unravel 9 in (22 cm) of the wire and whip the junctions; 7 x 7 wire can be divided into 2 x 2 and 1 x 3 to produce three strands. Unravel about 1 in (2.5 cm) of the rope, 1, and, meshing the wire and rope strands as evenly as possible, whip the rope firmly to the wire. Tuck in the wire strands against the lay, taking care not to kink the wire, 2. Tape and tuck the rope and protect the whole length with an overall whipping, 3.

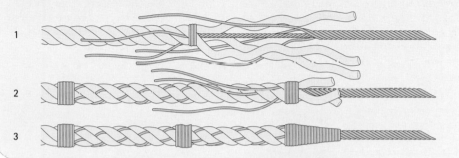

Mooring warps are usually made from eight strands, with two pairs running clockwise and two pairs anticlockwise. When splicing, the clockwise strands must be worked anticlockwise. Tape the ends of each pair of strands a different color for clockwise and anticlockwise. Unlay three turns and put a whipping around the clockwise strands, 1. Tuck the uppermost clockwise pair, pointing to the left of the rope, down between the clockwise pair, 2. Tuck in the left pair and the two remaining strands, as shown, 3.

WHIPPING AND SEIZING TECHNIQUES

Working with twine is an ideal way to introduce younger crew members to the skills of seamanship. As most heat sealing tends to break down after prolonged use, many owners are now taking up the whipping twine, palm, and needle as their predecessors did. All whippings should be made against the lay of the rope to stop it twisting open. Take 18 in (46 cm) of thread and, beginning 1 in (2 cm) in, lay a loop of thread along the rope in the direction you are working and cover it with tightly wound thread. Put the end through the loop, pull the protruding thread, and cut both ends to form a simple and secure whipping.

An alternative way of joining ropes or making eyes, if it is not possible to splice them, is to lash them together with thin twine using a lot of tight turns. Known as

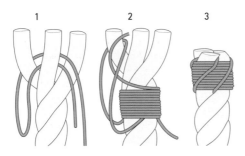

For a sailmaker's whipping, open a 3-strand rope and thread a loop of whipping thread loosely around one strand, **1**. Close the strands and wind the thread tightly around the rope, thread the end between the strands, and bring the loop back over its original strand, **2**. Pull the loop tight with the bottom end of the whipping. Tie the thread tightly to the top end with a reef knot, but make two or three twists to form the final part of the knot, **3**.

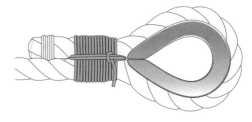

To form an eye with seizing, make a loop in the end of the seizing and attach it securely around the doubled ropes. Wind it around, using a marlin-spike hitch (see below) to tighten the turns. Make about eight turns, then loop the seizing around one of the points of the eye or lead it down inside the seizing through the looped end and tie an overhand knot.

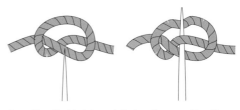

A marlin spike hitch is made by inserting a marlin spike into the loop of a slip knot so that more power can be applied when whipping or seizing the end of a rope, since twine is hard to grip firmly.

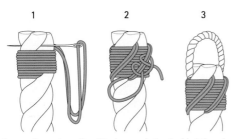

For a palm and needle whipping, push the doubled thread under one strand. Wind the thread to the top, take in another strand, and tighten, **1**. Lead the thread down to the base and back until the three grooves are filled. Finish with half hitches, **2**. To make a halyard strop, make a sailmaker's whipping and stitch a loop across the top, **3**. This is also the best whipping for braided line. You begin with two stitches through the rope, make a tight whipping, and finish with three alternating stitches at the top and base of the whipping, passing the twine over the whipping between each stitch and moving around the rope's circumference in 120° increments.

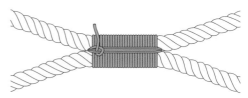

To join two ropes together at regular intervals use a crossed seizing. This is made in the same way as seizing an eye, but two or three turns are taken around the center. Finish with two half hitches or by sewing the seizing into one of the ropes.

seizing, this is particularly useful when joining braided ropes. Another method is to stitch through both parts.

Having fun and playing with rope will help you to understand it better. You can often collect offcuts from your local chandler. Youngsters lucky enough to go sailing regularly could have their own bosun's bag containing many different samples of rope.

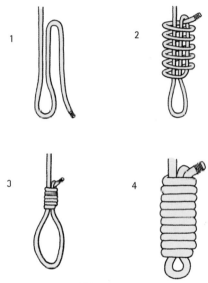

A **hangman's knot** will keep a young crew occupied for quite a while. Loop the end of the rope and double it back, **1**. Make 13 round turns with the rest of the rope's end and pass it through the loop at the top, **2**. Tighten up the round turns so that they grip firmly, **3**. Now you have a running noose, **4**.

A **running figure-of-eight** knot is useful for scooping up a floating object from shallow water, or even for tying parcels. Loop the end, twist it round in a figure-of-eight, and tighten.

Blocks and tackles

Before the days of winches, blocks and tackles were used to lift heavy loads, to hoist sails, and move spars. On modern boats, the best example of blocks and tackles is the mainsheet system, which has blocks and ropes to reduce the pull transmitted to the helmsman. The power of a purchase is calculated by counting the number of lines coming from the moving block or blocks. The simplest mechanical advantage is gained by using one pulley block on the load to be moved, such as the boom. It halves the effort required to pull the boom in and so has an advantage of 2:1, **1**. The bottom block here acts as an anchorage and turning block for the rope. A further advantage is gained by inserting another block at the moving point, to produce a 3:1 purchase, **2**. A fourth block with its own anchorage point will double the leverage power to 6:1, **3**, and may be used for a kicking strap/vang. These can be multiplied further by adding another 2:1 known as "cascading," to result in 12:1.

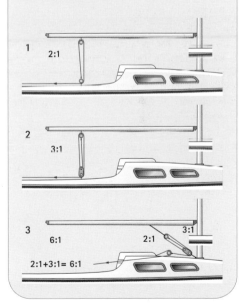

A **blood knot** is used to attach a hook or swivel to a fishing line. Loop the line through the eye, make four or five round turns, bring the end down, and tuck it back through the eye. Tighten it gently.

WIND AND POWER

CHOOSING SAILS

A conventional bermudan rig for the average cruising boat requires the minimum of a mainsail and one headsail. With a furling headsail, this is probably enough for most of the season. However, it is always worth carrying a small second jib for safety, rather like carrying a second anchor, just in case the furling genoa tears.

Anyone cruising one weekend and racing the next may need more sails. The furling headsail does not lend itself so well to racing because as it rolls up the sail tends to become fuller, which is not ideal when sailing to windward. Several sizes of headsail would, therefore, be necessary.

The minimum wardrobe for occasional weekend racing is a mainsail, medium-weather genoa, a No. 2 and No. 3 genoa, and a spinnaker (see p.29) of medium weight. For cruising or racing offshore, a storm jib is essential, both to comply with the rules and for safety.

The movement in sailing today, however, is towards ease of handling. As the conventional bermudan rig involves the expense of a large crew and a full wardrobe of sails to achieve maximum efficiency, new solutions have been sought.

Fully battened mainsails and in-mast mainsail furling systems, together with better cut roller reefing genoas are increasingly being specified. These give a good account of themselves to windward as well as being controllable from the cockpit.

Other more unusual rigs include the Freedom style rig. Here the mast is supported in the deck alone and is unstayed. The sails can either have wraparound luffs or more conventional bolt rope grooves or tacks. The junk rig (see p. 28) is also set on an unstayed mast, but differs in that the sail extends forward of the mast as well as aft and uses full-length battens to support the sail itself.

When buying sails, beware of sales talk circulated by manufacturers. Invest in strong, well constructed sails that may be expensive, but should remain in good shape for seven or eight years. For cruising, choose a good-weight cloth in preference to plastic laminate which is more fragile.

The gaff rig is the traditional working rig for European trading and fishing boats and is now enjoying a revival.

The wraparound "soft sail" reduces turbulence around the mast, which becomes a blunt but smooth leading edge to the aerofoil section of the sail. They are seen here on a laser dinghy but are also used on some larger vessels.

American schooners were generally trading vessels that evolved huge sail areas in order to boost their performance in the race back to port to sell their fish at the best prices.

Head
Luff
Leech
Seam
Foot

The vertical cut proved its high performance in top-class racing for many years.

The horizontal cut is the most popular for mainsails as there is no bias and so no extra stretch on the unsupported leech.

The cruising chute, which is smaller and more easily handled than the spinnaker, improves the downwind and reaching performance of family cruisers.

The leechcut, **1**, and the crosscut, **2**, are the most common designs for headsails.

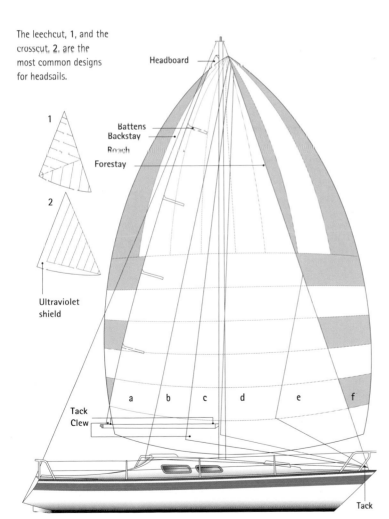

Headboard

1

Battens
Backstay
Roach
Forestay

2

Ultraviolet shield

Tack
Clew

a   b   c   d   e   f

Tack

a The mainsail takes more wear than any other sail so must be cut for strong winds. Battens wholly support the curved leech (roach).

b The medium-weather genoa needs a high enough foot to give good visibility ahead and on the leeward side.

c The No. 2 genoa, which reefs to a No. 3, is useful in strong winds, but this is a compromise.

d Alternatively, use a No. 3 genoa.

e The storm jib must be in heavyweight cloth, preferably fluorescent orange.

f The cruising radial-head spinnaker is made of light, shock-absorbent cloth. Avoid white to prevent eye strain.

HOW A BOAT SAILS

A boat will not sail straight into the wind, but needs the sails to be full on one side or the other to make it move efficiently through the water.

The angle to the wind determines the sheeting position of the sails and which sails to set. The ideal angle for the wind to strike a sail depends on its shape, the type of boat and the tautness of the rigging. However, in all sailing vessels and on all points of sail, the sails need to be trimmed to keep the boat sailing at this optimum angle.

The strength of wind dictates the amount of sail area to be set. The wind exerts a constant pressure of 1 lb/sq ft (4.9 kg/sq m) in a 16 kn or Force 4 (29.6 kph) breeze. However, if the wind speed increased to 35 kn or gale Force 8 (64.8 kph) the pressure rises to almost 5 lbs/sq ft (24.4 kg/sq m).

To keep the same amount of pressure on the boat in Force 8 as in Force 4, and so prevent the boat heeling excessively, the size of sail will have to be reduced.

Sails should be reduced equally to prevent the boat becoming unbalanced. Too much main and not enough jib creates weather helm, which pushes the boat up into the wind because the center of effort is too far back. If there is too much headsail and not enough mainsail, the driving force is too far forward and the boat bears away from the wind.

The keel prevents the boat moving sideways when under sail. It also provides stability as well as preventing most sideways slip. Thus, since the boat cannot move sideways through the water, the resulting forces drive it forward.

The angle of heel is important to the speed of the craft. An excessive angle of heel causes the boat to slow down, even though it may appear to be going faster. It is, therefore, more efficient and more comfortable to keep the boat on a reasonably even keel. The ballast on the bottom of the keel provides a righting lever counteracting the pressure of the wind on the sails, and prevents the boat sailing on its beam ends.

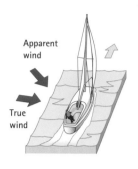

Apparent wind

True wind

The apparent wind is a combination of the true wind and the wind created by the movement of the boat and feels strongest when the boat is close-hauled. When sailing away from it, the wind feels lighter than it really is. If a 17.25 mph (15 kn) wind is blowing and the boat is sailing at 5.75 mph (5 kn) downwind, an apparent wind of 11.5 mph (10 kn) blows over the deck.

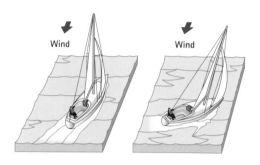

Wind · Wind

Above: Sails have to be trimmed to create a **smooth air flow** over them. When bearing off the wind, the sheets are eased so that the sails maintain their angle as the boat turns.

Below: **When beating**, or reaching, the sails interact to create a slot effect. The compressed wind flows fastest over the curved back of the mainsail and forces suck the boat forward.

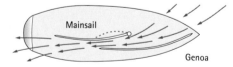

Mainsail

Genoa

COE

CLR

The correct **center of effort** (COE) is the balancing point of the sail area in relation to the balancing point of the underwater hull shape, or **center of lateral resistance** (CLR). Once this is achieved a boat should sail with a small degree of weather helm.

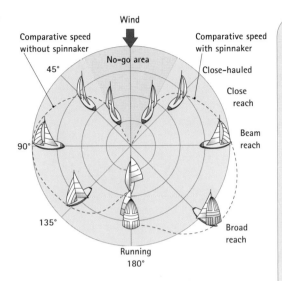

Wind

Comparative speed without spinnaker

No-go area

45°

Comparative speed with spinnaker

Close-hauled

Close reach

Beam reach

90°

135°

Broad reach

Running
180°

Points of sailing

The relative speed of any sailing boat is determined by its point of sail or angle to the wind.

1 Too close to the wind, in the "no-go" area, the sails luff, or shake, and the boat moves slowly.

2 Close-hauled or beating at 40–50° off the true wind, speed increases as the sails are pinned in tight and at the optimum angle.

3 On a close reach (70°), the sheets are eased out and the boat sails more easily.

4 On a beam reach, at right angles to the wind, speed increases.

5 A broad reach (135°) is the fastest point of sailing, if extra sail is set.

6 Running, or sailing downwind, the sheets are let out to a maximum, and unless more sail is set or the wind kept on the quarter, the boat will slow down.

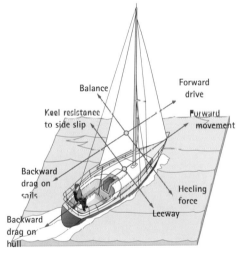

Balance

Forward drive

Keel resistance to side slip

Forward movement

Backward drag on sails

Heeling force

Leeway

Backward drag on hull

The boat's speed increases as it moves from close-hauled to reaching. Beyond a broad reach, the apparent wind reduces and the boat slows down unless a spinnaker or cruising chute is set to boost it. A dead run is the slowest point of sailing, unless it is blowing very hard.

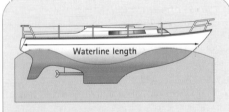

Waterline length

Maximum hull speed

In theory maximum hull speed is 1.3–1.5 times the square root of the waterline length and is reached when the waves are the same length as the hull—a wave peak at both bow and stern. Today's lighter boats can exceed this speed by planing on the water surface.

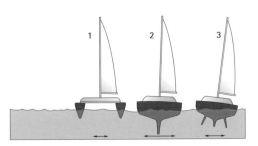

1 2 3

1 A catamaran's width gives it initial stability, but once beyond 90° it is difficult to right.

2 A cruising boat only heels to a moderate angle because of its hull shape and outside ballast.

3 Alternatively, a cruising boat's stability can be achieved by ballast on twin bilge keels and possibly a central stub fin. The same leverage is produced with less draft.

SETTING THE SAILS

The starting point of any day's sail is the proper rigging and setting-up of the mainsail and jib on to the spars. Care taken at this stage will prevent snags arising later, such as battens flying out when the sail is flapping.

The first consideration is the weather, especially when you are short-handed. Light winds in the early morning may freshen during the day, requiring a change of headsail, so if short-handed it is advisable to choose the foresail best suited to the maximum wind speed forecast for the day.

The tack of the jib is fastened to the bow fitting with either a pin, a hook, or, for good visibility below the sail, a short tack pennant (length of wire). The luff of the foresail is either hooked to the forestay or fed into a forestay-mounted luff groove, which eliminates the turbulence created by hanks.

Once the sails are bent on, the sheets and halyards attached, and the boat facing into the wind, the mainsail is hoisted first. If, however, the tide is flowing against the wind use the jib to get under way.

Having hoisted the sails, check the tension. Some cruising boats never seem to have the jib adequately tensioned. If it is slack, horizontal creases will run off the luff and a scallop will form between each hank so that the boat sails badly to windward. Wind on enough halyard to eliminate this. Don't worry, so long as everything is in good order, nothing will break! It is always easier to pay out an over-tensioned halyard than to tighten one; the harder the wind, the tighter the halyard should be. If the wind drops, ease off the halyard until the crease just disappears; if it increases tighten the halyard progressively. The luff on the mainsail works in the same manner.

Each headsail is rigged in exactly the same way. The plungers of the hanks should be on the same side on all the foresails. This avoids confusing the tack with the head, and so hoisting the sail upside down, particulary at night. It also reduces the chances of twisting a hank. Always check that the halyard is not twisted round the forestay before

hoisting. Once a furling headsail has been hoised onto a forestay, the halyard can be made fast and tidied away for the season, save for the occasional check. To unfurl, carefully pay out the control, which will be led aft to the cockpit, while winding in the leeward sheet. To furl, reverse the process, taking care to maintain sufficient gentle tension on the sheet to ensure a neat roll.

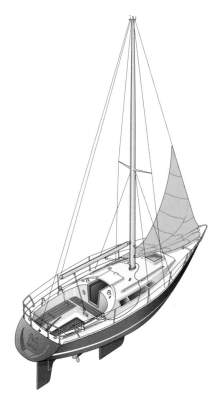

To set the jib, take the bag forward and attach the tack to the bow fitting. Hank the sail on to the forestay, beginning with the bottom hank and taking care not to twist any hanks. Attach the sheets to the clew with a bowline, not a shackle or snapshackle, as these can injure anyone unlucky enough to be hit and may detach themselves when tacking. Use separate sheets rather than an endless one. Attach the halyard to the head of the sail, lead the sheets through the fairleads and aft to the cockpit, then secure the end of each sheet with a stopper knot. To hoist, pull hard on the halyard until the head of the sail reaches the top of the forestay, then cleat both halyard and the leeward sheet.

The sails act as the engine of a sailing boat. To achieve maximum power, the outhaul tension on the mainsail and the halyard tension on both sails must be sufficient to allow the sails to set wrinkle-free. The sheet must also be tightened until the luff of the sail just stops shaking and the tell-tales (see p. 49) are streaming horizontally.

Sail care

Sunlight is a sail's worst enemy, so cover the sails when they are not in use. An ultraviolet guard (see p. 43), fitted down the leech of a roller headsail, will protect the exposed part from the weathering effect of the sun and from dirt and grit. Mildew, which discolors, is prevented by storing sails dry and by hand-washing twice a season.

Check all sails regularly for chafe, particularly where they press on deck fittings or rigging, at reef points, batten sleeves, and the foot of the headsail. Stick-on reinforcing patches can be used where necessary.

Stowing sails

To stow the mainsail, start at the leech and flake it on to the boom, left and right, in about 18 in (46 cm) folds, while pulling the leech aft. Secure with a sail tie and continue to the luff. Lash to the boom with sail ties or shock cord.

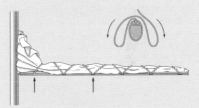

The headsail, neatly rolled and fastened, can be temporarily stowed along the lifelines. To stow below, flake it into a length, **1**, then if not using a "sausage" bag, roll from luff to leech, **2**. Take care not to crease the leech. Pack in a clearly marked bag.

Topping
lift

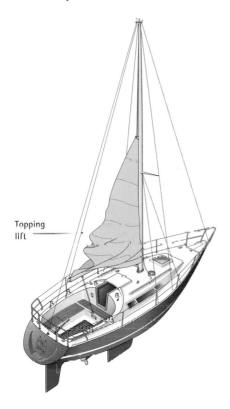

To rig the mainsail, take the bag to the mast and slide the clew of the sail into the boom. Attach the tack to the gooseneck. Fasten the clew to the end of the boom and tension the clew outhaul. Attach the halyard to the head of the sail. Fit the slides into the sail track, starting at the head. Fit the stop into the end of the sail track. Fit and secure the battens. When hoisting, check the halyard is running free. Slacken the topping lift so that all the leech tension is taken on the sail itself. When lowering, always tension the topping lift before releasing the halyard. Mark each batten with its pocket number; insert the thin end first and put stiffer battens in lower pockets.

CLOSE-HAULED

Close-hauled is the most challenging point of sailing, and the most difficult in which to get the best out of a boat. As it is impossible to make the boat sail directly into the wind, the only way to travel quickly to windward is to climb up into the wind by a series of tacks (zigzags).

The crucial question when sailing to windward is how close to the wind to sail and this is a matter of trial and error. The normal tacking angle—the difference in compass heading between one tack and the other on a cruising boat—in average conditions is about 80–90°.

Some designs, particularly twin-keels, will tack through 90–100°. High-rigged, deep-keeled racing yachts may tack through about 70–80°. The angle depends not only on the shape of the sails and the boat design but also on the wind strength, the air temperature, tide, and height of the waves.

The aim when beating is to point as high as possible, while maintaining the fastest possible speed. If the boat points higher, it approaches its destination more directly, but sails more slowly through the water. If it points farther off, it moves through the water faster, but covers more ground.

Tacking through 90° at a water speed of 5.75 mph (5 kn), the boat sails directly to windward at 4 mph (3.53 kn); pointing higher at a tacking angle of 80°, the water speed may drop to 4.6 mph (4 kn) and the boat's speed directly to windward or velocity made good (VMG) falls to 3.5 mph (3.06 kn). It often pays to sail farther off the wind and go faster, since it requires a lot of concentration and a well-rigged boat to point high and still maintain speed. When sailing long distances, the wind is likely to change before you arrive, so, everything else being equal, choose the tack that is closest to the desired course when setting off.

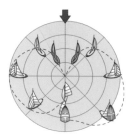

The closest course most boats can sail to the wind is about 40–45°. The sails are sheeted in as far as they will go without pinching. The apparent wind is strong and the boat tends to heel.

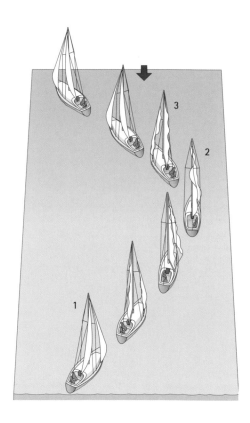

To tack, crew A uncleats the headsail sheet and holds it on the winch ready to let go, 1. Crew B holds the weather sheet with one clockwise turn around the winch ready to pull in. Three more turns will be needed for the final tensioning. Check that the winch handle is in its holder. When all crew are ready, slowly luff the boat up into the wind, 2 and 3. As the headsail comes aback, cast off the leeward sheet, push the tiller hard over and as the boat comes through the eye of the wind, haul in the other sheet.

1 Sails sheeted in tight.
2 Crew on windward side help to counteract heeling.
3 Kicking strap adjusted so that top batten of mainsail is in line with boom.

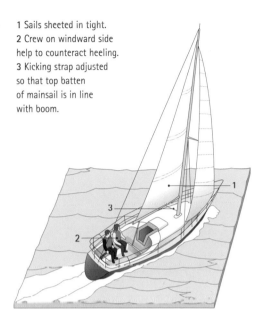

The optimum speed at which to tack is dictated by the design of the boat and can be established by watching the speed at every turn. The idea is to keep the speed as high as is possible throughout the maneuver, which means tacking slowly; a fast tack will stop the boat. It is important not to haul in the sheets too quickly immediately after a tack, but to ease the last few inches in slowly until the optimum speed is reached.

Fitting the tell-tales

Tell-tales give a visual indication of the flow of air over the sails and hence their trim, and are particularly useful on the headsail. To fit tell-tales, take some threads of wool about 18 in (46 cm) long, make several small holes in the sail with a hot needle (to seal the fabric) and pass the wool through—until 9 in (23 cm) appears each side—tying a knot on each end. Position them 12–18 in (30–46 cm) abaft the luff edge and midway between the seams to avoid the wool catching on the stitching. The tell-tales on each side should stream aft. If the windward one flutters when the boat is close-hauled, it is pointing too high; when reaching, the headsail needs to be sheeted in slightly. If the leeward tell-tale flutters when the boat is close-hauled, it is too far off the wind; when reaching, the sail is too taut. Mainsail leech tell-tales should fly horizontally but will stall if the sail is oversheeted or is "hooked," perhaps due to too much kicking strap/vang tension.

Position midway between seams

12–18 in (30–46 cm) from luff

If the sheets are pinned in too tight and the heeling angle of the boat feels suddenly extreme, **ease the sheets** to reduce the sideways pressure on the sails.

Take into account that a boat makes most **leeway when close-hauled**. A deep-keeled boat may only make 2–5° leeway, a twin-keeled boat may deviate by as much as 15°.

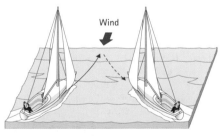

If the boat stops as it goes about (it gets "into irons"), try **reversing the tiller** by pulling it towards the intended direction of sailing. This pulls the stern over to one side and the sails should fill again. Then back the jib by pulling the sheet you have just released and ease the mainsheet. When the bow is 20° off the wind, you can sheet in the jib.

REACHING

Reaching is the fastest point of sailing. In heavy weather it is essential to set the right amount of sail area to prevent excessive heel and to balance the rig to keep weather helm to a minimum. A reefed mainsail with a relatively larger headsail will move the center of effort of the sail plan forward. This reduces the pull on the helm and also the heeling angle of the boat, and should allow the boat to gain maximum speed very quickly.

In fair weather a spinnaker can be set, although in very light winds a light-weather headsail is preferable since it will not collapse when the boat rolls to leeward. If a spinnaker is set, the luff tension (the height of the outboard end of the pole) is crucial. As a general rule the two clews of the sail should be an equal height off the deck. As the wind rises, the pole should be raised. When the spinnaker collapses, either down its entire leading edge or in the middle, you've got it right.

The spinnaker should not be over-trimmed on a reach; the sheet should be eased until the leading edge just begins to fold, and then sheeted in again slightly to keep the sail at its optimum angle.

In heavy-weather reaching, all the crew should be aft and up on the windward side. This helps to keep the boat upright and the stern down so that the rudder is more effective and the bow out of the water, thus reducing the boat's weather helm to give the helmsman more control.

In very light weather the reverse should happen; the crew should be up forward of the mast and on the leeward side. This keeps the bow down, lifting the flat sections out of the water, so reducing the wetted surface. Increasing the weight to leeward causes the boat to heel slightly, with the result that the sails take up their natural shape through gravity.

On a beam reach the apparent wind attacks the sails at an angle of 90°. On a close reach, this decreases to 70°; on a broad reach, it increases to 135°.

The correct trim of the sails is crucial, so watch the tell-tales and the luff of the sails carefully. As soon as the boat is on course, ease out both the main and jib sheets until the sails begin to flutter, then haul them in just beyond the point where they stop shaking. At this point the sails should be pulling most efficiently. If the mainsheet is eased out too far, causing the wind to

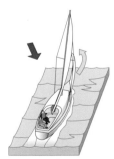

When luffing up into the wind, put the helm down to leeward and sheet in until the tell-tales flutter and luff begins to shake. Then bear off a fraction.

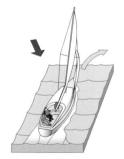

When bearing away, pull the helm to windward and ease the sheets out to increase the flow of wind over the sails and to prevent stalling.

1 Crew aft on windward
side (heavy weather)
2 Sheets eased
well out

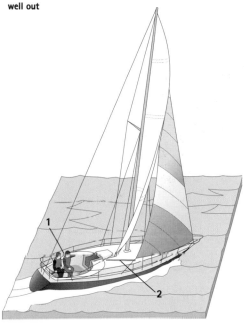

Wind direction

Before setting off, the wind direction can be
determined by using any of the following indications.
1 A burgee, a windsock, wind indicator, or racing
flag, attached to the head of the mast, where the
sails and rigging do not distort the wind direction.
2 The position of sails on other boats underway
indicates the direction of their apparent wind.
3 Flags, smoke, and trees on the coast blow away
from the wind.
4 A wind vane or electronic indicator reveals the
true wind when stationary and the apparent wind
when sailing.
5 Wave direction in the open sea and cloud
movement can be misleading.

strike the mainsail's lee
side, all driving power will
be lost. The solution is to
ease the sheets. If both
sails are sheeted in too far,
the boat will heel sharply
and slow. If the wind draws

ahead, tighten the sheets; if
it moves farther aft, ease
them. On a broad reach, the
boat-to-wave angle may
cause it to yaw so
anticipate, rather than
fight, the boat's movement.

Weather and lee helm

Neutral helm

Lee helm

Weather helm

Weather helm, the
tendency of a boat to
come naturally head-to-
wind when left on its
own, is a safety feature
that slows and eventu-
ally stops the boat if the
helmsman has to leave
the tiller. Its effect is
stronger while reaching
than on any other point
of sailing and can be
reduced by increasing
the foresail area. Lee
helm, the opposite,
occurs when the center
of effort (COE) is too far
forward of the center of
lateral resistance (CLR).
The green dot represents
COE and the yellow CLR
(see also p. 44).

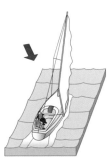

If a squall hits and there is
no time to luff up or bear
away, let fly the sheets to
reduce the angle of heel.
The effect will be
immediately apparent.

On a reach, the traveler
should be as far to leeward
as possible and the sails
correctly trimmed so that
the tell-tales stream aft,
flat against the sail.

BEFORE THE WIND

Off-the-wind sailing is a bit like cruising down the trade winds. Direction is not limited, it is dry, and usually much warmer since the apparent wind is less. Steering is not so critical and more sail area (eg. spinnaker) can be set.

A course, appropriate to your direction and the tidal stream, will dictate the wind angle to the boat. If it is between 90° and 180° and there is sufficient manpower on board, a spinnaker can be set. This is the ideal wind angle to use this sail, and it should be set with just the mainsail, the genoa being lowered and secured on deck.

The cruising chute (the style of spinnaker) can be used efficiently up to Force 3 with the wind 70–100° off the bow and up to Force 4 or 5 with the wind at 100–135°. If the wind is dead astern, it can be used in a Force 6 (see Beaufort Wind Scale p. 212). It is usually set flying, with no other sails other than the main, and is easily handled by a small crew.

If the wind is blowing very hard, a genoa or jib can be set with full or reefed mainsail, and with the wind forward of 135° it can be used on the same side as the main. Once the wind is aft of 160° the headsail can be goosewinged (see p. 216), preferably with a whisker pole if the boat is rolling heavily. This is a good downwind, heavy-weather rig and, as the wind increases, the same format can be maintained by reefing the mainsail and setting a smaller headsail.

With the wind dead aft, the crew should split into two parties to balance the boat. In light winds they should sit amidships and as far outboard as possible on each side, to act as wing ballast and reduce rolling. When the wind freshens, they should move farther aft to keep the stern down, while maintaining an even distribution of weight.

Running can be the most hazardous point of sailing because of the risk of gybing and the true wind always being stronger than it seems.

Downwind sailing ranges from a broad reach at 135° to a dead run at 180°. With the wind way aft, the sails act like parachutes rather than aerofoils.

Broaching occurs when the boat becomes overpowered, heels and rudder control is lost. The boat then luffs, and heels excessively. To prevent a broach, slow the boat, sail a lower or less aggressive course, or let the mainsail twist off at the top by easing the mainsheet.

Rolling can be reduced by tightening the kicking strap to hold the mainsail flatter and to stop the top twisting. Also try sheeting in the main.

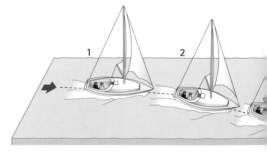

Gybing involves swinging the boom over nearly 180° to the other side of the boat. In a controlled gybe, the helmsman checks the new course is clear, and bears slightly off the wind, 1, then orders "Stand by to gybe" as he pulls the tiller over, hauls in hard on the

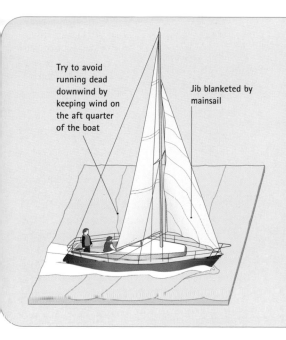

Try to avoid running dead downwind by keeping wind on the aft quarter of the boat

Jib blanketed by mainsail

1 The mainsail, not the boom, should be at right angles to the boat when the wind is dead aft.

2 Keep the wind over on the quarter opposite the mainsail by 5–8° and if necessary tack downwind to stay on course; the increase in speed more than compensates for the slightly longer distance sailed. This also guards against going into an involuntary gybe.

3 Move the crew aft to counteract the weight of the wind pushing the bow down.

4 Remember the apparent wind is less than the true wind and reduce sail area before turning into the wind.

5 The topping lift should be tensioned a little to give more fullness to the mainsail and to prevent the boom dragging in the water.

6 If the boat has runners, keep the leeward one slack.

7 In a multihull, it is significantly faster to tack downwind than to sail dead before it.

When sailing downwind the helmsman should watch the wind and steer carefully to avoid an accidental gybe. In a fluky wind, or if the boat is rolling heavily, the wind may catch the leech of the mainsail, forcing the whole sail to slam across, damaging both boat and crew. A boom preventer leading to the foredeck can forestall this. If the jib is not boomed out, it will warn of an imminent gybe by filling on the opposite side to the mainsail. To derive some driving force from the jib, it should be boomed out, so that the boat sails goosewinged.

Drop keel

Drop-keel or centerboard boats are ideal for cruising and are becoming increasingly popular, particularly as trailer sailers. With the centerboard up, they fit into shallow anchorages and sit firmly in a dry berth or on a trailer. When the centerboard is lowered, the keel is deep enough to make the boat very efficient to windward. In some boats, the keel can also be angled aft, which, when reaching, puts the center of lateral resistance (see p. 51) farther aft, so reducing the amount of weather helm and the chances of broaching. When running, if the centerboard is raised, some boats will plane over the water.

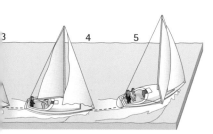

mainsheet, and cleats it, 2. The crew release the jib sheet and haul it in on the other side. 3 As the boom swings over, it is held firm by the mainsheet, 4, and the crew move to the other side. The mainsheet can now be paid out and the sails trimmed on the new tack, 5.

SPINNAKERS AND CRUISING CHUTES

Spinnakers have been known to intimidate, baffle, and enrage many good crews and significantly raise the volume in the cockpit! Because they are largely un-supported, having no one edge supported by a sail or stay, they can become unruly if allowed to take command. However, it needn't be a cause of anxiety.

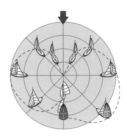

A spinnaker can be hoisted from a close reach to a dead run to boost the boat's speed downwind.

To set a spinnaker rig the sheets and guys at the same time as you rig the other sails before a day's sailing. If you prefer to launch from the pulpit simply clip the snap shackles onto the pulpit on each side so that they are easily reachable when the time comes.

A safer method is to launch from the leeward rail where the blanketing effect of the mainsail can be used to advantage. In this case clip the two sets of sheets and guys together so that they can be pulled round the front of the forestay onto one side or the other as needed. Make sure the halyard will be easily to hand—it too could be clipped to the sheets and guys.

Using the fasteners sewn onto its outside, attach the bag, or "turtle," containing the sail to the pulpit or guard-rail. Open the bag and pull out the three corners that will be lying on top if the sail has been properly packed. Connect the shackles to the sail.

Raise the spinnaker pole at the mast end and secure. Connect the guy (on the windward side) to the pole end and raise the pole using the uphaul, making it secure with the downhaul. Go to the mast ready to haul on the halyard. The cockpit crew should be ready with someone tending the sheet and another the guy. A third should be following you up on the halyard if this is led aft.

Hoist the sail quickly—nothing is so effective for broaching a boat than a part hoisted spinnaker suddenly filling with wind. The pole angle should then be set—a good rule of thumb is to have it at right angles to the apparent wind direction. Lower the genoa.

A popular means of handling spinnakers aboard short-handed cruisers is to use a "snuffer"—a sock type arrangement from which the spinnaker can be deployed or collapsed.

Cruising chutes were developed in large part as a means to escape much of the unruliness of spinnakers. No pole is needed with the sail having a tack—like a genoa, which is also likely to be attached at the foot of the forestay. The sail is set in the same way as a genoa but without attaching to the forestay. As with the spinnaker, launching from the leeward rail rather than the pulpit will be safer.

Gybing is far easier, but make sure the new sheet is reeved around the front of the forestay.

Asymmetric spinnakers are in some ways a development of the cruising chute for racing boats. They are usually tacked to a sliding pole, or bowsprit, which emerges straight out from the bow, allowing more sail area to be set.

Hoisting the spinnaker before the genoa is lowered helps to prevent the spinnaker from setting before the halyard is fully hoisted. Raising the genoa before lowering the spinnaker also helps make for lighter work.

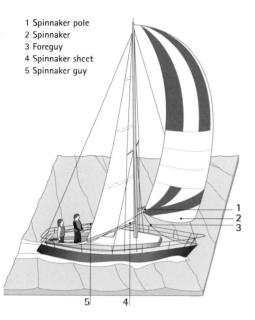

1 Spinnaker pole
2 Spinnaker
3 Foreguy
4 Spinnaker sheet
5 Spinnaker guy

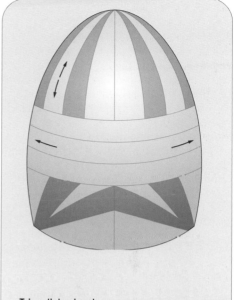

When cruising, the safest way to lower the spinnaker is to bring the boat round to a dead run and let the spinnaker guy go so that the pole goes up against the forestay. Ease the spinnaker boom lift to bring the pole within arm's reach.

The moment the crew forward unclips the spinnaker from the guy at the end of the pole, haul in the spinnaker sheet behind the mainsail, on the lee deck. Pay out the halyard at the same rate as the crew and gather in the sail.

Tri-radial spinnakers

The most common spinnaker is the tri-radial. It provides an efficient shape combined with a long life due to the fact that panels of cloth are cut in the directions of stress. Always be aware that spinnaker cloth is a lot less durable than normal sailcloth and care must be taken to ensure that it doesn't come into contact with sharp edges, particularly split pins or wire.

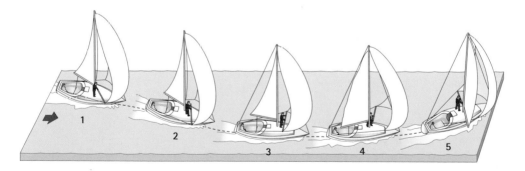

Gybing the spinnaker should be undertaken only with sufficient crew on board. When it is blowing hard and there are few hands on deck, it is worth considering lowering the spinnaker, gybing, and resetting it. End-for-end gybing is the best method for boats up to about 30 ft (9 m). Run off the wind until it is virtually dead aft and square the pole so that the sheet is let out as far as possible, 1. Unclip the inboard end of the pole, take it across and attach it to the sheet on the other side, 2. Unhook the outboard end from the original guy and push it across to attach it to the mast, 3. Gybe over the mainsail and, at the same time, pull in the old sheet (now the new guy) to draw the pole square across the boat, 4. Ease out the old guy (now the new sheet), 5.

LIGHT-WEATHER SAILING

Light-weather sailing can be satisfying and enjoyable. However, to make a boat move at a reasonable speed, the maximum sail area must be set and the weight of the sails kept down to a minimum.

Few yachts are fitted with a full wardrobe and, as a precaution, most tend to have more sails that are suitable for heavy weather. So when the wind is light, set the largest and lightest sail on the boat, such as a cruising chute or large genoa.

It can be frustrating to use the spinnaker in very light winds, especially downwind or if the boat is rolling, unless the spinnaker boom can be kept well forward by bringing the wind round on the quarter or beam, to prevent the sail collapsing.

A common mistake in light winds is to pull the sheets in too hard, particularly when going to windward. Instead they should be eased out until the boat points a further 10° off the wind than usual to get the boat moving. Both the mainsail and headsail halyards need to be slackened to produce more fullness in the sails. The mainsail will also fill and generate more power if the outhaul is eased off, the traveler brought to windward, and the boom pushed out at least 2¹/₂–3 ft (75–90 cm) away from the centerline. Adjust the twist of the sail using the sheet and the kicking strap/vang to take account of wind sheer.

The most effective way to get the boat moving is to sail free for a few minutes, then gradually head up so that the apparent wind increases, which will allow the boat to make way on its own created wind. Some momentum can be maintained if the crew sit on the leeward side. This encourages the boat to heel, and the sails to fill.

Light airs call for patience, a keen eye for signs of gathering clouds or increased wind on the water, and a gentle hand on the tiller.

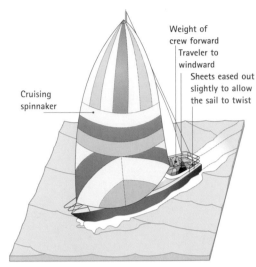

Cruising spinnaker

Weight of crew forward

Traveler to windward

Sheets eased out slightly to allow the sail to twist

On a calm day, there is likely to be more wind along the coast: the sea breeze starts to blow on to the land at about 11 a.m. If the early morning wind is off the land, the sea breeze will come in around noon. It blows hardest close to the land and tails off about 10 miles (16 km) out to sea, so it is worth hugging the coast to be sure of wind. This phenomenon is at its most powerful in late spring and early summer when the difference in temperature between the cold sea and the warmer land is greatest. At night, the sea breeze dies off and an hour or so later, the land breeze starts blowing off the land. Again it is strongest close to the shore and does not reach out quite as far as the sea breeze.

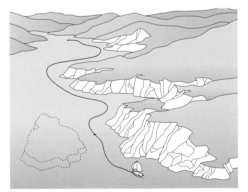

When coastal cruising, take advantage of the old saying, "the wind will always follow the sun." In the northern hemisphere, the sea breeze will veer (change direction) during the day, so that on a south-facing coast, it will go round to a south-westerly or even a westerly direction before dying away. In the southern hemisphere, it will back eastwards.

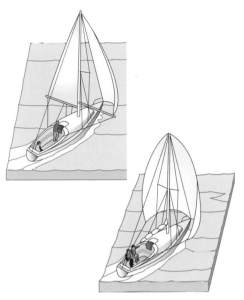

A **spinnaker** in use in light-weather conditions.

To create a large and firm sail area, pole out the No. 1 genoa on the opposite side to the mainsail. A boom preventer, running from the end of the boom to the foredeck, holds the mainsail to one side and prevents a gybe.

Another alternative for sailing dead downwind if you have two spinnaker or whisker poles on board, and a double luff groove up the forestay, is to sail "wing and wing." Two genoas, one set each side (goosewinged) are each poled out. Be careful if you try this in confined waters, because if a sudden change of course is needed, you'll have your hands full.

Motor sailers

If the sails will not fill, the only way to make any headway in still weather may be to use auxiliary power. With the sails up and the wind forward of the beam, speed can increase usefully with low engine revs. Using motor and sail simultaneously can also result in a saving of as much as 20 percent on fuel.

Motor sailers are designed specifically for this combined propulsion, although their performance in either mode is inferior to that of a yacht or a power boat. The advantages of the modern motor sailer for cruising are additional comfort and leisure, particularly for the less active, speedier passages and easy maneuverability.

Checklist for light-weather sailing

Bright sunlight and heat can affect an unconditioned crew, so watch out for symptoms such as headaches, tiredness, nausea, or fever and take action immediately.

1 To avoid sunstroke (symptoms are sickness and fever), wear a hat or keep the head wet. A wide-brimmed hat tied under the chin is advisable for young children.

2 To avoid dehydration (lethargy), make sure that a large quantity of non-alcoholic liquid is consumed. Salt must be taken during the day and is best taken with food or a little water rather than as salt pills.

3 Remember the reflection of the sun off the water speeds sunburn and that children have sensitive skin. Rinse salt off the skin and apply sunblock.

4 Use the easy conditions to teach children how to take the helm, tie knots, etc. Try to avoid focusing attention within the boat for too long. Make sure you keep an eye on the horizon to help avoid seasickness.

LEISURELY CRUISING

Long-distance cruising should be leisurely and enjoyable—so it helps to have a full crew to share the work. But most long-distance trips today are made short-handed, perhaps with only two or three people on board.

Even so, if thought has been given to the appropriate equipment and supplies, a small crew need not be overstretched. A good self-steering system, and the right food and water are a start.

For extensive sailing, the most popular rigs have been the ketch, yawl, and schooner as a wide range of small sails can be set, which reduces the strains and weight on any individual sail. However, improved sail-handling systems mean that many blue-water cruisers are now sloop rigged.

Roller-reefing gear is a useful and now almost universal addition. A maximum-sized genoa, which can be furled or reefed by one person, eliminates the need to both carry extra sails and change them each time the wind strength varies.

In-mast furling gear (see p. 60) fitted to the mainsail provides easy reefing and gives a wider choice of mainsail sizes.

On most long-distance trips you will encounter the trade winds, particularly on the Azores to West Indies route, known as the "milk run." As the trades blow from dead astern at Force 4 to 6, as much sail as possible should be set forward of the mast by booming out the headsails. These can both be set flying or with one hanked to the forestay.

Twin foresails hanked to a twin forestay and boomed out from the mast is another labor-saving and efficient system that works well, even in squally weather, since the sails balance each other. To counteract the roll of the boat, however, it is best to double-reef the mainsail and lash the boom amidships.

Autopilots

These will be tiller pilots, as shown below, or a permanent unit fitted to the wheel steering mechanism. They detect deviations from a pre-set compass course and move the helm one way or the other. Since they are powered by the boat's electrical system, the batteries need to be recharged every day by running the engine. Small solar panels, designed to recharge the batteries automatically, can now charge up to 4 or 5 amps. They need no upkeep, can be easily mounted on the deck, are flexible, and often nonslip.

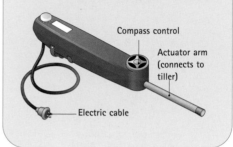

Compass control

Actuator arm (connects to tiller)

Electric cable

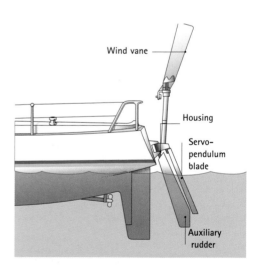

Wind vane

Housing

Servo-pendulum blade

Auxiliary rudder

Mechanical wind vanes, which need no extra source of power, provide the most reliable form of self-steering. Their one drawback is that when the wind direction alters, the boat's heading follows. Some types, such as that shown above, overcome this with a compass that holds the boat on course when the wind shifts. A servo-pendulum magnifies the wind direction data from the vane and turns a large auxiliary rudder.

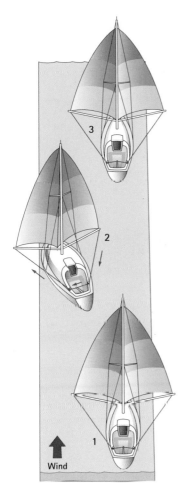

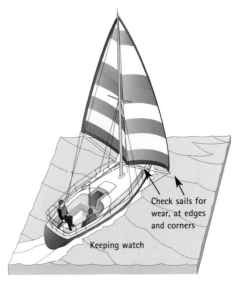

Check sails for wear, at edges and corners

Keeping watch

The times of watches depend on the number of crew and length of trip. Ideally, there should be two people on deck, but with only two on board, two hours on, two hours off is the normal maximum by night, with longer watches of three to four hours by day (see p. 212).

In the early days before self-steering gear, many sailors used various improvised systems. When running, the sheets of the boomed-out jibs can be taken back through blocks and lashed to the tiller or wheel, **1**. When the boat turns too far to port, **2**, the leeward or starboard sail flaps and takes the weight off the tiller line, automatically allowing it to swing to port so bringing the boat back on course, **3**. Similar, more old-fashioned systems, which link the sheets of the mainsail and jib to the tiller, can be used.

Checklist for leisurely cruising

1 You may wish to choose colored, not white, sails to prevent glare hurting the eyes.

2 Watch out for chafe caused by hard wear. Areas to watch on the rigging are the spreader ends, the back edges of the spreaders where the mainsail rubs, and also where the wire stays and shrouds attach to fittings. Baggywrinkles (plaited rope yarns) wrapped around the shrouds at the end of the spreaders or any area where the sails rub, are a safeguard against chafe.

3 Watch all sheets for fraying and turn end-to-end if the inside strands begin to wear. Ease or tighten the halyards every day to move the point at which they come out of the masthead. Carry extra maximum-length halyards to replace any that break.

4 Inspect sails regularly for stretch, chafe, mildew, ultraviolet damage, or frayed stitching.

5 Check for dried-out sealant around bolts or screws; it can cause leaks.

6 Run the engine periodically to recharge the batteries and to check that it is working. Carry spare parts for the self-steering gear. Check the bilges regularly.

7 To calculate the quantity of food to take, list consumption for an average week and multiply by the estimated number of weeks at sea, adding extra for emergencies.

REEFING FOR HEAVY WEATHER

Heavy weather is hard, challenging, and can be dangerous if you are not properly prepared. As most people do not seek it out, it is vital to ensure that every precaution is taken in advance and that the necessary safety equipment is always on board in case the unforeseen should happen.

First it is essential to reduce sail sufficiently and in good time to control the boat reasonably well. Reef the mainsail and change the headsail down, or take in a few rolls, to a sufficiently small size to withstand the anticipated wind strength.

The time to reef is as soon as it occurs to you that perhaps you should. If the boat is starting to feel overpowered and/or is sailing on its ear (leaning heavily), reef. If you wait for ten minutes to see if the wind eases, it will probably increase to spite you and the task of reefing will be that much harder.

In extreme weather a boat may often be safer in deep water with plenty of sea room, so it is sometimes wiser to grit your teeth and ride out a storm at sea than to risk trying to enter a harbor where the waves may be more treacherous, particularly if there are rocks, a bar, or an ebbing tide. Navigation may also be difficult if visibility is affected by the weather.

Often the biggest problem with heavy weather is that the crew gives up trying to cope with the difficult conditions before the boat. It is therefore vital that the boat is made as easy to handle as possible and the crew are properly provided for.

Efficient and easy-to-use reefing systems prove their worth in these circumstances.

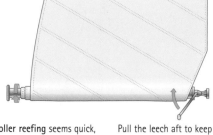

Roller reefing seems quick, neat and easy, but rarely gives you a well-set sail. To reef, release the halyard and remove the kicking strap from the boom.

Pull the leech aft to keep the foot wrinkle-free. A claw ring fitted over the reefed sail provides an attachment point for the kicking strap.

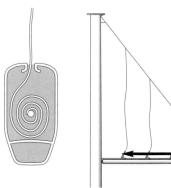

In-mast furling mainsail systems are common on cruising boats. There is a trade off in sail area as the sail cannot be properly battened so has little or no roach (curve from head to clew), although solutions are being sought. There is also a stability trade off as these systems add to the weight aloft.

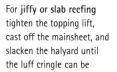

For jiffy or slab reefing tighten the topping lift, cast off the mainsheet, and slacken the halyard until the luff cringle can be

attached to a hook at the gooseneck. Pull on the reefing pendant, to pull the leech cringle to the boom, and cleat the line.

Tighten the halyard and release topping lift. Tie the loose sail using the reefing pendant.

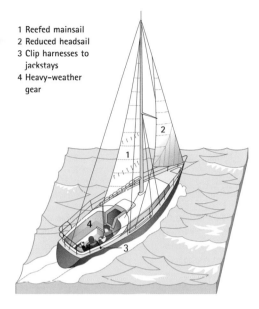

1 Reefed mainsail
2 Reduced headsail
3 Clip harnesses to jackstays
4 Heavy-weather gear

Clothing

The ideal heavy-weather clothing is warm but not bulky: a thermal suit next to the skin, a sweater and quilted jacket, and a good set of loose-fitting oilskins with elasticated or sealed wrists and waterproof pockets.

Most body heat is lost from the extremities, so keep them warm and dry with waterproof gloves that still allow the fingers to work shackles, knots, etc.; two pairs of knee-high socks, the inner pair of normal wool, the outer of water-repellent wool; and non-skid rubber boots. Wear a towel around the neck and a woollen or thermal material hat: wool takes longer than synthetics to become saturated, but also takes longer to dry.

- Woollen hat
- Scarf
- Sweater
- Snug wrists
- Gloves
- Waterproof jacket
- Warm trousers
- Oilskins
- Woollen socks
- Sailing boots

1 Reef early to avoid strain on the gear and crew.
2 Maintain the boat's balance by reefing the mainsail and jib in equal proportions. The feel of the helm will tell you if it is right
3 Sail close-hauled to bring the boom inboard when reefing.
4 Sail downwind to change the foresail. This keeps the deck drier and steadies the boat.

5 Clip harnesses to toe rails or jackstays to leave both hands free.
6 Stand to windward of the sail when reefing.
7 When points reefing, be sure not to confuse the points on one reef with those on another.
8 Shake out a reef by reversing the reefing procedure. Always untie reef points before the luff and leech.

A roller-reefing headsail saves sail changing. It is cut so that the sheets lead aft at a constant angle.

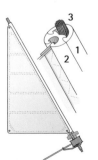

To convert a boat to roller reefing, a headfoil, with attached drum, 1, and a groove for the headsail luff, 2, is fitted around the forestay, 3.

To reef a genoa, usually No. 2 to a No. 3, attach both sheets to a higher cringle. Fix the parallel luff cringle to the bow fitting, tie the points, and re-hoist.

RIDING OUT A STORM

Techniques for handling a boat in heavy weather depend on its design. Some will heave to, others lie better a-hull; some will ride to a sea anchor, and some have to run before the wind. The only way to find out the best method for your boat is to try it out.

Some of the most seaworthy boats ever designed for heavy-weather sailing were the Bristol pilot cutters. They had the ability to heave to under a staysail only and, as they were very long-keeled, could lie to a sea anchor. A short-keeled boat will sail over the top of the anchor and can cause the anchor warp to foul the propeller or the rudder.

In a modern cruising boat, it may not be possible to lash down the tiller and heave to under a staysail with much safety, so it is advisable to sail the boat at about 80° off the wind, slowly, with just enough steerage way to luff up or bear away to avoid the worst of the waves.

If the wind becomes uncomfortably strong and you have sufficient sea room, it is often best to run before the wind under bare poles or with a storm jib. Although small, the storm jib that hanks to the forestay does help to control the boat. It gives a little steerage way, and often reduces the rolling of the boat.

When it is really blowing hard, the circumstances often dictate the best course of action. If the gale is blowing along the course you want to take, it is possible to sail downwind at a reasonable speed under a storm jib.

Although noisy and uncomfortable, lying a-hull is often a safe way to ride out a bad storm. This is simply a question of lowering sails, lashing the boom to the deck so it cannot move, sealing up all the hatches and going below until the storm passes. The tiller must be lashed to leeward so that the boat is always trying to come into the wind. It will make 1.1–2.2 mph (1–2 kn) downwind and probably a little headway.

Breaking waves pose the greatest threat to a boat in heavy weather. A freak wave in a bad ocean storm can cause a boat to pitchpole, stern over bow. Pooping, when a wave breaks over the stern and fills the cockpit, is a more likely hazard. To prevent this, slow the boat and keep the main hatchway closed.

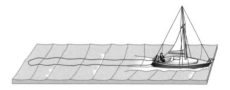

When running before a storm, or approaching a lee shore, the boat's headway can be reduced by streaming warps over the stern. Five or six 180 ft (30 fm) warps, joined together and towed in a loop in the boat's wake, will slow the boat and may prevent pooping.

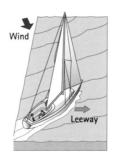

To heave to, ease the mainsail, back the headsail, and lash the tiller to leeward. The boat will sail slowly, making a lot of leeway. Yawls and ketches may lie better under mizzen only.

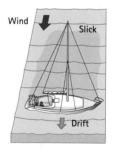

Lying a-hull under bare poles with the helm lashed to leeward, the boat finds its natural angle to the wind. The hull moves to leeward, creating a slick on the weatherside to smooth the sea.

1 Storm trysail
2 Hatches closed
3 Personal flotation
  devices (PFDs or life
  jackets) and heavy-
  weather clothing
4 Stowed mainsail
5 Jackstays

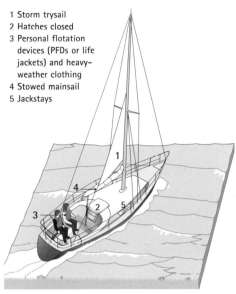

Anchors

A canvas sea anchor is streamed from the boat by a long warp (never chain) and, ideally, a slack tripping line, even though it may tangle with the warp.
A Bruce anchor can also prove light enough to make an efficient sea anchor, but only in deep water.

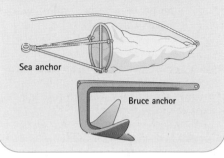

Sea anchor

Bruce anchor

The trysail, when combined with the storm jib, helps to stabilize the boat in even the strongest winds. Often neglected, since the conditions make it difficult to rig any sail, the trysail nevertheless allows the mainsail to be lowered completely. It is fed into the mast above the furled mainsail, via the sail track gate. It is set loosefooted and sheeted down to either side of the boat, like a jib. To withstand the wind force, the sail is reinforced, particularly at the corners, and triple-stitched along the seams.

Checklist for riding out a storm

At the first sign of heavy weather, or when gale warnings are issued (indicating a Force 8), start preparing for a storm.
1 Double check that everything is well stowed below and lash down anything loose on deck, including the tender. Fasten cockpit lockers. It is a good discipline to imagine the boat upside down.
2 Make sure the boat is watertight. Close and fasten all the hatches. Close the ventilators. Turn off the seacocks to the sink and toilet.
3 Rig the jackstays and issue personal flotation devices (PFDs or life jackets) and safety harnesses to each crew member, although this should be done before any voyage.
4 Make sure all the crew take seasickness precautions, put on extra clothing, and have a good meal before the heavy weather arrives, in case the wind takes several hours to subside. Prepare hot drinks or soups in a Thermos.
5 Make sail changes in good time. Have stormsails and flares ready.
6 Clear cockpit drains. Ensure the bilge pump works. Run the engine from time to time.
7 Listen to the shipping forecasts.
8 Keep an eye on the boat's position and a good lookout on deck.
9 Organize a strict rotation of watches (see p. 212).

Wind

Drift

Wind

Drift

With a sea anchor streamed from the bow and a riding sail set on its mizzen mast, a ketch will lie close to the wind and drift to leeward. Sternway, however, may strain the rudder.

A sea anchor streamed from the stern allows the boat to follow its inclination to head downwind. It may prevent a broach, but could hold the boat too tight and stop it riding the waves smoothly.

RULES OF RACING

When taking part in a boat race, the participants agree to be subject to the racing rules, which take the place of International Regulations for Preventing Collisions at sea, or "Col Regs" as they are called (see pp. 124–125). The racing rules are produced by the International Sailing Federation (ISAF), in which each country is represented by its national authority. They are revised every four years. They are based largely on the "Col Regs" but differ from them in several important respects, particularly when boats are rounding marks or obstructions. When a boat that is racing meets a boat that is not, the "Col Regs" apply to both of them.

A boat when racing is bound by the racing rules from the time she intends to race until she has left the vicinity of the course. However, she can normally be penalized for breaking a rule only when the incident occurs after the preparatory signal (usually five minutes before the start of the race) and before crossing the finishing line.

A boat that touches a mark of the course during a race may exonerate herself by sailing well clear of other participants and making a complete 360° turn. A boat involved in an incident with another boat that accepts that she is to blame may sail clear and make two complete penalty turns, known as a "720 penalty." When neither accepts the blame for an incident, one or both may "protest" by shouting "protest" and by prominently displaying a red flag, and leaving it displayed until the end of the race.

The protesting boat must then submit a written protest to the race committee, explaining her grounds for doing so.

For most match racing events, such as the America's Cup where only two identical boats are racing, there are umpires in an umpire boat that accompany the competitors, and they respond immediately to any claim by one boat that the other has infringed a rule. When a protest occurs the umpires

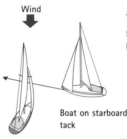

Wind

Boat on starboard tack

Boat on port tack

The boat on the port tack should keep clear of the boat on the starboard tack.

Windward boat

Leeward boat

When two boats on the same tack are overlapped, the leeward boat has right of way over the windward boat.

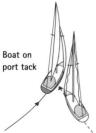

Boat on port tack

Boat on starboard tack should not alter course

A boat that holds right of way must not alter course to hinder another boat that is keeping clear.

Tacking boat

Boat on a tack

A boat that is tacking should keep clear of one that is not. When two boats are tacking at the same time, the boat on the port side should keep clear. A boat should not tack into a position that will give her right of way if it causes a give-way boat to alter course before the tack is complete.

display a green and white flag when no penalty is necessary or a blue or yellow flag to indicate which boat must take a penalty turn. The penalty has to be taken after starting even if the incident

occurred before the start, but can usually be taken any time before the finish of the race. Umpires are also now used on the water in some short offshore events in which ocean racers take part.

Outside boat must keep clear

When rounding a mark or passing an obstruction, the outside boat must give room to the inside boat. However, when two boats are on opposite tacks at a windward mark, the port tack boat keeps clear of the one on the starboard tack.

When a give-way boat does not keep clear, and there is a collision involving damage, the right-of-way boat may be disqualified as well as the give-way boat if she could have taken avoiding action but did not do so.

Leeward boat

A leeward boat has the right to protect her wind by luffing to windward. If she does so she will give the windward boat room to keep clear.

The two **International America's Cup Class yachts** *Team New Zealand* and the Italian challenger, *Prada*, racing neck and neck during Race 5 of the America's Cup held in Auckland.

ENGINE BASICS

When choosing an engine the basic decision for most pleasurecraft owners is between gasoline and diesel. Gasoline engines are lighter, smoother, less noisy, and cheaper than diesel but they use expensive, potentially dangerous fuel, and need reliable electrical ignition systems. Diesel engines use a smelly but cheaper fuel and can remain reliable, despite periods of non-use. Few gasoline engines are fitted as standard today.

Both types are available in 2- and 4-stroke form; 2-strokes are lighter and use more fuel, and are generally employed where light weight is important. Thus 2-stroke gasoline outboards are often used for small, fast sports boats, and 2-stroke diesels in large, fast motor yachts.

The next consideration is the type of drive. The traditional, straight drive system uses a propeller installed permanently under the boat and connected more or less directly by a shaft to an engine fitted inside the hull. This has the advantage of simplicity, but the propeller may be vulnerable and hard to get at. If the boat is of a size to take the ground regularly, or to be trailed, it may be much more sensible to fit an inboard/outboard drive. On boats under about 25 ft (7.6 m), it is probably much easier to fit an outboard gasoline engine, clear of the accommodation.

An increasingly common and inexpensive installation in lightweight sailing boats is the sail drive (see p. 71), where a gasoline or diesel inboard engine is mounted through the hull bottom on a fixed outboard-type leg. Stern drives are used for power boats.

Two other factors should influence choice. Remember that the bigger and heavier a boat is, the bigger the propeller needed, regardless of the speed and power of the engine. Secondly, maintenance is important if you desire a high-performance and long-lasting engine. If you seldom use your boat choose outboard gasoline or inboard diesel.

Outboard engines are convenient and cheap for smaller boats, the lower maintenance costs offsetting the heavier fuel consumption. Bracket mountings usually allow them to be lifted clear when sailing or even stowed below decks.

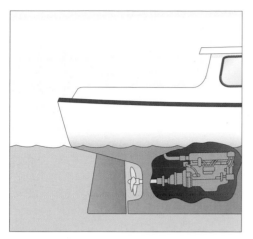

The straight drive is the simplest installation, with minimum loss of power. The engine is connected directly to a shaft and propeller, which can be well protected from damage in an aperture, above, or in the open, supported by one or two shaft brackets.

Crowded marinas and harbors, like The Hamble (UK) pictured here, make an auxiliary engine essential.

Propeller operation

A marine propeller works by the action of each blade creating thrust from its aerofoil-type section along the line of the shaft—in a similar way to an airplane propeller.

The slim two-bladed propeller is slow moving, like a glider, and gives highly efficient thrust for small power. It is, therefore, used for comparatively large hulls driven by small engines, and usually needs a reduction gear to reduce shaft speed.

With more power, the blade area has to increase and, with faster engine speeds, it is necessary to reduce the overall diameter to prevent too fast a tip speed: the resultant need for blade area has led to the three-bladed propeller, often with quite broad blades.

Three-blade propeller   Two blade propeller

The effect of centrifugal action throws the blades of a folding propeller out into their working position when the shaft is turned. The blades of variable pitch propellers can be set in a number of positions, usually including reverse and a feathered position to reduce drag.

Folding propeller   Variable pitch propeller

HOW MUCH POWER?

The power required to drive a boat at any given practical speed increases with its weight, and for the same weight, decreases with length. The potential maximum or economical cruising speed varies greatly with the type of hull.

Heavy displacement hulls—some motor launches and most older-style sailing yachts—are limited by the wave train they set up around themselves, and are at maximum speed when traveling essentially on one wave. Modern light displacement sailing boats and faster launches are shaped so as not to build up stern suction at speed. This means more power can be used to drive the hull up and on top of the single wave, so that it is partially supported by the effect of speed as well as buoyancy. Beyond this semi-planing range, boats shaped and powered for it can climb over the single wave until the bow drops and they plane along, supported more by water pressure than buoyancy.

Whatever the hull, a quite modest increase in speed can require a great deal of extra power and fuel. However, in deciding the engine power needed, some further allowances must be made. First, to meet local conditions, such as tide races, where extra speed may make the difference between getting home or not. Second, windage and rough seas increase hull resistance anything from 10–50 percent, and extra power may be needed to compensate where these factors are important. Again, if high speed is important, 10 percent drop-off in output must be allowed for as the engine gets older. High ambient temperatures can cause a drop of up to 15 percent.

Any increase in engine power must be taken into account in the propeller design, since the extra loading from wind and seas may cause a breakdown of the flow over the blades, and may necessitate an even greater power allowance.

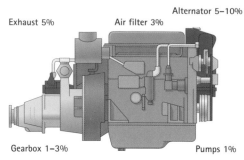

Exhaust 5% Air filter 3% Alternator 5–10%

Gearbox 1–3% Pumps 1%

Listed engine output is usually given for a standard engine with essential accessories, in ideal conditions. In practice, the climate is not likely to be ideal and the fuel may have less caloric value. Power will also be taken from the engine by the generator and any pumps, etc. There will be further losses in a reduction gearbox and from bearings and glands. The propeller will have a propulsive efficiency of about 50 percent.

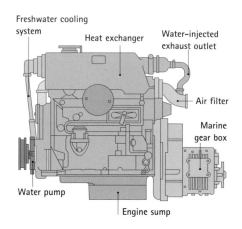

Freshwater cooling system
Heat exchanger
Water-injected exhaust outlet
Air filter
Marine gear box
Water pump
Engine sump

The true marine engine has a large, heavy cast iron block with wide galleries to prevent caked salt obstructing the saltwater cooling system. Although reliable, such engines are much less economical than an automotive engine adapted for marine life. Marinizing entails replacing all the aluminum castings with marine-grade aluminum alloy, and arranging a closed-circuit fresh water cooling system, cooled in turn by pumped saltwater. Other changes involve redesigning the engine sump, fitting a marine gear box and exhaust elbow, and adjusting the carburetors or injectors.

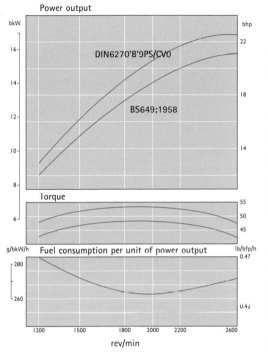

Power output

Torque

Fuel consumption per unit of power output

rev/min

Speed potential

Differing power requirements for boats can be compared by taking the square root of the waterline length as a proportion of the speed. A displacement hull will be powered economically at $\sqrt{v}/L$ of about 1.0 (5.7 mph or 5 kn/25 ft or 7.6 m WL) with a maximum speed potential of about 1.5 (8.6 mph or 7.5 kn/25 ft or 7.6 m WL). A semi-planing hull has the same economical speed but maximum potential up to 3.5 (20 mph or 17.5 kn). A planing boat will have a speed potential from 23 mph (20 kn) up and, as it will have got over the "hump" in climbing its wave, has an economical cruising speed of 25.3 mph (22 kn), or possibly more.

Typical engine sizes fitted on new boats

Length (ft)	Displacement (lb)		Engine (hp)
16	900	1800	2–4
20	1250	6000	4–8
25	4000	10000	6–12
30	8000	18000	10–30
35	14000	25000	20–40

Electrolysis

Any metal object in saltwater or even in a salt atmosphere takes up a particular value of electrical potential. An electrical current is set up with any other metal object of a different potential through the salt electrolyte, and the natural circuits can be greatly increased by electrical currents from the boat's fittings. The flow is from the high potential, or cathodic, item to the low potential, or anodic, fitting, which is subject to corrosive attack. The potential of different metals can be listed in a galvanic table, with stainless steel, titanium, and nickel near the cathodic end and aluminum alloys and zinc near the anodic end. Any metal will deteriorate in saltwater in the presence of one of higher potential. Lumps of low-potential metal, such as zinc, are often fitted to hulls as sacrificial anodes to attract corrosive forces away from more valuable items such as bronze or aluminum propellers.

Power curves in makers' brochures give maximum output over the range of revolutions. The top curve shows how power is developed as engine revolutions increase. The middle graph shows the range of revolutions over which the engine delivers the most torque. The lower graph marries fuel consumption to revolutions. It can be seen that at about 2,000 RPM the engine develops high torque for low fuel consumption.

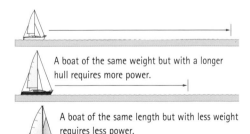

A boat of the same weight but with a longer hull requires more power.

A boat of the same length but with less weight requires less power.

The heavier of two boats of the same size and windage requires more power to reach a specific speed. For craft of the same weight, hull length is the governing factor, the shorter boat needing more.

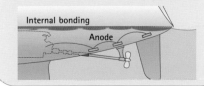

Internal bonding

Anode

ENGINE INSTALLATIONS

Most engines and installations start out as reliable units, but they need protection and maintenance if they are to remain so. Good access to all parts is, therefore, important.

The majority of engines are fitted on flexible mountings, since it is not practicable in light boats to provide the massive bearers necessary to absorb vibration. As the engine itself is vibrating freely, the connections to it must also be free to flex. The propeller shaft too has to absorb the movement, usually by a short intermediate shaft fitted between two flexible couplings. However, if the engine is infrequently used, a flexible stern gland, sometimes with a flexible coupling, can be a successful compromise.

Safety in the fuel systems starts with electrical grounding of the filler plate and tank and fuel lines, to eliminate the possibility of sparks from static electricity. The fuel piping should be strong and well protected, and the flexible connection to the engine should have a five minute fire rating. Cut-off cocks for the tank should be easy to reach from outside the machinery space. Marine fuel is often dirty and contaminated with condensation, so fuel lines must have big filters and tanks must be cleared of water regularly.

Some engines are air cooled, but most use a pumped sea water supply with an inter-cooler to cool a fresh-water system. Some or all of this water can be injected into the exhaust to cool and silence it.

Exhaust lines must be looped up high or fitted with water traps to ensure that sea water cannot run back into the engine, despite heeling, and cooling-water outlet pipes must have special valves for the same reason.

All engines need plenty of air, both for consumption and for cooling, and a power fan should be installed to increase circulation in the engine compartment, if necessary.

Flexible mountings

Most engines are fitted on flexible mountings to insulate the hull from noise and vibration. The type of mounting, 3, is chosen to suit the vibration characteristics of the engine and varies from hard to quite soft. Other connections must suit this free movement, eg., shaft arrangements, 1, vary from a single flexible coupling, 2, to twin universal joints with an intermediate cardan shaft. Usually a thrust bearing is needed on the propeller shaft to take the load off the mounts. Pipe connections for fuel and water need a final flexible section; those for the exhaust are usually made with a bellows joint.

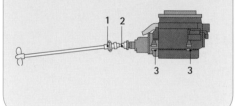

Exhaust systems

Exhaust lines usually inject engine cooling-water into a high elbow close to the manifold by means of a self-draining pipe, sometimes with a muffler, to an external outlet. Water injection silences and cools, reducing the need for elaborate insulation. When the exhaust is discharged through the bottom, close to the engine, using a small auxiliary exhaust pipe to prevent back pressure affecting the engine, the exhaust smell on deck is reduced.

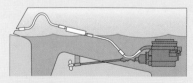

Wet exhaust: engine below waterline

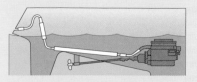

Dry exhaust: engine below waterline

The modern diesel engine is still comparatively large, heavy, and slow running. It needs heavy mountings, shaft and propeller, a well-maintained fuel system, and good sound insulation. Care should be taken to prevent the diesel smell from pervading the boat.

Stainless steel or **ungalvanized mild steel tanks** are usually fitted, as diesel attacks zinc coating. The supply line is taken from a bottom sump to avoid airlocks.

Easily changed **duplex-type filters**—more than the engine-maker requires—should be used.

Water separators help to protect against condensation in both shore supply and the boat's own tanks.

Ideally, **fuel lines** should be solid, and clipped to sturdy structures, to reduce movement. Ensure that any joins are low and airtight.

High-compression engines need plenty of air, preferably trunked to the air inlet, with a fan sucking more air into the engine room itself.

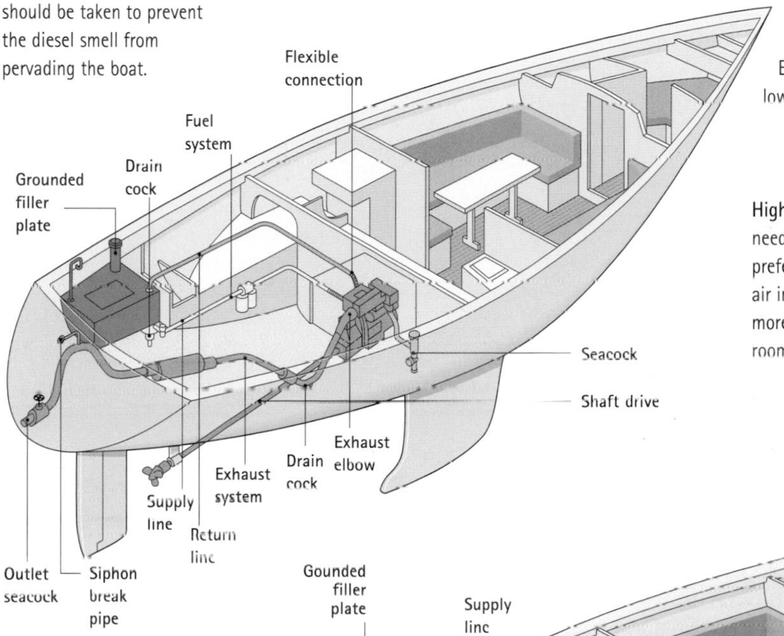
Flexible connection
Fuel system
Grounded filler plate
Drain cock
Seacock
Shaft drive
Exhaust elbow
Drain cock
Exhaust system
Supply line
Return line
Outlet seacock
Siphon break pipe

Saildrive units are popular aboard modest sized cruisers as they are easier to fit, require considerably less maintenance, and usually run much more quietly and with less vibration than conventional prop shaft-type systems. Saildrives have their propeller units mounted directly to the underside of the engine with the complete installation sitting on conventional engine mounts. A rubber gasket where the prop unit penetrates the hull prevents water from flooding into the boat.

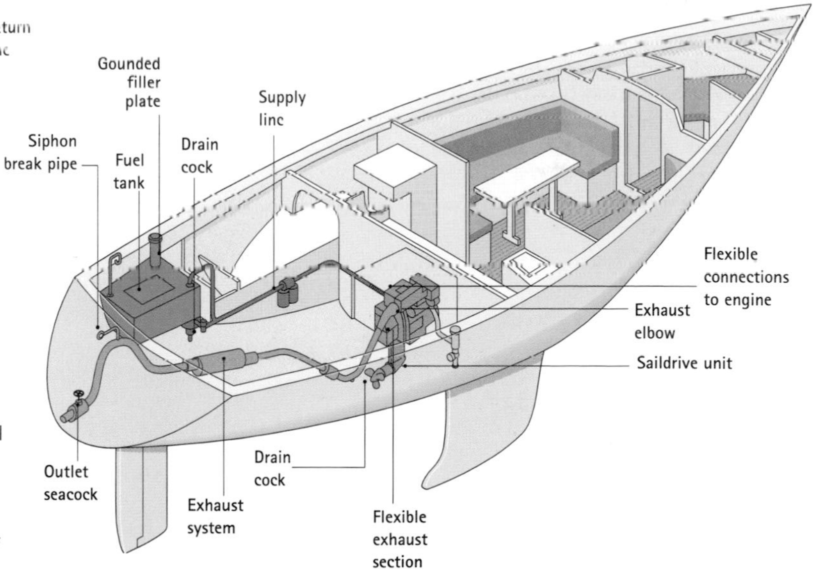
Gounded filler plate
Supply line
Siphon break pipe
Fuel tank
Drain cock
Flexible connections to engine
Exhaust elbow
Saildrive unit
Outlet seacock
Drain cock
Exhaust system
Flexible exhaust section

For minimum drag, **propeller shafts** are made thin, often of aluminum bronze or stainless steel. Shaft bearings are commonly rubber, and water-lubricated.

Most engines are cooled by filtered saltwater. Some use a **heat exchanger** arrangement to a closed-circuit freshwater system in the engine.

Install batteries carefully: they contain sulphuric acid and give off explosive hydrogen when charged. Too much engine heat reduces their life.

HANDLING UNDER POWER

Boats are generally used under power in crowded anchorages and marinas, or when sea or weather conditions are difficult, so it is essential to know how your craft will handle.

Any boat hull slides through the water and rarely goes exactly forward or backward; it is also susceptible to the effects of wind, sea, and tide. Although the hull is turned slightly by the movement of the rudder, it is the increased water pressure, induced by this movement on one side of the bow or keel, which produces the greatest turning moment. Under power, this effect can be boosted by the strong thrust of the propeller jet stream, deflected to one side by the rudder.

When turning slowly in close quarters, a quick burst of power against the rudder will swing the boat without producing much headway. Also useful at such times is the paddle-wheel or prop walk effect of the propeller, which makes the turn appreciably tighter in one direction than the other.

The mechanics of steering astern are the same as those for ahead, and a good astern-steering form must have suitable hull surfaces. The modern sailing boat with a fin keel is usually particularly good. The effect of the propeller stream is much reduced but the prop walk can prove useful.

In really bad weather, the boat under power alone is best motoring slowly into the wind and sea. In gale force conditions, when you have to run with the waves, you may have to go astern occasionally to prevent the boat broaching.

The boat under sail can improve its state by running the engine, even quite slowly. In light airs, an extra push from the engine will dramatically improve the airflow by increasing the apparent wind.

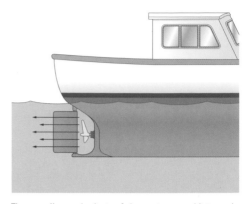

The propeller needs plenty of clear water around it to work efficiently. This means that it should have the minimum of hull obstruction in front of it and that the blade tips should have good clearance from the hull.

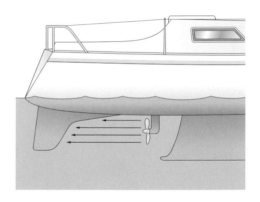

A modern sailing boat is very easily steered. The propeller is only required for propulsion. In a less maneuverable vessel, such as a heavy long-keeled boat, the propeller jet stream should pass the rudder to improve steering.

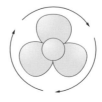

A propeller that rotates clockwise walks the stern to the right unless counteracted by gentle rudder action.

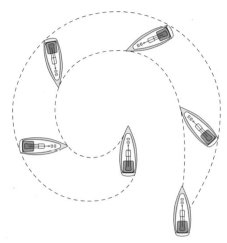

Turning circles vary from boat to boat, and from port to starboard, depending on hull steering qualities, propeller rotation, and thrust deflection. At full speed, most modern boats will turn in two boat-lengths. A boat slips side-ways as it turns, but it will, typically, behave as shown in the illustration above.

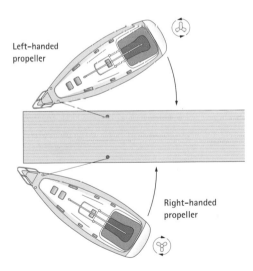

Left-handed propeller

Right-handed propeller

A propeller that turns clockwise when viewed from aft is termed right-handed; one that turns anticlockwise is left-handed. Most gasoline engines have right-handed propellers, and many diesel engines left-handed propellers. A propeller tends to paddle the stern of the boat in the direction in which it turns. In both docking positions shown above, the boat is brought alongside by using propeller thrust deflected by the rudder.

Engine failure

Most engine failures result from fuel contamination, a blockage in the water-cooling system, or the effects of a line caught around the propeller. If unable to carry on under sail, the boat should be anchored for repairs, and the engine switched off. A propeller can sometimes be freed if one person, well aft, pulls hard on the line while another turns the fly-wheel in the right direction by hand. When anchoring is impractical, a drifting boat can employ windage and tidal streams to retain some control over the direction of drift; tide against wind can be used to push the boat far enough sideways to reach shallower water or avoid an obstruction.

In a flat calm and strong tide, the anchor or any weight can be lowered until it just drags along the bottom, slowing the rate of drift. The tidal flow past the hull can then be used to slew it around bows on to the current, and induce a line of drift with a strong sideways effect.

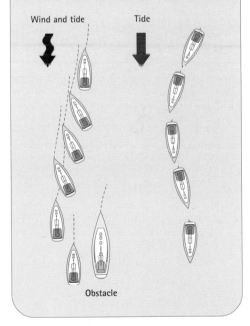

Wind and tide   Tide

Obstacle

CRUISING

CHOOSING A CRUISER

Your choice of boat will depend on where you plan to keep it and what you aim to do with it. Deep-water marina berthing, for example, imposes different requirements than shallow or drying moorings, and the boat that needs four experienced people to handle it would not suit a couple with three young children. Since moorings are in high demand in many areas, it is wise to confirm the availability of a mooring before buying a boat—or to buy a suitable second-hand boat, complete with a mooring.

Trailer sailers overcome this problem, but to be big enough for open-water cruising, say 25 ft (7.6 m) as an absolute minimum, they are normally so cumbersome and time consuming to rig that launching and recovery become daunting tasks. Furthermore, a substantial towing vehicle is required.

Long-keeled hulls are often regarded as the traditional choice for a cruising boat, but while they tend to keep the course well, they are also heavy to turn. Modern hulls, with long fin keels and a separate rudder, can be just as stable as long-keeled hulls, but much lighter to steer and more maneuverable.

If you need a boat that handles well going astern, a spade rudder is better than a rudder supported on a skeg. The skeg type, however, is usually stronger and better protected when sailing or motoring ahead, which represents 99 percent of the boat's cruising time. The remaining 1 percent spent reversing can be embarrassing, however, if things go wrong.

Cruising catamarans often pay higher rates in marinas, but can moor in shallower waters. They should give quicker and smoother passage times than monohulls of the same length.

The fin keel is the normal design for a modern performance cruiser. The fin must be long enough, fore and aft, to support the boat when drying out against a wall in a number of European harbors. The rudder may be of spade type, shown above, or mounted on a skeg.

The twin keel takes $^2/_3$–$^3/_4$ of the water depth needed for a fin keel. But it will stand upright only if the bottom is hard and level. It is noisy to windward due to water slamming under the hull and will not sail as well as a fin keel version.

The lifting keel boat opens up possibilities for new sheltered cruising grounds and shallow moorings. Drafts can be reduced dramatically when the keel is raised and this also provides an easy way of freeing the boat if grounded.

The long-keeled hull usually has lots of storage space, but heavy displacement tends to make it slower and heavier to maneuver than other types, and it demands a more powerful rig to drive it. It has, nevertheless, a comfortable motion.

Trailer tips

Try to avoid putting wheels in the water because if salt-water gets into the hubs the bearings will be ruined. Furthermore, by the time the boat can float free, the trailer may be so deep in the water that the towing vehicle must be unhitched and a rope used to join the two together. The best solution is to carry a wheeled cradle on a tipping section of the trailer. The cradle may also fit some standard car-recovery trailers, should you not want to purchase a trailer initially. The boat must be very well secured to the trailer and everything carried aboard must be padded against chafe when on the road. Even a 22 ft (6.7 m) boat will require a powerful car (say 2$^1/_2$ liter engine) to pull it, and remember the clutch has a hard life. You must allow for on-board stores when calculating weight—and don't go anywhere without a spare wheel.

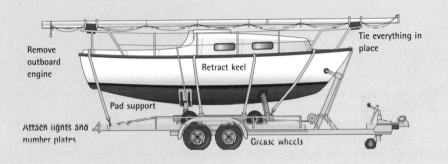

Remove outboard engine

Retract keel

Tie everything in place

Pad support

Attach lights and number plates

Grease wheels

Multihulls

The motion of a multihull is quicker than in a monohull, but the boat rolls through a smaller angle. A major attraction of multihulls is that it offers more accommodation. However, it is easier to capsize a catamaran than a trimaran when under sail, although in severe conditions, if the boat is just left to drift, the opposite may be true. Experience will tell how much sail the boat can carry safely. Multihulls offer fast passages, ample deck space, shallow draft, and level drying out—which few monohulls can match. The speed advantage—say 8 mph (7 kn) against 5.75 mph (5 kn) may not sound much, but in a 60 mile (96 km) passage it could save 3$^1/_2$ hrs and mean an easy daylight arrival. Further, if confronted with a 1.75 mph (1$^1/_2$ kn) adverse tide, a 20 mile (32 km) passage would take 3 hrs 40 mins against 5 hrs 40 mins. In very light airs, however, the multihull may well be slower.

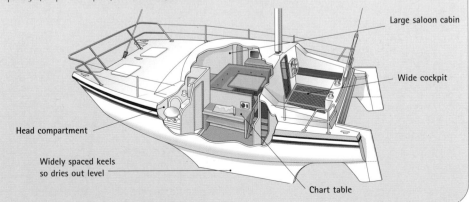

Large saloon cabin

Wide cockpit

Head compartment

Widely spaced keels so dries out level

Chart table

LAYOUT BELOW DECK

Below deck a minimum of sitting headroom is essential, though a little more height makes it easier to get dressed and move around. There should be good handholds for safe movement—always two within reach from any point—and lee cloths or lee boards on bunks to allow the crew to sleep comfortably in the windward berths while on passage.

There needs to be room for all except the watchkeepers to rest without using the berths forward of the mast since these normally suffer too much motion at sea. This may limit the size of your crew for a passage, but there is no fun in forcing people to grow cold and tired in the cockpit due to lack of space below.

The more people there are, the more gear and stores must be stowed. Sleeping bags and clothes take up a surprising amount of space, even when packed into soft waterproof holdalls. It is best to allocate each person a locker that can be reached at sea without disturbing a sleeper when warmer clothes are required. All lockers must be dry or clothes must be kept in sealed polyurethane bags. Oilskins are best hung up inside out to drip without causing annoyance; the head (toilet compartment) is often a good place if there is no wet locker.

The most convenient position for the head is aft by the hatchway as it saves struggling through the saloon—an advantage for anyone suffering from seasickness. The galley and navigation area also need to be near the hatch, so a compromise may be necessary.

Ideally, lighting should include fluorescents for working areas, such as the galley, to allow plenty of light with little battery drain. Bunk lights provide less harsh lighting elsewhere. Galley lights should be colored red or be well shaded so that they do not shine out into the cockpit.

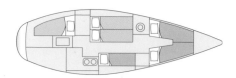

Ideas on the layout for a boat evolve with changes in fashion and the ability of the designers to find new ways of using the space available. A conventional layout for a cruising boat of about 30 ft (9 m), shown above, includes more berths than can be used comfortably while under way. These are useful when moored or for a long stay. The boat is wide enough to allow access to the fore-cabin past the head.

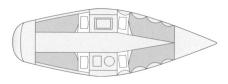

The layout of a racing boat is intended to keep weight out of the ends of the boat, so that it performs well in a seaway, while providing secure sleeping berths for brief snatches off watch. Total weight and thus comfort are kept to a minimum. Even the navigator may be expected to work with primitive facilities.

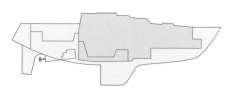

Headroom usually decreases as you move forward, due to hull shape and the angle of the coach/cabin trunk roof and deck. Flatter-bottomed, more performance orientated boats have less depth below water than traditional boats, so they must have a high coachroof or sides to provide acceptable standing room. Even more important than headroom is space to lean back comfortably against the saloon back rests.

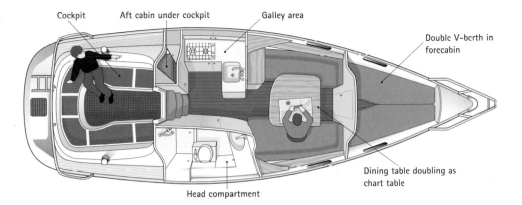

Cockpit   Aft cabin under cockpit   Galley area

Double V-berth in forecabin

Dining table doubling as chart table

Head compartment

This is a typical 33 ft (10 m) **cruising boat layout.** The cockpit should be spacious enough for the whole crew. It should be roomy below deck, with good headroom and a feeling of space. The raised dinette table seats four. The table should have good fiddles to stop the plates sliding off and, ideally, a separate central storage area for various items, such as salt, jam, etc. The dinette arrangement allows for a double berth in the saloon, with the table lowered to seat level with backrest cushions on top. For those who prefer more privacy, the forepeak affords a comfortable double berth when moored, but would not be used under way. At least one additional cabin will be available aft, which extends below the cockpit. Stowage is mainly under the bunks in dry, well-lined lockers.

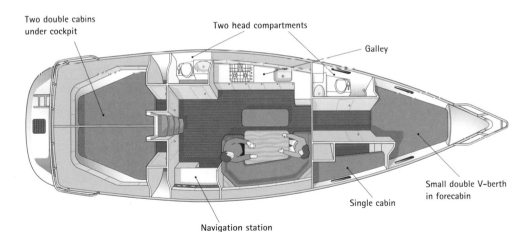

Two double cabins under cockpit

Two head compartments

Galley

Small double V-berth in forecabin

Single cabin

Navigation station

A larger boat can make different use of the space. The cockpit is designed so that, when seated, it is comfortable to brace yourself against the opposite seat when the boat heels. This internal layout has more volume, with its capacious saloon and uncluttered arrangement. It sleeps six comfortably in three cabins. In the saloon the couch opens out into a double bed, providing two further berths while still leaving a single couch and a large quarter berth. The forecabin provides an ideal berth for two children. The galley is well situated by the main hatchway to allow good ventilation.

THE GALLEY AND HEAD

Galley lighting needs to be bright, obscured from the cockpit, and well placed to provide good illumination over the cooker, worktop, and sink. The cooker requires a heat shield above it and must be gimballed or have high fiddles for use at sea. A strap is essential to keep the cook secure in a seaway, while leaving both hands free for work.

Sink drains need to be large, but it is best to wash up in a bowl because the sink plug can be pushed out by the pressure as the boat negotiates large waves, allowing your hot soapy water to vanish. Water consumption is always a problem in boats and pressure systems positively encourage overuse. A seawater hand pump in the galley helps to preserve precious freshwater, since much food preparation can be done in saltwater. It is also a good plan to involve the cook when water containers have to be carried in harbor!

Increasingly, electric fridges are fitted, although these do drain the battery quickly. Use space below the galley floor for cold stowage of vegetables and drinks.

When buying food for an organized menu, remember to include stocks of dry food—biscuits, nuts, fruit, chocolate, cheese, and cake—for convenient sustenance in bad weather. Simple hot drinks are always welcome, but soups are more nutritious and keep hot longer than coffee in cold weather. A pressure cooker, ideally an automatic one, saves gas, time, and a lot of dish washing. Contrary to popular belief, eggs last for weeks, and canned butter will keep indefinitely until opened. If canned food is to be stored in a potentially wet area, write an abbreviated or coded description on the top of the can and remove the label. It may float off later, choke the bilge pump, and give rise to countless mystery meals.

The head, so called because it was traditionally located at the bow, or head, of a boat, needs good handholds and permanent ventilation. Easily accessible inlet and outlet seacocks are also important as water tends to syphon back when the boat heels if these are not closed.

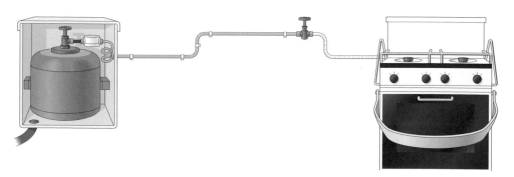

Meticulous care must be taken when **installing a gas system** to avoid explosions. Flexible pipes should be kept very short and replaced at the first sign of deterioration. If at all possible the rigid pipe should be kept in one length, but if a branch pipe must be taken to a heater,

for example, check the joints periodically. As gas is heavier than air, a drain overboard must run from the bottom of the locker. There must be easy access for disconnecting and changing the bottle, and a valve shut-off near the stove and at the bottle. Mark each one clearly.

Safety and economy are the watchwords when **cooking with gas**. Always turn off the tap at the galley end of the supply pipe after use and have a clear "open/closed" indicator. Beware of drafts from the hatchway, which can easily extinguish a simmering flame.

A pressure cooker and vacuum flask both save gas. A folding oven is available for stoves without one, and if there is no grill, a toasting rack can be fitted over the burner. Useful additions are a bolt to lock the cooker upright in harbor and another to keep the oven door shut.

The head should have instructions for use clearly displayed. Make sure that everyone on board, especially visitors, knows how the system works. It is good practice to keep the seacocks closed when the head is not in use. Ease of access and clear labeling are essential.

Most cooks like plenty of light and fresh air in the galley and also to be in contact with what is happening on deck. As a result, most galleys are L- or U-shaped and tucked just inside the main hatchway. If the worktop area extends across and below the hatchway, ensure that a reliable and positive separation exists between food and descending feet.

Water

1 Conserve freshwater by using seawater for washing up—then rinsing in fresh. Dish-washing liquid works well in saltwater.

2 If the cook insists on more capacity, it is possible to add extra freshwater tanks. Flexible plastic ones that adopt the shape of the hull are easiest to install, but must be initially cleaned as recommended by the manufacturers. Provided a vent pipe is fitted, they can be linked to the existing water-filling and supply lines. It is tempting to position them in otherwise inaccessible corners, but remember to keep the weight out of the ends of the boat and balance the load each side of the centerline.

3 If you use the pressure water system at sea, have a back up pump in case the electrical system fails.

Stores

1 Canned food is a convenient way of buying in bulk. Foil/packet and freeze-dried meals are considerably lighter, and although more expensive, have reasonable flavors without the effort of "dressing-up" bland canned food—a great advantage when rough seas make cooking a chore.

2 When provisioning for a trip, work out one person's average consumption for a day, multiply by the number of crew and number of days, changing the basic ingredient type for variety. Fresh food, salads, fruit, bread, milk, and cheese can be bought at ports of call. In spite of ravenous appetites induced by the sea air, you will almost certainly have too much. Remember to take plenty of fruit juice to supplement water intake and avoid dehydration.

Children

At sea, children's food needs to be fun and more of a treat than onshore, to distract and entertain them. Between meals nibbling helps to keep morale and energy high. Allow a good mixture of sweet and savory, since sailors of all ages often find their tastes change at sea.

PERSONAL SECURITY

There *must* be as many personal flotation devices (PFDs) and safety harnesses on board as there are people. Children must have equipment that fits them safely. This should be issued to everyone before leaving port so that it can be adjusted to fit before it is needed, and kept in individual kit bags if necessary so as not to get mixed up.

Buoyancy aids of the type you might wear for inshore dinghy sailing are not good enough for sailing at sea. Always look for a buoyancy rating on a life jacket. A life jacket (PFD) with a minimum buoyancy rating of 34 lb is suitable for general use at sea. In some countries the buoyancy rating is given in Newtons. A rating of 150N (Newtons) is equivalent to 34 lb. There should be a whistle, built-in harness, and ideally a light. Inflatable jackets are more comfortable and so more likely to be worn. The advice is always to check carefully what you are taking on board—and always buy from a recognized supplier.

Self-inflating life jackets, which should be regularly inspected, inflate on immersion in water and are becoming more common, but many prefer the type where you have to pull the red tab. Those that can only be inflated by mouth must have integral closed-cell foam buoyancy as well.

Crotch straps are a very good idea— they may feel slightly uncomfortable at first, but they stop the inflated jacket riding up around the wearer's neck when in the water, keeping the head higher out of the water.

Sprayhoods are now offered as an option and are worth considering— hypothermia is accelerated by the effect of seas breaking over the face.

Practice putting on your harness with your eyes shut—it's usually a dark night when you need it. Safety harnesses built into oilskin jackets are an option, although they add considerable weight.

At *minimum*, always wear harnesses when the boat is reefed, and at night. Life jackets (PFDs) should always be worn by non-swimmers and by everyone on board at night and in fog.

Safety harnesses are no good unless they are worn. There is a normal reluctance to put one on, partly because of the effort, partly bravado, and partly because of the implied risk. Built-in harnesses have the attraction that if the weather is cold or wet enough to wear heavy-weather gear the harness is included automatically. The only further effort required is to attach the safety line.

Life jackets that incorporate a safety harness are a good idea for children. Preventing them from falling overboard must always be the prime factor.

Safety on deck

1 Casualness on deck at sea can lead to injury or even a fall overboard. Always hold on with at least one hand. Do not leave anything loose on deck that may be tripped over and avoid leaning nonchalantly against the backstay.

2 Conventional spring carbine hooks that used to be standard on tethers can be disengaged from an eye plate if they are twisted sideways. The double closing type, shown below, requires a positive action to release the safety bar before the spring catch can be opened. It cannot, however, fit around large diameter fastenings.

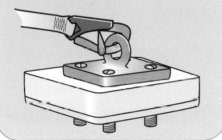

Jacklines and U bolts

All boats should have purpose-fitted safety harness attachments. These can be either U-bolt fittings in key places, or a pair of jacklines that the crew can clip onto while allowing them to move freely along the length of the boat. Ideally, have both. Always avoid clipping them onto the guardwires as these are rarely intended as safety harness attachments.

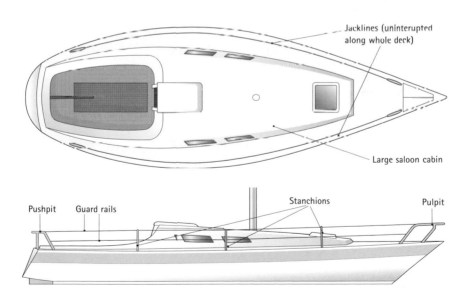

Jacklines (uninterupted along whole deck)

Large saloon cabin

Pushpit   Guard rails   Stanchions   Pulpit

Wear a safety harness for even the simplest of deck jobs. When a piece of gear you are holding gives a sudden hard tug, the confidence inspired by a clipped-on harness is immense. The harness safety line should not be long enough to allow you to go overboard to leeward when clipped on to the weather side. There must also be eye plates by the hatchway so harnesses can be secured before going on deck.

Try not to put heavy sideways loads on **stanchions** or **guard rails**, however well fitted. They are vulnerable to determined levering. Hook your harness safety line to a **windward jackstay**, which runs from right forward to right aft on each side of the boat. Nonslip material is available in various grades and types of grip and in different colors. Stick it in strips on hatches and smooth areas.

STAYING WARM AND DRY

Many people make the mistake of going to sea before preparing for the cold and wet. It is no fun being cold on a boat, so give some thought to your attire. Depending on the weather, clothing can consist of a thermal undersuit, probably of polypropylene, then a quilted or pile middle layer, with foul-weather gear on top.

The aim of all this gear is to "wick" moisture—perspiration or condensation— away from the skin. These inner layers are infinitely warmer, lighter, and less restricting to wear than a pair of jeans and two sweaters.

Breathable foul-weather gear is now available that allows the perspiration out, without letting water in. They are made from hard-wearing material and are inevitably more expensive, but are now the first choice of the serious sailor.

On most nonslip decks almost any type of training or sports shoe should give a similarly good grip, although leather moccasin types are the fashion; these are a little more expensive, but are salt-resistant and very comfortable. Boots must have a good grip to resist lurch on the foredeck in bad weather. Do avoid wearing shoes with black soles, no matter how soft the material, as these can leave marks on teak and fiberglass decks that are difficult to remove.

Some people like to pack their boots full of socks—others like an air gap for warmth; each system works for different people. Similar gear is available for children, who must be kept warm and comfortable, because if they are miserable no one is going to enjoy the trip.

Always take at least one change of clothing and keep shore-going clothes to a minimum. Pack everything in easily stowed soft bags, not a suitcase. Large polyethylene bags are useful for keeping spare clothes dry as well as for storing wet clothes later.

Foul-weather gear
If you plan to spend only daytime at sea, coastal suits will do well. Some people prefer all-in-one outfits, but they are inconvenient if you want to shed layers, so two pieces are usually a better bet for cruising. At night, the benefit of heavy-duty oilskins (foul-weather gear) soon makes itself felt. As well as obvious items, such as attached hoods with adjustable fastenings, good oilskins have no seams where they will be under tension and exposed to heavy spray, and have doubling patches on seats and knees that provide discardable protection against chafe on deck. There should also be fastenings at the wrist and ankle to stop water getting in. A fly makes life easier provided it is watertight.

1 **Polypropylene** long johns and long-sleeved T-shirts make good undergarments, with thermal socks and balaclava.
2 If the weather demands it, the next layer is a thin quilted garment or fleece. The salopette-type is very comfortable and convenient.
3 The outer layers should give warmth and protection from damp.
4 On goes the jacket, ideally complete with a harness. Fasten wrist and ankle straps.

Children and safety

Children and adults who cannot swim should put on life jackets (PFDs) before going down the marina pontoon (so should all the crew if embarking by dinghy). At sea, well-secured safety harnesses must be worn on deck and a responsible adult should ensure that they are fastened to a strong point—not just a guard rail—since the jerk of even a child falling can be very severe. Explain to children in advance which ropes are likely to run out suddenly, when tacking for example. Keep a calm atmosphere and children won't worry.

ARRIVALS AND DEPARTURES

SUCCESSFUL MOORING AND DOCKING

Too often, skippers find themselves fazed by the crowded conditions (and the omnipresent spectators) when it is time to exercise their skills at mooring and anchoring. A little practice soon produces an understanding of the factors affecting the handling of the boat at slow speeds.

Maneuvering under sail is one of the purest forms of sailing, although now, regrettably, it is becoming the province of those who like to frequent uncrowded anchorages, because many harbor authorities now actively discourage sailing in the waters under their jurisdiction. All mooring and anchoring maneuvers, under sail or power, must be undertaken slowly, accurately, and with intelligent use of wind and tide.

Find out which way your propeller turns. At very low boat speeds, or from stationary, it will act partly like a paddlewheel and this "propwalk" effect will move the boat sideways one way or the other. Get a feel for this by engaging the engine when stationary in open water. Once you are used to it, propwalk can be used to good effect when berthing.

Many marinas are located in estuaries where the tidal stream must be taken into account when planning to berth or to leave. Tidal streams can be overlooked in the apparent shelter of a marina complex, so when using an unfamiliar berth or boat, check the tidal flow on a mooring buoy or pile.

When reversing, always operate the engine gently unless your boat has a folding propeller. Designs with a "fin and skeg" keel and rudder configuration are not generally very good at going astern. Boats with spade-rudders, however, are more responsive.

Before attempting to approach or leave a mooring, weigh up all the observed variables against the known turning characteristics and drifting attitude of your boat. Determine potential danger areas and make your plan known to everyone involved.

Downwind, jib only

Crosswind, mainsail only

Upwind, both sails

Mooring under sail requires slow speeds. The boat's angle to the wind dictates which sails to use. An upwind approach is best carried out under both sails. On a reach, when the wind acts as a controllable accelerator, use the mainsail only. When approaching downwind, a small, easily lowered headsail provides some control. Whenever possible, however, luff up and moor under mainsail only.

The boat's stern swings out when turning, in the same way as a supermarket cart. When going astern the bow swings wide. Use this "skidding" effect to slide into or out of a marina berth.

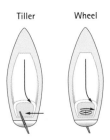

Tiller   Wheel

When reversing to starboard, push the tiller to port or turn the wheel to starboard.

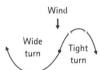

When approaching or leaving a mooring, remember that the boat turns in a wider circle when turning into the wind than when turning away from it.

When turning towards a weak tide, the boat will swing out, etching a figure 9 in the water.

When turning towards a strong tidal stream, the boat is forced into a tight turn.

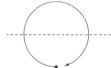

Modify turns to account for the tidal flow. In still water the boat will make a perfect circle once well started in its motion.

Circling away from a weak current elongates, rather than compresses, the turn into a figure 6.

A boat is pushed downstream while it turns when circling away from strong tides.

Checklist for docking

1 Use all the boat's equipment to aid you. Ropes and fenders are your principal allies; your worst enemy is speed.

2 Always have an escape route in case things go wrong. It should take you away from the dock, allowing time to look again at the correct approach. It is more seaman-like to abandon a bad approach than to crash. Make your approach to a dock into the wind or current, whichever is more significant, if possible. Approach at a 20° angle in normal cirumstances, but make the angle steeper when your berth space is limited, and be prepared to use docklines to warp your boat alongside as necessary.

3 Sailing boats are notoriously unpredictable when going astern. Use reverse as a brake, or to kick the stern into a berth or away from an obstruction. To steer in reverse, push the tiller away from the direction you wish the stern to go or turn the wheel towards it. Try facing the stern to orientate yourself. All other things being equal, docking a boat with a right-handed propeller port-side-to will enable you to kick your stern into the dock when you reverse the engine.

4 Determine the natural drifting tendencies of your boat by experimenting under bare poles.

5 In tidal waters, establish the state of the tide, and check docklines frequently.

MOORINGS AND DOCKS

Most marinas offer alongside berths in finger pontoons. Some, however, have pairs of piles (fixed wooden or metal stakes driven into the sea bed), which provide fore and aft attachment points. In many harbors, tidal estuaries, and creeks, traditional mooring buoys are still used.

Before approaching any dock, ensure that no ropes are hanging over the side. Start the engine and check the water, gears, and fuel. Lower the sails.

Prepare bow and stern lines by passing an end outside the lifelines and rigging and back through the fairleads to a cleat or mooring post at the bow and stern. Loosely coil the free ends of the warps and lay them on deck amidships.

Securely fasten the fenders on the side they will be needed, and lay the boathook on the coach/cabin trunk roof. Modify your approach to allow for the wind and tide.

If planning to dock at a marina, you could use your VHF radio to book a berth, so you will know exactly where to make for.

Enter cautiously along the row opposite your berth to allow a wide swing in. When the boat's beam passes the end of the pontoon/slip, two of the crew can leap ashore with bow and stern lines, and a short burst astern should stop the boat. Securely cleat the bow and stern lines, rig springs, and, if necessary, breast ropes, then adjust fenders for position and height.

Before leaving, ensure dues have been paid, warm the engine, and brief the crew. Release bow and stern lines last and reverse slowly out of the berth, collecting shore crew on the way. Clear, coil, and stow warps and clean and stow fenders.

When docked in a raft, perhaps six deep, obtain the cooperation of boats either side and slip out in the same direction as the strongest element: wind or tide.

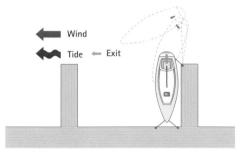

To leave a finger pontoon when wind and tide are both moving across the exit of the berth, rig a doubled line from the stern cleat to the end of the windward pontoon and reverse. When the bow is almost clear, snub the doubled warp around a sheet winch and turn the tiller to swing clear. The line will run clear when one end is freed.

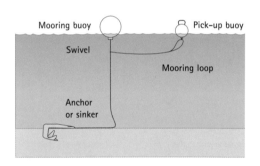

Approach a swinging mooring so that the crew can hook the small pick-up buoy aboard and secure the chain to the bow cleat. Point into the strongest element to coincide with the heading of moored boats. If they face in all directions, try a downwind approach.

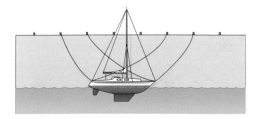

Plan to arrive at a tidal wall near high tide to get the lines ashore easily. Check the water depth at low tide and the position of ladders. Protect the boat with fenders, fender boards, and anti-chafe and, if berthing outside another boat, secure your own lines to the jetty.

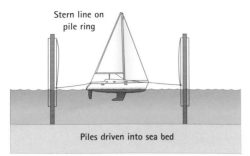

Stern line on
pile ring

Piles driven into sea bed

When mooring to piles, approach against the strongest element, usually the tide. Slip a doubled stern line round the downtide pile. As the bow reaches the uptide post, slip the bow line through the mooring ring. Haul in on stern line and pass through the ring. The boat lies between the two posts.

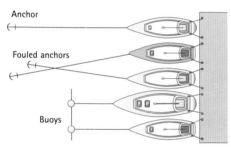

Anchor

Fouled anchors

Buoys

In non-tidal waters, such as the Mediterranean, boats are usually moored stern-to-quay/dock. Reverse slowly towards the line of buoys parallel to the quay and attach a bow line. Haul on the line running to the quay and secure the stern lines to the quay. Alternatively, drop a bow anchor well out and swing the stern to the quay.

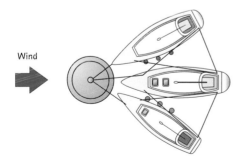

Wind

To leave a large mooring buoy when sandwiched between two boats, release your neighbor's stern-line, then your own line from the next boat. Motor slowly ahead to push the windward boat. As a leeward gap forms, release the bow line and reverse out.

Tools of the trade

A sensible number of dock lines required is: two lines twice the length of the boat (bow and stern lines); two $1\frac{1}{2}$ times the length of the boat—usually the strongest pair—(springs); and two the same length as the boat (breast lines). The lines should be reasonably stretchy. Nylon lines are ideal and three-strand is preferred, although braided also works. Use plastic tubes or old sail material to protect the warps from chafe, particularly where they rub against the quay/dockside.

1 Stern line	4 Aft spring
2 Aft breast	5 Fore breast line
3 Fore spring	6 Bow line

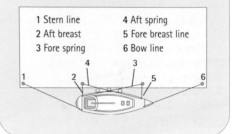

Fenders

Fenders absorb the shock when coming alongside and protect the hull once docked. They should be attached to cleats, toe rails, cabin-top grab rails, or stanchion bases, but avoid attaching to the lifelines because this imposes unnecessary stress on the guard rail. Each should be fitted with a 5–6 ft ($1\frac{1}{2}$–2 m) line. Always keep a minimum of six fenders on board—they may be needed on both sides.

When docking alongside a quay/dock, particularly one with buttresses, attach a ladder or plank of wood outside the fenders so that the board rests against the quay.

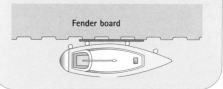

Fender board

CHOICE OF ANCHOR

As marinas with parking facilities have burgeoned, anchoring skills have sometimes been neglected.

But as sailors gather experience, they might wish to venture away from protected marinas to the independence of anchorages in more remote areas—and as a result anchoring assumes greater importance.

As a rough guide, the standard equipment for a cruising boat should be a large main anchor, rigged with a chain, and a smaller kedge anchor, with a short length of chain and a long nylon warp. The strength and high-stretch properties of nylon minimize the snatching loads experienced in rough conditions.

The main anchor should weigh 1 lb (0.5 kg) for every 1 ft (30 cm) of boat length and the kedge about 20 percent less. There is no substitute for weight, despite marked advances in design.

When cruising, carry two different types of anchor to suit the conditions of the sea bed. For example, to equip a 30 ft (9 m) boat for cruising in the Caribbean or the English Channel, you might choose:
• a 30–35 lb (14–16 kg) CQR main anchor with 30 fm (54 m) of chain;
• size ⁵⁄₁₆ in (4.5 mm) and an 18–20 lb (8–9 kg) Bruce kedge anchor with 3.3 fm (6 m) of chain; and
• size ⁵⁄₁₆ in (4.5 mm) and 55 fm (100 m) of braided or cable laid nylon warp, size 1⅛ in (18 mm).

If you are venturing into rocky or weedy anchorages, take a 2 lb (11 kg) fisherman's anchor.

Chain is sold by the length, and sized in inches or millimeters across the metal of the link, while rope is sized in inches–circumference or millimeters–diameters, so use conversion charts when ordering. Anchor winches are designed to accept a specific size of chain, so order both together.

The Danforth, an American design, holds well in mud, sand, and river mouth silt, but is unreliable in rock and weed. Its crown design and flat flukes make it easy to stow but often hard to break out from the sea bed.

The traditional fisherman's anchor is useful when cruising in areas with rocky sea beds. As only one fluke digs into the sea bed, it relies on its own weight and that of the rock it snags for holding power, and it may drag in loose sand.

1 A bow shackle passes through the last link in the anchor chain and the pin is secured with non-corrosive wire.

2 A swivel inserted at any join in the anchor cable, allows the system to turn freely. (Also see p. 98.)

The CQR "plow" anchor is designed to burrow beneath sand, mud, weed, shell, and overlying gravel, as well as into mixed sand and rock. The hinged, angled shank encourages the anchor to bite, although it often takes a while to hold. It is a popular all-rounder.

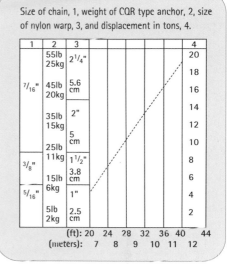

Size of chain, 1, weight of CQR type anchor, 2, size of nylon warp, 3, and displacement in tons, 4.

1	2	3						4
	55lb 25kg	2¼"						20
7/16"	45lb 20kg	5.6 cm						18
								16
	35lb 15kg	2"						14
		5 cm						12
	25lb 11kg							10
3/8"		1½"						8
	15lb 6kg	3.8 cm						6
5/16"		1"						4
	5lb 2kg	2.5 cm						2

(ft): 20 24 28 32 36 40 44
(meters): 7 8 9 10 11 12

The Bruce anchor, designed to secure the giant North Sea oil rigs, slices deep into sand or mud with its semi-circular flukes. Light to handle and with high holding-power-to weight, it is efficient on short scope but may drag in rock.

Joining rope and chain

To join rope to chain when the rope is too thick to go through the last link, unravel about six turns. Loop strands **1** and **2** through the last link and unravel strand **3** six turns more. Lay strand **2** into 3's place. Join strand 2 and 3 with an overhand knot and tuck in strand 1.

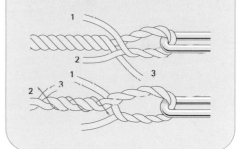

3 A D–shaped shackle is used to join each length of chain. The rounded end faces the anchor to prevent fouling when it is let out. (Also see p. 98.)

4 Mark the anchor rope and chain with, for example, one knotted cord or colored stripe for each 30 ft (9 m).

FOREDECK FITTINGS

In severe conditions, the loads imposed on bow and deck fittings are enormous, especially if the yacht is pitching into a confused sea. It is essential, therefore, that when your equipment is put to the test, every part of your anchoring system is up to the job. Equipment is only as strong as the weakest link, so choose each element carefully.

Some production boats are not fitted with adequate bow fittings, capable of receiving the chain or warp from any angle. Even quite substantial fittings may not be adequately secured to the hull with bolts and backing pads. This may not matter in normal situations, but can become critical in extreme conditions, so check and, if necessary, reinforce all the attachment points.

Ideally, a bow fitting should have two large rollers divided by a substantial metal fence. The sides should be high enough to accommodate the largest chain and a large-diameter drop-nose pin should be added to prevent the chain jumping out.

When buying a boat, check that the bow fitting is sited so that the chain does not foul the forestay fitting as it is hauled in, particularly if there is an anchor windlass.

Once the anchor has been laid, the rope or chain is wound around a cleat or bollard. Rope can be tied with a bowline. The end of the rope or chain must be secured to a large through-bolted eye by means of a light line that can be easily cut away in an emergency. In theory, you should never let your chain out so far—but it happens!

It is becoming common practice to stow either a Bruce or a CQR anchor in the bow roller, to which it is attached by a steel pin. The chain can be fed down to the locker below through a navel pipe. It may have a watertight cover, or a hinged cover with a slot for a link of chain.

Securing chain
Chain must be secured to the boat so that it will not slip, yet can be easily released, even under load. For this purpose, a post or bollard is preferable to a cleat. Take two turns around the bollard, 1, then take a loop under the taut chain and slip it over the bollard, 2. Cleats used for securing chain, 3, should be large and mounted on a wooden pad to raise them above the deck. Take one turn round the cleat then twist a loop of chain over the front end of the cleat, 4.

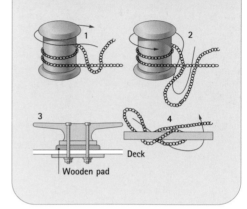

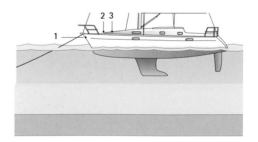

The anchor chain is led on board through a bow roller 1, and is held in place by a large-diameter pin or a chain pawl. After it has been hauled in, by hand or windlass, the anchor is secured to a post or cleat on the foredeck, 2. In many boats the chain is fed below through a navel pipe, 3. The last link of the chain is secured to a metal eye bolt, with a light line, which can be cut in an emergency.

Ideally, **a bow fitting** should have two large rollers with a dividing metal fence. High sides to the fitting and a large diameter pin should prevent even the largest size of chain from jumping out.

A windlass, hand operated, as shown above, or electric, takes away the strain of hauling in an anchor.

Pulpit stowage, as shown above, in a molded deck well, leaves the anchor ready for use, with chain and warp attached. The end of the warp should be secured to a cleat or eye in the well.

The anchor, once hauled in, can be conveniently stowed in the bow roller for ease of handling and held by a strong steel drop-nose pin.

Checklist for anchoring

1 When dropping anchor, do not stand on the chain or rope, and beware of bights.

2 When paying out or hauling in, never take a turn around your hand.

3 Sit on the foredeck with feet braced against the base of the pulpit. Try to pull by straightening your legs, not bending your back.

4 Never cleat chain or rope with a half hitch; it will often jam.

5 Always buy chain that has been tested for strength and calibrated.

6 Be sure the chain locker is well ventilated, as the anchor will bring plenty of slime aboard.

7 The working anchor should be let out over the port bow in the northern hemisphere, since the wind will veer as a low front passes. If a second anchor is let out over the starboard bow during the blow, the two cables will then not cross as the boat swings round.

8 Stow the anchor warp loosely in a well or rolled up on a reel.

HOW TO ANCHOR

Careful preparation is needed before dropping the anchor over the side. First the anchor must be freed from its stowage and positioned, ready for release at the right moment. As you will usually anchor under power, the mainsail should be loose-stowed, all the ropes brought inboard, and headsails removed from the foredeck to give ample space.

If the chain has been detached from the anchor, shackle it on and secure the pin with wire or thin line. If you are using a windlass, make sure you know how it works. If paying it out by hand, flake about 33 ft (5.5 fm) of chain along the deck ready for anchoring. If using rope attached to chain and the anchor, ensure that rope that has been flaked into a locker is free to run out.

Your final approach to your chosen spot should be into the strongest element so that when the anchor is released, the boat drifts away from it. Never drop the anchor at the spot where you wish the boat to end up.

If you are anchoring in a rocky area or one that is known to contain debris, it may be wise to rig a trip line to the anchor and attach a float that will show at high water—usually a fender with ANCHOR written on it. In crowded anchorages, however, it is unwise to use an anchor buoy since an unwary newcomer is likely to moor up to it or catch it in his propeller. It you still want a line, lash it to the chain and bring it back on board.

Watch out for local styles of anchoring when venturing into new cruising areas. You may be accustomed to laying two anchors, up and down, in a strong tide but find when you cruise in foreign waters that it is customary to lay anchors across the tidal stream. If its swinging pattern is different, your boat will cause chaos with neighboring boats at the change of tide.

Anchoring for a short stay to eat a meal or sit at a favorite anchorage highlights the value of a second anchor. Its light weight, short length of chain, and nylon warp allow younger members of the crew to practice their skills. In a crowded anchorage, ask your neighbors if they are using chain or rope. Do likewise to follow their swinging patterns.

For a short stay of a few hours, between two and three times anchor chain to water depth is usually enough if you are staying on board. If you extend your stay, you will need to lay your main anchor and more chain.

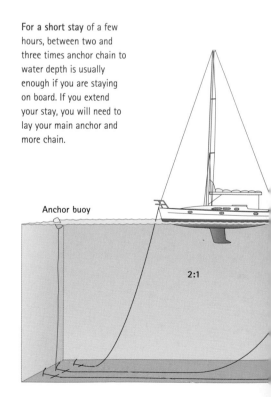

Anchor buoy

2:1

96

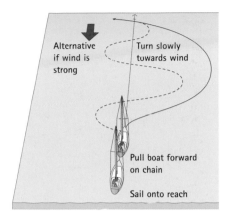

Alternative if wind is strong

Turn slowly towards wind

Pull boat forward on chain

Sail onto reach

When it is time to leave, and the boat is pointing towards the wind, try leaving under sail. Hoist the mainsail and haul in enough chain to break out the anchor and cleat it. Sail the boat in a broad arcs, tacking and sailing slowly towards the anchor,

until the chain begins to slacken and can be hauled in, followed by the anchor. As the boat sails on, stow the anchor gear and set the headsail. It would be well to practice this in seclusion before trying it out in front of spectators!

Choosing an anchorage

Seek an anchorage sheltered from the wind and waves by land and offshore reefs. Consult the chart for good anchorages (indicated with an anchor symbol), water depths, and tidal information. Use the echo sounder to verify the depths and, since anchors hold best on flat surfaces, to locate areas free from ridges, holes, and slopes. The chart should tell you the nature of the sea bed, but if not you could use a lead "armed" with grease to collect a sample of the sand, shingle, mud, weed, or coral on the sea bed. If it doesn't pick anthing up, look for any marks on the lead that may have been made by rock.

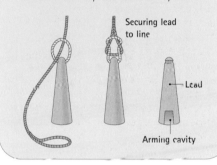

Securing lead to line

Lead

Arming cavity

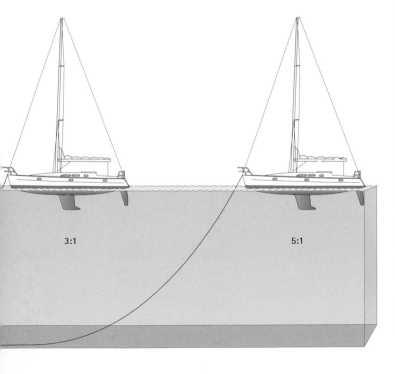

3:1

5:1

The water depth and amount of chain paid out (the scope) determine the angle of pull on the anchor. For an overnight stay, if strong winds are present, or if the tidal current is strong, let out at least four times and preferably five times the water depth at high tide in chain. Choose a well-protected anchorage, check every shackle and pin, and set the anchor firmly by going astern. This will also take out slack in the chain on the sea bed. The weight of the chain gives extra stability to the anchor and ensures horizontal pull, free from stretch or tugging. To hold the boat steady in gale conditions, a second anchor is often advisable.

TWO ANCHORS FOR SECURITY

Problems can arise when strong winds and tides are opposed, causing the boat to swing wildly around its anchor. If more than 1.2 mph (1 kn) of tide or 17 mph (15 kn) of wind is expected, drop a second anchor to allow the boat to lie securely between two fixed points.

However, the use of two anchors requires careful planning and preparation. In case you have to weather a gale, carry a large mooring swivel to which both anchors can be attached without risk of tangling the chains. This method does, however, mean that the anchors take the strain alternately rather than together.

To take the strain on both anchors simultaneously, lay the ground chain across the wind or tide, having prepared trip lines for both anchors. The easiest method is to lay the kedge with its long warp first and then motor across the wind or tide. When the warp runs out, drop the main anchor and, as the boat swings back toward the kedge, veer the chain and take in the slack of the kedge warp until the boat lies midway between both anchors. Then attach the warp to the chain and release the chain until the knot is about 10 ft (3 m) below the surface.

The last anchor down is normally the first to be taken up. If the mooring swivel is used, the smaller anchor may have to be retrieved with the trip line. When it is stowed, haul the swivel aboard, cleat the chain, and bring in the buoyed rising chain. Once the swivel is removed from both ground and rising chain, shackle the chains together before stowing. Haul in the rest of the chain and the anchor.

Anchoring is another traditional skill to suffer from the proliferation of marinas. To anchor under sail, first determine the depth and nature of the bottom and then drop and stow the headsail. Once abeam of the anchorage, gently turn head to wind, drop anchor as the boat comes to a standstill, and lower the mainsail.

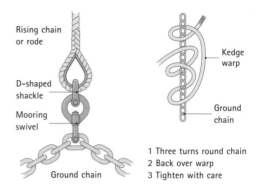

Rising chain or rode

D-shaped shackle

Mooring swivel

Ground chain

Kedge warp

Ground chain

1 Three turns round chain
2 Back over warp
3 Tighten with care

A 270-ft-long main anchor chain made up of three 90 ft (15 fm) lengths joined by D-shackles can be **split up to set two anchors.** Remove one of the three lengths and shackle a mooring swivel to the center of the remaining 180 ft (30 fm) length to form the ground chain. Connect the 90 ft length to the free end of the swivel to form the rising chain. You can also use an anchor rode in place of the rising chain, shown above left. If you lack a shackle-and-swivel attachment for the rising chain or warp, tie the kedge warp to the main anchor's chain, shown above right.

Anchoring under power

If precision is required, anchor under power rather than sail. Start the engine, lower the sails, and motor gently against the wind or tide to help slow the boat and give greater control when neutral is engaged. When the chosen point is reached, and the boat almost stationary, drop anchor. The wind or tide will push the boat back away from the anchor, pulling it along the sea bed until it digs in. A powerful burst astern will check that the anchor is holding well. When leaving under power, plan your course, brief the crew, and motor forward to break out the anchor.

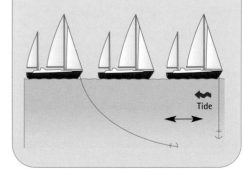

Tide

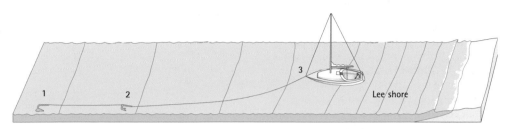

If gale force winds are blowing you on to a lee shore, it is safer and cheaper to anchor as a last resort than to run the boat on to mud flats or rock. Use the anchors in tandem: drop the kedge, **1**, attach its cable to the crown of the main anchor, **2**, and lower both. Veer

most of the chain and cleat, **3**. Attach a mooring swivel to the end of the chain, and fasten two warps to the inboard eye of the swivel. Take the warps back to the main winches, which are designed for heavy loads, then secure.

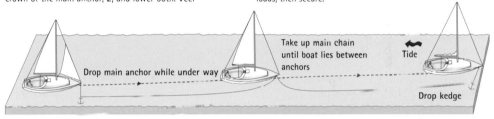

To lay two anchors, drop the main anchor while underway and allow the boat to drift until it has dug in (shown above). Shackle the second anchor to the ground chain, attach a trip line (as shown below), and drop the anchor. Motor upwind, taking up the main chain until the boat lies between the anchors.

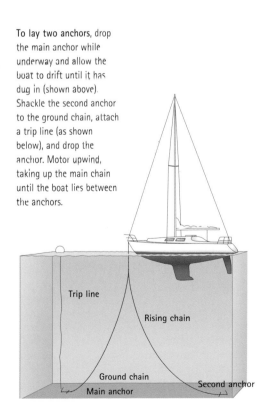

Checklist for anchoring

1 Approach your anchorage against the strongest element—wind or tide. Have anchor and cable ready on deck in good time.

2 Always anchor at least two anchor scopes (lengths of cable lowered) from any other boat, and, if anchoring with chain, allow yachts with nylon rope a wider berth.

3 The boat that anchors first has "right of way."

4 To test if the anchor is holding, pull gently on the chain or warp. If a grating, snatching action can be felt, the anchor is skimming over the bottom, probably on its side.

5 Even though the anchor appears to be holding, it may drag when the tide changes—take regular bearings or transits.

6 A thick warp is easier to pull on than a thin one.

7 When using nylon warp, guard against chafe.

ANCHORING EMERGENCIES

Anchoring skills are often learned the hard way, so, whenever possible, anchor a good distance from other boats. This allows more room for maneuver, more time to react if you drag, and an easier departure.

A dragging anchor can be the cause of a lot of damage so always check that the anchor is holding. If it isn't, try letting out more warp or chain; if it still will not set, it must be hauled up and dropped elsewhere. Transits (aligned landmarks) or compass bearings can also be used to indicate any movement from the original anchoring position.

In fog, rough weather, or potentially dangerous situations, it may be necessary to organize anchor watches where one member of the crew is constantly available to check transits and bearings to ensure that the boat is not drifting.

When the anchor will not leave the sea bed, you have a fouled anchor. Let out some rope or chain and motor in a circle, keeping tension on the warp, and occasionally go astern away from the anchor. If fouled under a rock or in a crevice, it will come free. If this does not work, and there is some give in the chain, winch it in and release it suddenly. If the offending obstruction was rope or chain, the anchor may then fall free.

Power cables can be a hazard, so if the chart shows these or you can see yellow diamond shapes on the shore line, do not anchor. If you do foul a power cable, buoy the last 90 ft (15 fm) of chain and report to the local harbor master to find out if the wire is "live." With old cables, once you are sure it is safe to do so, haul in the cable to get the wire as close to the surface as possible. Somehow slip a rope under it to hold it and lower the anchor free.

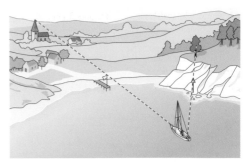

A visual reference can determine if the anchor is dragging. Once the anchor is set, and the boat settled, line up two stationary objects. Take another transit at right angles to the first. Draw a circle on the chart around your position of a radius equal to the length of cable out. If the transits put you outside the circle, you are dragging, not swinging.

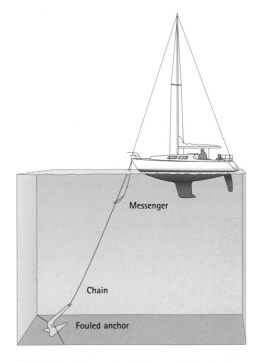

Messenger

Chain

Fouled anchor

If a fouled anchor cannot be freed by motoring round it in a circle, try using a messenger. Lower a loop of chain with a very large shackle on a line down the cable. Shake it about until it reaches the anchor and slips over it. Attach a buoy to the last 90 ft (15 fm) of chain if it is detachable and drop it over the side. Motor fast away and try to jerk the anchor out in the opposite direction with the messenger line.

To dampen the snatching action when a boat is anchored in waves, **shackle an anchor weight or another anchor over the chain**. Slide it down on a line until it lies midway between the sea bed and the surface. This "angel" makes a curve in the cable, so relieving the vertical pull on the anchor and reducing the chances of dragging. A set of weights and a custom-built traveler may be a useful investment if you are serious about cruising.

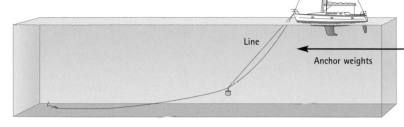

Line

Anchor weights

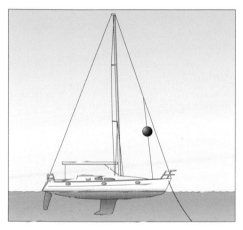

In daylight you must, by law, display a black spherical ball forward of the mast when at anchor.

Laying a second anchor

The yacht's tender can be used to lay a second anchor. Flake the warp into the tender so that it does not increase drag as you row away. When enough cable for the depth is in the tender, make fast the other end to the boat. If the anchor is very heavy hang it under the tender with a rope strop secured with a slip knot (see below). Row or motor upwind or tide as quickly as possible, then across to the anchor point, release the slip knot or lower the anchor to the sea bed. The tender may also be needed to retrieve a firmly entrenched anchor.

1 Form bight with one rope
2 Thread second rope through bight, and around it
3 Then through under itself and tighten. Pull to release

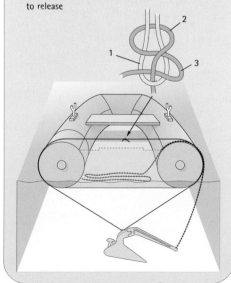

At night, carry an all-round white anchor light in the same position.

NAVIGATION AND WEATHER

USING A COMPASS

Position on the Earth's surface is generally expressed in terms of latitude and longitude. In coastal navigation and pilotage, however, the position of a vessel is more often identified in relation to the coastline or seamarks, such as buoys and light vessels, or perhaps the nearest danger point.

There are two basic, fundamentally different ways of determining position at sea: by dead reckoning (DR), which is the application of direction and distance traveled to the boat's last-known position; and by fixing the position in relation to outside objects, such as points of land, the sea bed, satellites, or astronomical bodies.

Because the knowledge of the course steered, the distance run, and the effects of wind and tide will necessarily be approximate, the accuracy of the DR or estimated position needs to be updated, whenever possible, by fixes.

Direction at sea is measured in relation to north, nowadays clockwise through 360°. Charts are oriented to true north, the direction of the Earth's geographical North Pole. The magnetic compass, however, which is used to

steer courses and take bearings, points towards magnetic north.

The difference between true and magnetic north at any place is known as the variation. Compass north may vary from magnetic north because magnetic interference within the craft causes deviation. The difference between true (chart) north and compass north, the sum of variation and deviation, is known as compass error and must be allowed for in all chartwork.

Distance (or speed) at sea is measured by some form of log. The unit of distance is the international nautical mile of 6,076 ft (1,852 m); speed is measured in knots, that is, one nautical mile per hour.

Longitude is measured in degrees, minutes, and seconds of arc east and west from the prime meridian, which runs through Greenwich, England. Latitude is measured in arc north and south of the Equator, as viewed from the Earth's center.

Degrees and minutes of longitude represent the angle at the center of the Earth between any longitude and the Greenwich meridian. Each degree of latitude is divided into 60 minutes, each of which equals approximately one nautical mile (6,076 ft/1,852 m).

An **onboard compass** gives rapid and clear visual confirmation of a boat's direction. For tiller steering it is usually mounted on the bulkhead as shown above, but a mounting on the pedestal is better for wheel steering.

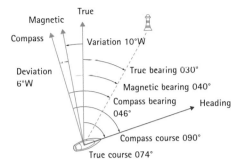

To establish compass error, observe a known true bearing, such as a transit marked on the chart or, for example, a distant lighthouse. Suppose it is 030° true, and the magnetic variation (from the chart) is 10°W, then magnetic north lies 10° west of true north, and the magnetic bearing of the lighthouse will be 040°. The bearing is then taken by pointing the boat directly at the lighthouse and reading the steering compass, which reads say, 046°. Deviation is thus 6°W.

Deviation

Compass north may differ from both magnetic and true north because of magnetic interference within the craft itself. The extent of deviation varies with the heading, and is named east or west of magnetic north. When compass north is east of magnetic north, add the deviation to convert from compass to magnetic bearings. Large compass errors are corrected by a qualified adjuster and the residual deviations recorded on a card, as shown below. Modern flux gate compasses can include automatic deviation correction. If you can adjust a magnetic compass so that the residual deviation on all courses is no more than 1–2°, this deviation can be safely ignored.

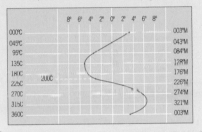

Compass location

The compass should be sited as far as possible from sources of magnetic interference, such as metal, electronic, and electrical equipment. The higher the compass, the further it will be from the influence of the engine and iron ballast keel and, on a steel boat, from the hull. It must be located at least 3 ft (0.9 m) from switches and any instruments containing magnets. A tiller-steered boat almost always uses a bulkhead-mounted steering compass, and a wheel-steered boat almost always uses a binnacle-mounted steering compass.

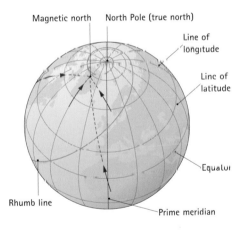

Variation, the difference between true and magnetic north, with its annual rate of change, is given on each compass rose on a chart. Variation is west if magnetic north lies west of true, and vice versa. To convert magnetic bearings to true, add the easterly variation and subtract the westerly.

Projecting the curved surface of the Earth on a flat map involves some distortion. The Mercator chart is constructed so that a course can be laid off as a straight line that will cut all meridians at the same angle. Drawn on the globe this "rhumb line" would spiral towards the poles.

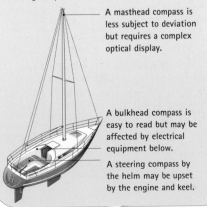

A masthead compass is less subject to deviation but requires a complex optical display.

A bulkhead compass is easy to read but may be affected by electrical equipment below.

A steering compass by the helm may be upset by the engine and keel.

FIXING A POSITION

A position line is an imaginary line at some point along which the observer's position must lie. The intersection of two position lines fixes the position, although three produce a more reliable fix. All methods of position fixing, whether astronomical, by visual compass bearing, etc, yield position lines, albeit from widely different sources. Position lines from any source can be combined to produce a fix.

The greater the angle of intersection of two position lines, the less will any error in either of them affect the accuracy of the fix. For two position lines a right-angled cut is ideal; for three, 60°.

Position lines obtained at different times can be advanced (or retarded) to a common time by applying the course-made-good and distance run between observations. This running fix is used in coastal navigation when only a single object is visible, or in astronomical navigation when, say, the altitude of the sun is taken at successive intervals so that its bearing will have changed sufficiently to produce a good cut. A running fix is generally inferior to simultaneous observations because the course and distance are seldom completely accurately known.

Some idea of the accuracy of each of the position lines will enable an estimate to be made of the accuracy of a fix. In general, because none of the position lines will be entirely accurate, the intersection of three position lines will result in a "cocked hat," the size of which will give an indication of the reliability of the fix. The position will not necessarily lie within the cocked hat and the cautious navigator will assume a position near to it, biased towards the nearest danger.

In coastal navigation, the most frequently used position lines are those obtained from visual compass bearings.

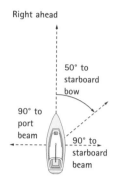

A relative bearing is the angle between the boat's heading and the direction of the object. A beam bearing, or an object in line with the port or starboard beam, is 90° from the boat's heading, not 90° from the course-made-good. A bearing that is 50° to starboard is known as "Green Five Zero."

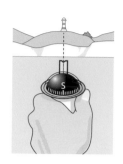

To take a compass bearing, identify a landmark on the chart, sight it through the ring or V of the compass and read off the bearing. Correct it from magnetic to true and lay it off on the chart. The closer the object, the more accurate the position. A hand-held compass is easier to use and more accurate for this task than a fixed steering compass.

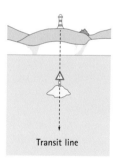

A highly accurate transit or range line, can be obtained from any two charted objects that are aligned one behind the other from your position. Simply draw a line from the far object through the nearer object on your chart, and extend it seaward. You are on that line.

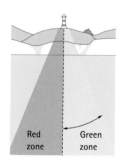

At night, sectored lights can help to indicate position. If the boat crosses from, say, the red sector to the green, a position line can be drawn along the change-of-color line as indicated on the chart or in the Light List.

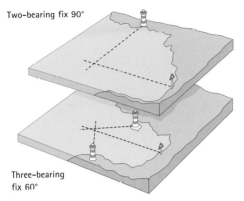

Two-bearing fix 90°

Three-bearing fix 60°

The compass bearings of two or more landmarks onshore will fix the boat's position. When using only two position lines, they should cross at a broad angle for accurate results.

Three bearings will give a more reliable fix. Ideally the three marks should be about 60° apart, and never less than 30°. The position lines will rarely intersect at one point but will form an error triangle or "cocked hat."

Sea horizon distances

Distance measurement of an object gives a circular position line that can often be combined with a bearing to give an instantaneous fix. Thus, a vertical sextant angle of an object of known height combined with a compass bearing of the object provides one of the quickest and most reliable fixes. Given the height of the object and the observer's height of eye, the sextant angle is converted into distance by means of a table (see p. 211) or by calculator. The top of the object, or the light in the case of a lighthouse, is brought down to the shoreline immediately below it.

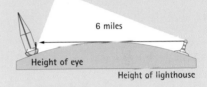

6 miles

Height of eye

Height of lighthouse

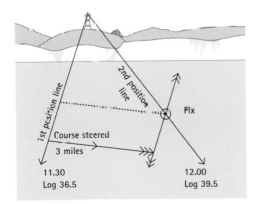

1st position line

2nd position line

Fix

Course steered

3 miles

11.30
Log 36.5

12.00
Log 39.5

A running fix can be obtained from a single landmark by observing two bearings with, say, half an hour's interval between them. Read the log at the time of the first bearing, steer a steady course for half an hour, take a second bearing, and read the log for distance traveled. Plot

the two position lines and the course-made-good. Draw a line through the second position line parallel to the first at a distance along the course-made-good corresponding to the distance sailed. The intersection of the position lines will be the fix.

Estimating distances

Distances at sea can be hard to assess, as short distances are often over-estimated and long distances foreshortened. The following clues give a rough distance guide, as seen from 7 ft (2.1 m) above sea level in good conditions and with a moderate sea.

3 statute miles (4.8 km)—Horizon.

2 miles (3.2 km)—Large buoy just visible: small buoy lost: windows are dots.

1–1½ miles (1.6–2.4 km)—Rigging of a large vessel visible.

1 mile (1.6 km)—Color and shape of large buoys visible: small buoys are shapeless: people are dots.

450 yards (411 m)—Man seen walking or rower pulling.

250 yards (228 m)—Tide ripples round buoys.

100 yards (91 m)—Faces visible.

The distance of a boat from a cliff can be determined by the number of seconds it takes for a blast on the fog horn to echo:

1 sec = 200 yards (183 m).

USING THE CHART

A boat's course is the direction in which it is moving, but because of the set (direction) of cross-currents or tidal streams and leeway due to crosswinds, the course will not necessarily be the same as the heading. The course-made-good is the direction followed between fixes; the track, which may involve a number of courses, is the path followed by a vessel over the Earth's surface.

Dead reckoning (DR), which is the determination of position by keeping an account of the courses steered and distance run, is usually worked out on the chart, although the DR position may also be obtained by using tables or a calculator.

Two of the main problems in chartwork relate to finding the estimated position when the effect of tidal streams or current and leeway are taken into account, and, its collorary, finding the course to steer in the same situation to make good a certain course.

Tidal stream information is obtained from tidal stream atlases that show, in relation to high or low water, the hourly rate/drift and set of the stream; similar information is often tabulated on the chart. Leeway is generally estimated from experience of the boat in different conditions. A rough idea of leeway angle can be obtained by comparing a bearing of the wake with the course steered.

When working from the magnetic rose on the chart or with a special plotter set to the magnetic variation, only deviation of the compass need be taken into account. However, it should be remembered that tidal stream information is given in true, not magnetic directions. Whether you choose to work in true or magnetic, be consistent to prevent errors creeping in. Working in magnetic usually saves you from making one calculation, and therefore potentially one error.

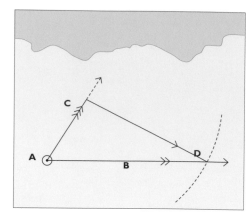

To find the course to steer to make good a certain direction, pencil in the required course on the chart (**AB**). Then plot the rate/drift and set of the tide or current to establish how far it will push the boat in, say, 1 hr (**AC**). With the dividers set at the distance the boat will travel in 1 hr, intersect the required course at **D**. The course to steer, allowing for tide, will then be **CD** and the distance made good in 1 hr/**AD**. Allow for leeway when necessary by steering upwind of the course to steer.

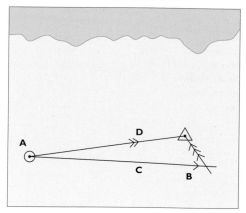

To find your estimated position, plot the course steered (**AC**) from the last known position (**A**). Modify the angle to account for leeway and mark the dead reckoned position (**B**) to correspond with the logged or estimated distance traveled. Plot the set and rate/drift of the tidal stream **BD** to indicate the effect of the current (for the time it took to sail **AB**). The point D is the estimated position (**EP**) and AD, the course- and speed-made-good. The logbook must be kept up to date with details of distance traveled and course steered. Whenever an accurate fix is obtained, the old **EP** can be ignored.

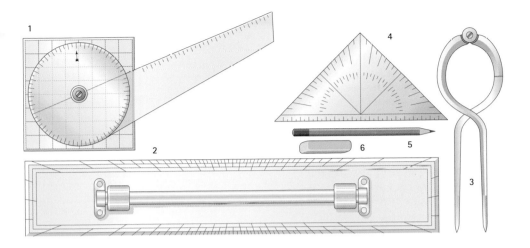

The chart table should measure at least 24 in x 30 in (61 cm x 76 cm) Basic equipment includes up-to-date charts, a nautical almanac, which includes tide tables, pilot books, a log book, and a note pad. A practical selection of plotting instruments would consist of: a navigational plotter, 1, which is above all useful for plotting magnetic bearings; a roller rule, 2, or parallel rule that can be rolled or walked across the chart with one hand to lay off courses and bearings; a pair of dividers, 3, for measuring off distances; and a navigational set square or navigational protractor, 4 Soft pencils (2B), 5, a sharpener (not shown), and a square eraser, 6, that will not roll are also indispensable.

MARK	COURSE & DISTANCE	REMARKS
⚓ 18 ft	↑	spire ⌀ chimney pier Lt 065°M
No. 4 ⏢ R 200°M	1.5 miles / a/c 125°M ↑	F.S ⌀ TOWER LEADS TO ⚓
No. 1 ⏢ R.W. 1 mile	2.6 miles / a/c 085°M ↑	
FAIRWAY ⏢ R.W. 1/2 mile	0.5 miles / 015°M	Tidal stream astern 2.0 kt.

Chart symbols

The chart symbols, below, are a universal form of shorthand when plotting a course. Use the 24-hr clock, eg., 18.30, not 6.30 p.m. Symbols in blue represent those used in the US.

+ ⊙	Dead Reckoning position	⟫	Course-made-good
△ ▣	Estimated position	⟫⟫	Tidal stream
⊙ △	Fix	⟶	Position line
↗	Course steered	⟨⟨⟩⟩	Transferred position line

Navigator's handbook

Electronics can fail so prepare a back-up in the navigator's handbook. To read the sequence above, start at the bottom. Leave fairway buoy to port, 1, distance 1/2 nautical mile (804 m); steer 015°M for 0.5 miles. No. 1 buoy, 2, is now 1 mile (1.8 km) abeam to port. Alter course to 085°M for 2.6 miles (4.8 km), until No. 4 beacon, 3, is abeam to starboard, bearing 200°M. Alter course to 125°M to bring flag staff and tower in transit which leads to anchorage in 1.5 miles (2.8 km). Anchor, 4, in 18 ft (3 fm or 5.5 m) of water when spire and chimney are in transit and pier is bearing 065°M.

THE LANGUAGE OF CHARTS

Visualize a light within a globe throwing the shadows of coastlines on to a cylinder. The cylinder is then rolled to produce a flat surface. This is the basis of map projections.

The problem of the nautical chart is how to represent the spherical surface of the Earth on a flat piece of paper *without* distorting the features used by the navigator. Except in very high latitudes, for specialized purposes, or for harbor plans, the Mercator projection, which exaggerates the size and distorts the shape of areas far from the equator, is almost universally used at sea. One of its properties is that a straight line will intersect all meridians at the same angle.

The largest-scale chart should always be used. The larger the scale, the more detailed will be the information given. In addition, errors in plotting on a large-scale chart will cause less error in the position than on a small-scale one. Much of the information given on charts is expressed in standardized abbreviations and symbols, listed in the publications *Chart No. 1, Nautical Chart Symbols, Abbreviations, and Terms* (in the US) and *Symbols and Abbreviations Used on Admiralty Charts, Chart 5011* (in the UK). Because buoyage, lights, and other features change from time to time, charts have to be updated continually from *Notices to Mariners*, issued weekly. The date of publication of a chart is printed outside the bottom margin in the center or in the bottom left-hand corner, and new editions are shown to the right of it. Corrections are entered at the bottom left-hand corner.

Charts are published in the US and UK by the national hydrographic authorities with worldwide coverage, and the chart catalog shows what charts are available throughout the world.

Sailing Directions, or pilot books, are published by the same authorities and give information about local conditions, such as conspicuous landmarks, harbor approach courses, port facilities, and so on. They are a necessary adjunct to the charts, whose information is necessarily incomplete.

Chart symbols are grouped as follows: coastal and natural features, harbors and buildings, buoys and beacons, radio and radar, fog signals, dangers, depth contours, quality of the bottom, tides and currents, and the compass rose.

1 Radio mast exhibiting red lights.
2 Light beacon flashing every 3 secs, 16.6 ft (5 m) elevation luminous range 5 miles (9.3 km). Marks a shoal with 18 ft

11 Wreck showing part of hull at chart datum.
12 Sandy shore.
13 Depth contours indicate gradient.
14 Buildings.
15 Fort with flagstaff 102 ft (31 m) high.
16 Rocky bottom.

17 Light beacon flashing every 5 secs, 20 ft (6 m) elevation, luminous range 9.3 km (5 miles).
18 Light beacon flashing red every 5 secs, 29.5 ft (9 m) elevation, 8 miles (15 km) luminous range.

(3 fm) over it. Useful
day mark.

3 Mud.

4 Coral and shell bottom.

9.1 fm (55 ft) charted depth.

5 A patch of shallow water.

6 Beacon with quick flashing

light. Useful day mark.

7 23–33 ft (7–10 m) contour.

8 Wharves.

9 Church.

10 Flagstaff on coal
wharf building.

Cr.	Creek
Pass.	Passages
Chan.	Channel
Appr. Apprs.	Approaches
Anch.	Anchorage
Hr.	Harbor
P.	Port
Lndg.	Landing Place

Oil/gas platform

Lightship

Jade ▲ *No.5*
R   B

Names, numbers,
and colors of buoys
are shown as above

Rock which is uncovered
at LW (with drying height
above chart datum)

Rock that is awash
at level of chart datum

Underwater rock always
covered but with less
than 2 m over it at chart
datum, or a rocky area
the depth of which is
unknown but considered
to be dangerous

Obstn

Underwater obstruction
considered dangerous

Foul

Foul area, not dangerous
but to be avoided when
anchoring or fishing

RD

Non-directional
radio beacon

(Masts)

Wreck on which
masts only are visible

15 Wk

Unsurveyed wreck;
exact depth unknown;
considered to have
safe clearance at
depth shown

7₃ Wk

Wreck over which
the depth has been
obtained by sounding,
but not by wire sweep

5 Wk

Wreck that has
been swept by wire
to depth shown

Wreck over which
exact depth is unknown
but thought to be over
28 m (15.3 fm)

Wreck dring at LW

Overfalls and tide-rips

Eddies

Kelp

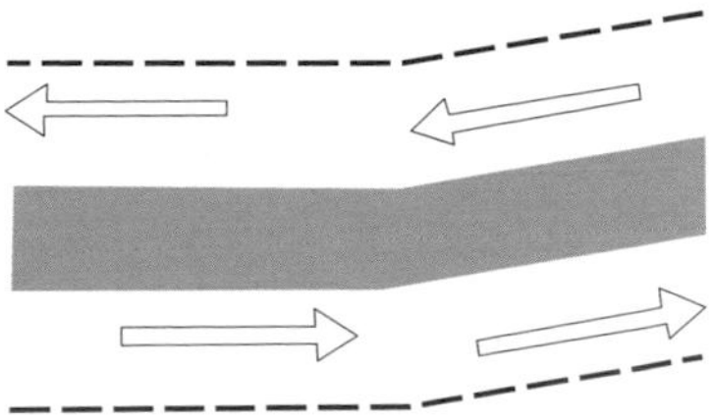

19 Coral reef.

20 66 ft (20 m) contour.

21 Flashing beacon
marking a shoal.

22 Black and red buoy,
flashing red every 1.5 secs.
Marks a patch with 27 ft
(8.3 m) over it.

23 Bearing line.

Reproduced from British
Admiralty Charts with the
permission of the Controler
of H.M. Stationery Office
and of the Hydrographer
of the Navy.

Traffic separation scheme: one-way
traffic lanes (separated by zone)

SOUNDING THE DEPTHS

Knowing the water depth, especially when used in conjunction with other information, can be valuable in many circumstances at sea, such as clearing a danger or making a landfall. Where the bottom configuration is distinctive or displayed on the chart as depth contours, a line of soundings can help to determine the boat's position.

Echo sounders give a continuous record of depth within the range of the instrument. An acoustic signal is transmitted to the sea bed by means of a transducer fixed to the ship's bottom, and the reflected signal received is converted into depth by measuring the time interval between transmission and reception—the average speed of sound through water being 4,925 ft/sec (1,500 m/sec). The display of depth can be presented in a number of ways: digitally, as a trace reproducing the bottom profile; on a cathode-ray tube; or as a flash on a circular scale.

The instrument measures the distance from the sea bed to the transducer, which is usually at the bottom of the hull. The sailor is unlikely to be interested primarily in this depth, but in one of two other measurements: the depth below the keel, or the actual depth of water above the sea bed. Most instruments have a keel offset facility, which adjusts the displayed depth to show depth below keel. If a negative offset can be set, then the instrument can display depth of water. The helmsman needs to know how the echo sounder is set up and the draft of the vessel.

The depth below the keel is the value most commonly monitored and the helmsman should regularly check that there is adequate clearance, especially close to shoal waters.

The depth of water is most useful for confirming position by comparing with charted depths, after allowing for the height of tide. An echo sounder with a graphic readout is best suited to running a line of soundings, since dramatic changes in the water depth are immediately apparent.

In very cold or freshwater, sound travels more slowly, so allow extra clearance since the actual depth will be shallower than indicated.

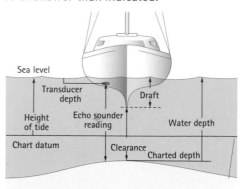

The depth of water on charts is given in fathoms and feet or in meters below chart datum, which is now usually the lowest predictable (astronomical) water depth. To estimate the clearance beneath a boat's keel from the echo sounder reading, add the depth of the transducer (if necessary) and deduct the draft of the boat. To estimate this from the chart, take the charted water depth, add the tabulated tidal height for the appropriate time, and deduct the draft of the boat.

The latest electronic echo sounders display depth up to 600 ft, 100 fms, and 200 m in a clockface display and/or LCD readout. The problem of weather-proofing is largely overcome by using a repeater in the cockpit, so allowing the main system to be sited in a sheltered position. An alarm, set to operate at any chosen depth up to 100 ft (16 fm), is useful in poor visibility, shallow water, or at anchor.

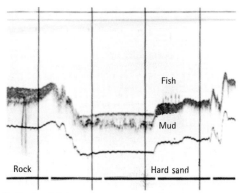

Fish

Mud

Rock

Hard sand

Unlike the digital sounders, the more elaborate **graphic recorder** provides a permanent depth record by tracing the contours of the sea bed with a stylus on a moving, sensitized- paper roll. It gives detailed information of the nature of the bottom; mud, hard sand, and rock are clearly defined. Shoals of fish are indicated as weaker signals.

Through-hull fitting

A **transducer** fitted to the ship's hull transmits the sound signal; although normally mounted on the outside of the hull, some models can be fitted inside to avoid cutting holes in the hull. Most give out an arc of sound over 45°, so if the boat heels more than about 22°, the signal will not aim directly at the sea bed. This produces a false reading. The solution for most cruising boats that are likely to heel more than 20° is to fit twin transducers, one for each tack, preferably with an automatic gravity switch. Position them forward of the keel and away from any areas of turbulence. If they are mounted too close to the keel the sound may be obstructed. Remember to calculate the vertical separation between the transducer and the bottom of the keel. This must be subtracted from the sounded depth to give depth below the keel, if not built into the instrument.

Sounding levels

The traditional way of sounding at sea used to be with the sounding lead: a leaden weight, generally "armed" with tallow to collect bottom samples, attached to a marked line. The hand lead is still widely used. The markings on the line, widely adopted with metrication of British Admiralty charts, are as follows:

Meters	Markings
1,11,21	1 strip of leather
2,12,22	2 strips of leather
3,13,23	blue bunting
4,14,24	green and white bunting
5,15,25	white bunting
6,16,26	green bunting
7,17,27	red bunting
8,18,28	blue and white bunting
9,19,29	red and white bunting
10	leather with a hole in it
20	leather with two holes in it
0.2	a piece of mackerel line

Using a depth sounder

In fog or off low-lying coastlines, a depth sounder can be invaluable for confirming an estimated position and to indicate position by successive soundings, with or without a bearing. It can also guide the boat into harbor or to a given destination by following a line of soundings. Choose a contour line on the chart, as seen below, and take continuous soundings, having made sure that no underwater dangers lie along the route. Soundings are, however, often difficult to interpret, and should be treated with caution.

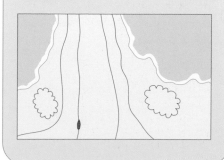

WORKING THE TIDES

The tides are caused by the attraction of the moon, and to a lesser extent the far more distant sun, on the waters surrounding the Earth. The tidal wave that carries the high waters around the globe is caused by the Earth's rotation.

The moving water itself is referred to as the tidal stream and the change in depth as the water piles up as the tide. A tidal day corresponds to the period of rotation of the Earth with respect to the moon, which is about 24 hrs 50 mins. Tides may be divided into three main categories: semi-diurnal with two high waters and two low waters each tidal day; diurnal with one high water and one low water each tidal day; and mixed tides, which vary from essentially diurnal to essentially semi-diurnal in character.

The seaman's principal interest in tides is in how to predict the times and heights of high and low water and the rate and set of the tidal stream. Tide tables give the times and heights above chart datum of high and low water for various Reference Stations (Standard Ports in the UK) and time differences for Subordinate Stations (Secondary Ports in the UK), as well as a means of determining heights at intermediate times.

Tidal streams, a coastal phenomenon caused by the vertical rise and fall of the tide, normally change direction every six hours. Their direction and strength are given in tidal stream atlases for both spring (high) and neap (low) tides, with a means of interpolating between them according to the range of the tide. Tidal stream information also appears on charts.

Meteorological conditions can have a pronounced effect on both tides and tidal streams. A prolonged strong onshore wind will increase the height of the tide and an offshore wind decrease it, and the tidal streams will be affected accordingly. A very high barometric pressure will lower the tidal heights.

Mean High Water Springs

Water level · Spring range · Spring rise · Neap range · Neap rise

MLW springs

Chart datum (LAT) · Drying height

Charted depths on modern charts are given in feet or meters below (and drying heights in feet or meters above) chart datum, which is usually (but not in the US) the lowest astronomical tide (LAT). Older charts show depths in fathoms, usually below mean low water springs (MLWS). The height of the tide is the distance between chart datum and sea-level, and the range is the difference between the height at high water and the height at low water. This range is greatest at spring tides, two days after a full and a new moon, when the sun and moon are in conjunction or opposition. When the sun and moon exert a right-angled force on the oceans, the water displacement, and thus the tidal range, is least. Mean high water springs

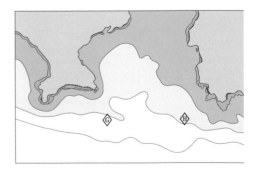

Diamonds marked on the chart indicate positions for which tidal stream data is available. The letter keys in with a panel on the chart where information for each of the 6 hrs before and after high water, springs, and neaps, is given.

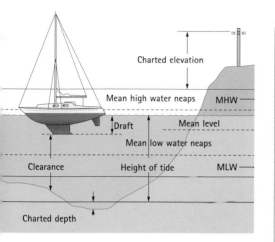

- Charted elevation
- Mean high water neaps — MHW
- Draft
- Mean level
- Mean low water neaps
- Clearance
- Height of tide — MLW
- Charted depth

(MHWS) is the average level of all high water heights, and mean low water springs (MLWS) of all low water heights, at spring tides throughout the year. US charts use mean high water (MHW), the average level of all high water heights, and mean low water (MLW), the average of all low water heights (both springs and neaps), over a 19-year period as the datums for charted elevations and charted depths, respectively. Metric charts use a separate chart datum. The mean high and low water levels at neap tides fall within the range of the springs. Drying heights covered at high tide, but not at low, are measured above chart datum and underlined on the chart, to distinguish them from soundings.

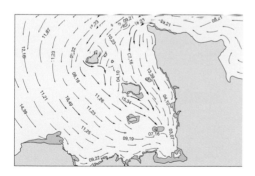

The tidal atlas of a given area indicates the direction of the tidal stream and its rate in knots. Pairs of figures, eg., 10.24, give the rate at neap and spring tides respectively. The atlas contains 13 small charts, one for each of the 6 hrs before and after high water at a Standard Port (such as Dover), and one for high water itself.

Tidal predictions

To find the height of tide at a particular place, consult the tide tables to discover the most recent high or low water at the nearest Reference Station or Standard Port, and its height. If you are nearer a Subordinate Station or Secondary Port, check the tables for the tidal time differences between the two. For example, if high water occurs 20 mins later at the Secondary Port add 20 mins. Work out the tidal range by subtracting the height at low water from the height at high. Note the difference between the time of the nearest high water and the time you require to give the interval (number of hrs) before or after high tide. Turn to the tidal curve diagram for the Standard Port and with reference to time between high and low water select the appropriate curve. Read off the factor where the interval cuts the curve. Multiply your tidal range by the factor to give the height of the tide above low water. Add this to the low water height (already gathered from the charts) to then obtain the height of the tide above chart datum at the time required. Before looking up tidal data, adjust the local time to the reference zone for the tables used, including summer or daylight savings time adjustment if necessary.

Twelfth's rule, below, gives a rough guide to the change of depth in a 6-hr tide.
The rate of rise or fall is:
1st hr—1/12 of range (10%)
2nd hr—2/12 of range (15%)
3rd hr—3/12 of range (25%)
4th hr—3/12 of range (25%)
5th hr—2/12 of range (15%)
6th hr—1/12 of range (10%)

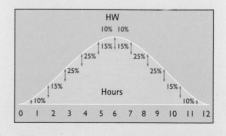

THE DISTANCE RUN

The difficulty in measuring distance traveled at sea is that the medium in which the craft moves is itself moving with respect to the Earth. Distance over the ground can be measured directly between fixes, but otherwise must be deduced from measurements of speed or distance traveled through the water.

A log is a shipboard device for measuring speed or distance through the water. In the towed, or taffrail, log a rotator is towed behind the vessel and turned by the flow of water past it as the vessel proceeds. The distance run, mechanically derived from the number of revolutions, is recorded, usually in miles and tenths of a mile, on a dial fixed to the taffrail. Although largely superseded by electronic bottom logs, it remains one of the most reliable logs.

The principle of deriving speed from a rotator is also used in the electronic log. Here the rotation of a small impeller projecting through the hull generates an electric current, the frequency of which will be directly proportional to the speed of the vessel. Such logs are highly sensitive and are generally integrated with other sensors that measure sailing performance.

In a pitot-static log, a pitot tube projecting through the hull detects the dynamic pressure in undisturbed water and, from this, the speed through the water is recorded automatically on a dial. The pitot log is apt to be unreliable at low speeds.

Another way of deriving speed from dynamic water pressure is by means of a small strut, usually raked aft and still found in a number of yachts' logs.

The electromagnetic log, housed beneath the hull, uses the principle of magnetic induction to detect the movement of the magnetic field as the vessel moves through the water. It is extremely accurate over a wide range of speeds, but can be affected by turbulence.

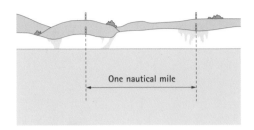

One nautical mile

Logs fitted to the hull should be calibrated by checking the recorded speed over a measured mile with a timepiece. Various measured distances around the coast are marked by transits and shown on charts. Several runs in both directions need to be made under power at a constant speed, and at right angles to the transits. The positioning of hull fittings for electronic equipment is important. Echo sounders and log transducers should be in the middle section of the boat to avoid turbulence but forward of the keel. Avoid using different metals together under water.

Chip log

A good homemade log is the "chip log"—a weighted triangle of plywood, approximately 6 in (17.7 cm) across. A towing line is attached to the top corner and short lines running from the bottom two corners are clipped to it with a peg. The towing line, always measured metrically, consists of 200 ft (61 m) of soft cord, knotted at 25.3 ft (7.7 m) intervals, starting some 30 ft (9.1 m) up the line. Drop the triangle over the stern and, using a stop watch, count the number of knots that run out in 15 seconds to check your speed (1 knot of speed = 15 sec/7.71 m).

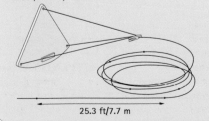

25.3 ft/7.7 m

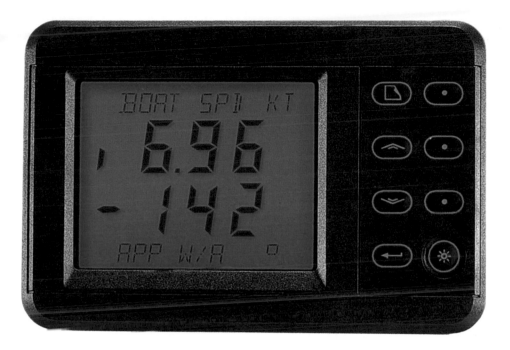

Electronic instrumentation has become commonplace aboard most yachts, with displays sited above and below decks. Basic systems will display boat speed, depth, wind speed, and wind direction. Some advanced integrated systems display a range of additional information, such as speed over the ground, average speed, velocity made good to windward, tidal rate, and, where a fixing system is interfaced, time and distance to a waypoint or the destination. The display here shows boat speed and, underneath, wind angle.

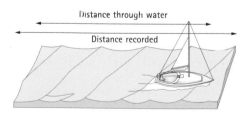

Distance through water

Distance recorded

Log readings are affected by sea conditions and boat speed, often resulting in underrecording at low speed and overrecording in heavy seas. An unsteady course will increase the distance traveled in relation to the intended course. Since the log reads the boat's speed or distance run through the water, the tides and currents must be allowed for, to determine the speed or distance-made-good over the ground.

Checklist for measuring distance

1 If you suspect the log's accuracy, check that the impeller, rotator, or pitot tube is not fouled by seaweed. Also check the power supply.

2 1.8 kph-1 kn equals one nautical mile per hour. Speed in knots equals distance in nautical miles divided by time in hours. Time in hours equals distance divided by speed. Distance equals speed multiplied by time in hours.

3 The Dutchman's Log requires no equipment and gives a rough speed guide. Throw any floatable object well ahead of the bow and start the stop watch as it passes the boat's stem. Stop the watch as it passes the stern.

4 Speed in knots is length of boat (distance) x 3,600 (seconds in an hour) divided by time in seconds x 6,076 (feet in a nautical mile).

THE USE OF RADAR

The size and weight of modern radar equipment makes it practicable for boats as small as 25 ft (7.6 m) overall. It can be used day or night and in fog as both a navigational aid and a collision avoidance device. It detects the range of an object by timing the interval between the transmission of a radio wave and the return of its echo.

The bearing of the object is determined by the direction of the antenna or scanner and the information is translated on to a map on the screen—a cathode ray tube plan position indicator (PPI), usually fitted by the chart table. In most yacht radars the PPI will be either a relative head-up display with the ship at the center and the ship's head pointing upwards, or either north-up or course-up. In the head-up mode stationary objects, such as buoys or anchored ships, appear to drift past the yacht as it makes its way towards the top of the screen. In larger ships with gyro compasses, at least one display will generally be in true motion where your own ship moves on the screen and static objects stay still.

The principal use of radar at sea is the avoidance of collision. It is by no means a simple problem because the movement of all ship echoes on the screen is relative. The movement of *both* ships in any encounter is key. Modern radar displays to some extent facilitate an understanding of the problem but, if the set does not do it for you, such practices as keeping a radar plot to ascertain the closest point of approach is highly desirable. The provisions of the Collision Regulations (see pp. 124–125) in relation to radar should be well understood and borne in mind.

The simplest use of radar for position fixing is by comparison with the chart. However, the radar picture of the coast will generally be difficult to interpret precisely because the echoing characteristics of points of land can differ widely from their appearance on the chart. A fix by radar can be obtained from the ranges of two or three identified objects or the bearings of two objects and a range, or of course the range and

bearing of a single object. However, radar ranges are generally more reliable than the bearings and visual bearings that are sometimes used with radar distances. With some systems the radar can be interfaced with GPS (see pp. 126–127) and advantage taken of the electronic link between range and bearing to, for example, mark a waypoint or a natural feature on the radar screen. The radar in this case must be linked to a fluxgate compass or gyro.

Radar transponder beacons, called Racons, are used to enhance the echoing characteristics of seamarks and landmarks around the coast, such as light vessels and lighthouses, and are marked on the chart. Since there is a slight delay in the signal, however, the boat's real distance from the Racon is slightly less than that indicated on the screen. Racons are used primarily for identification and generally have a range of about 10 nm (18.5 km).

Solid objects, such as ships, buoys, beacons, and land, show up as lighted areas on the screen and the water as dark. Compare this map with the radar screen opposite. High cliffs and even distant hills may be visible before an approaching fishing vessel or low-lying beach. So **choose prominent objects as marks for coastal navigation.** Remember that underwater dangers will not be picked up on the screen.

To establish your position by radar, refer to the local chart. Buoys marking a channel are often fitted with reflectors and look conveniently similar on the screen and chart. Radar beacons, marked on the chart as Ramark, appear as a line on the screen. Ships, islands, etc, often appear wider than they are, and a harbor entrance may only show up at close range. Consult the chart regularly for underwater hazards.

Radar reflectors

To alert other vessels to its presence, a boat needs a good radar reflector to boost any radar signals that bounce off it. The reflector works as a prism, presenting a series of right-angled corners to trap the signals and bounce them straight back, with as little loss in other directions as possible. It needs to be accurately constructed, strong, rigid, and not less than 18 in (45 cm) across the diagonal. Even a small increase in size dramatically increases the echoing area.

Site the reflector at least 15 ft (4.6 m) above sea level. Mount a bracket at the masthead, spreaders, or on twin triatic or backstays for a permanent fitting. To hoist temporarily, secure with shock cord or use a flag halyard to the spreader or up the backstay.

The octahedral-shaped reflector must be hoisted in the "catch rain" position, *not* point up. It is cheap and easy to stow, but loses efficiency when the boat heels.

The Firdell Blipper, which consists of a five-fold array of corners, accepts angles of heel up to 30° with little loss of echo. Lightweight and sealed in a plastic case, it will be picked up by most vessels at a good range; this depends on its size and height.

Units that combine radar and chart images make interpretation of radar echoes much easier and more reliable for modern sailors. The cursors on this split screen display are linked.

BUOYAGE SYSTEM

The buoyage system selected for use around the world is the IALA (International Association of Lighthouse Authorities) Maritime Buoyage System. There are two regions, A and B, in which the marks are identical. The colors, red and green, however, are used in region A to indicate, respectively, the port and starboard lateral limits of a channel when entering it, whereas in region B they indicate the reverse. Region B comprises the USA, Central and South America, Japan, and the Philippines; region A, the rest of the world. There are five types of mark: lateral, cardinal, isolated danger marks, safe water marks, and special marks. During the day, they are identified by the color and shape of the buoy and topmark, and at night by the color and rhythm of lights. Lateral marks indicate the port and starboard limits of a channel.

Cardinal marks, 4, are black and yellow with black double-cone topmarks to indicate where navigable water lies. If north, **5,** the cones point up; south, **6,** down; west, **7,** inwards; east, **8,** outwards. At night Cardinal marks exhibit quick or very quick flashes of white light: north, uninterrupted; east, groups of three; south, groups of six and a long one; west, groups of nine.

IALA Maritime Buoyage System for Region A

The **port-hand lateral markers** are a red can, **1,** or are spar-shaped bases, **2,** with a can-shaped top. The **starboard markers** are green conical with pointed topmarks, **3.** At night they flash red or green; respectively.

Isolated danger marks, 9, are striped red and black with two round black topmarks, and can be passed either side. At night they emit groups of two flashes.

Safe water marks, 10, are striped red and white with a round red topmark, and at night exhibit an occulting white light. Uncharted dangers are shown by cardinal or lateral marks.

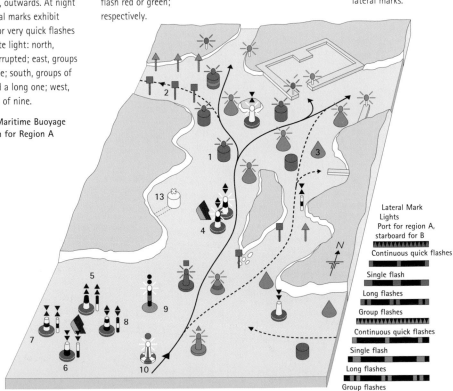

Lateral Mark
Lights
Port for region A,
starboard for B

Continuous quick flashes

Single flash

Long flashes

Group flashes

Continuous quick flashes

Single flash

Long flashes

Group flashes

Cardinal marks generally draw attention to shoal water, and the shape and color of the topmark indicates the side on which it is safe to pass.

Isolated danger marks are positioned above isolated shoals, rocks, or wrecks surrounded by navigable water. Safe water marks indicate that surrounding water is navigable. Special marks identify military, recreational, and traffic separation zones, as well as instruments or pipelines.

☐ IALA Maritime Region A
☐ IALA Maritime Region B

The USA, parts of Central and South America, and Japan, comprise region B, where the system is being gradually introduced to remove the confusion caused by the variety of traditional systems presently in use. The marks for regions A and B are almost identical, except that region B uses red to indicate the starboard side of a channel entered from seaward or from the conventional direction of approach, and green to show the port side.

The conventional direction for approaching the system is clockwise—north along the Pacific coast, south along the Atlantic, north and west along the coast of the Gulf of Mexico and in the Great Lakes, except Lake Michigan where it is south. The mnemonic, "red right, returning" is a useful reminder when entering the IALA B system.

A preferred channel may be indicated by a modified lateral mark—red with a green stripe if the preferred channel is to port, 11, green with a red stripe if it is to starboard, 12. (Or the reverse for region A.)

Special marks, yellow in both regions, 13, sometimes with a yellow X topmark, mark forbidden zones, such as cables, military areas, and spoil grounds.

IALA Maritime Buoyage System for Region B

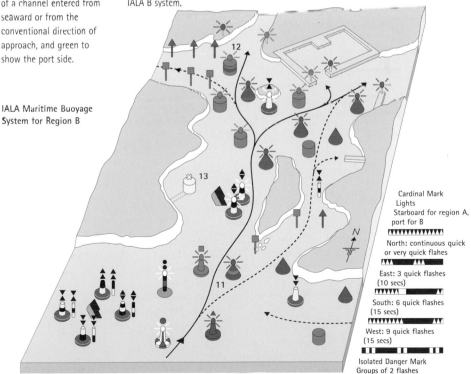

Cardinal Mark Lights
Starboard for region A, port for B

North: continuous quick or very quick flahes

East: 3 quick flashes (10 secs)

South: 6 quick flashes (15 secs)

West: 9 quick flashes (15 secs)

Isolated Danger Mark Groups of 2 flashes

NAVIGATING BY SEXTANT

Offshore, astronomical navigation provides the most generally available form of non-electronic position fixing. The apparent position at any moment of all visible heavenly bodies as seen from the Earth is tabulated in the *Nautical Almanac* and can be used in conjunction with a sextant and timepiece to establish position.

The coordinates given in the almanac are declination (Dec), which is analogous to latitude, measured north and south of the celestial equator, and Greenwich hour angle (GHA), measured westward through 360° from the Greenwich meridian. Time needs to be within about 1 sec since, at the Earth's rate of rotation, an error of 1 sec can produce an error in position of a quarter of a mile.

The fixed parts of the sextant are the frame, graduated arc, telescope, and horizon glass, which is half silvered so that the horizon can be viewed through the unsilvered part. The instrument should always be picked up by the frame, never the arc, and the delicate mirrors should never be touched except for cleaning.

The word sextant is derived from the arc which is 60°, one-sixth of a circle, but the mirrors double the reflection so angles can be measured up to 120°.

When the movable index arm is at zero the index mirror should be precisely parallel to the horizon glass.

The sextant altitude of the observed body must first be corrected to obtain the true altitude. The observer's height of eye produces a dip of the horizon for which the correction must be subtracted. Refraction of the light from the body observed, especially marked at low altitudes, must also be taken into account and combined corrections for dip and refraction are given in most nautical almanacs. When the upper or lower limb of the sun or moon are observed the correction for semi-diameter must also be applied.

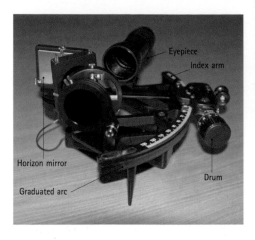

Eyepiece
Index arm
Horizon mirror
Drum
Graduated arc

To take an observation, view the horizon glass, and move the index bar along the arc until the body is visible. Turn the micrometer drum until the lower limb touches the horizon. Sway the sextant gently sideways through an arc about 20° either side of the line of sight to ensure that the exact point of contact is vertically below the body. The precise time to the nearest second is recorded, usually in GMT. The angle between the horizon, the line of sight, and the body is read on the arc for the degrees, and on the drum for the minutes. Read to the nearest half minute.

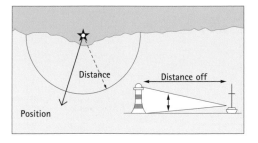

Distance
Distance off
Position

Distance-off can be measured by vertical sextant angle, if the height of an object, such as a lighthouse, is known. Given height of eye and the height of the object, Distance-off Tables or a calculator will give the object's distance. A bearing taken at the same time gives an accurate position fix. Ensure that the reading is corrected for any index error.

declination (15°–20°) same name as latitude

LHA	15° Hc d Z	16° Hc d Z	17° Hc d Z	18° Hc d Z	19° Hc d Z	Hc
0	61 00 ·44 180	62 00 ·44 180	63 00 ·44 180	64 00 ·44 180	65 00 ·44 180	66 00 ·
1	60 59 44 178	61 59 44 178	62 59 44 178	63 59 44 178	64 59 44 178	65 59
2	60 57 44 176	61 57 44 176	62 57 44 176	63 57 44 176	64 57 44 176	65 57
3	60 53 44 174	61 53 44 174	62 53 44 174	63 53 44 174	64 52 44 173	65 52
4	60 48 44 172	61 48 44 172	62 47 44 172	63 47 44 172	64 47 44 171	65 46
5	60 41 ·44 170	61 41 ·44 170	62 40 ·44 170	63 40 ·44 169	64 39 ·44 169	65 38 ·
6	60 33 44 168	61 33 44 168	62 32 44 168	63 31 44 167	64 30 44 167	65 29
7	60 24 44 166	61 23 44 166	62 22 44 166	63 21 44 165	64 19 44 165	65 18
8	60 13 44 164	61 11 44 164	62 10 44 163	63 09 44 163	64 07 44 163	65 05
9	60 00 44 162	60 59 44 162	61 57 44 162	62 55 44 161	63 53 44 161	64 51
10	59 47 ·44 161	60 45 ·44 160	61 43 ·44 160	62 40 ·44 159	63 38 ·44 158	64 36 ·
11	59 32 44 159	60 29 44 158	61 27 44 158	62 24 44 157	63 21 44 157	64 18
12	59 15 44 157	60 13 44 156	61 10 44 156	62 07 44 155	63 03 44 154	64 00
13	58 58 44 155	59 55 44 155	60 51 44 154	61 48 44 153	62 44 44 152	63 40
14	58 39 44 153	59 35 44 153	60 32 44 152	61 28 44 152	62 23 44 150	63 19
15	58 19 ·44 152	59 15 ·44 151	60 11 ·44 150	61 06 ·44 149	62 01 ·44 149	62 56 ·
16	57 58 44 150	58 53 44 149	59 49 44 148	60 44 44 148	61 38 44 147	62 33
17	57 36 44 148	58 31 44 147	59 25 44 147	60 20 44 146	61 14 44 145	62 08
18	57 12 44 147	58 07 44 146	59 01 44 145	59 55 44 144	60 49 44 143	61 42
19	56 48 44 145	57 42 44 144	58 36 44 143	59 29 44 142	60 22 44 142	61 15
20	56 23 ·44 143	57 16 ·44 143	58 10 ·44 142	59 03 ·44 141	59 55 ·44 140	60 47 ·
21	55 57 44 142	56 50 44 141	57 42 44 140	58 35 44 139	59 27 44 139	60 18
22	55 29 44 140	56 22 44 139	57 14 44 139	58 06 44 138	58 57 44 137	59 48
23	55 01 44 139	55 54 44 138	56 45 44 137	57 37 44 136	58 27 44 135	59 18
24	54 33 44 137	55 24 44 137	56 15 44 136	57 06 44 135	57 57 44 134	58 46
25	54 03 ·44 136	54 54 ·44 135	55 45 ·44 134	56 35 ·44 133	57 25 ·44 132	58 14 ·
26	53 33 44 135	54 23 44 134	55 13 44 133	56 03 44 132	56 53 44 131	57 41
27	53 01 44 133	53 52 44 132	54 41 44 131	55 31 44 130	56 19 44 129	57 08
28	52 30 44 132	53 19 44 131	54 09 44 130	54 57 44 129	55 46 44 128	56 33
29	51 57 44 131	52 46 44 130	53 35 44 129	54 24 44 128	55 11 44 127	55 59

Sight Reduction Tables for Air Navigation AP 3270 (=HO249) are the most suitable for small craft: Vol I is for stars, Vol II covers latitudes 0°–39° and Vol III, 40°–89°. To work up a sight, choose a position near your dead reckoning (DR) such that the latitude is a whole degree and the longitude, when combined with the Greenwich hour angle (GHA), will give a whole degree of local hour angle (LHA). Enter the tables at the page indicated by the latitude and declination of the body. Extract the calculated altitude Hc and azimuth Z. Then correct Hc for the odd minutes of declination using d and compare it with the true altitude.

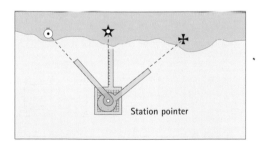

A horizontal sextant angle will provide an extremely accurate position fix. Three objects must be visible and the angle between them measured by holding the sextant horizontally. The easiest way to plot the bearings on the chart is to use a station pointer, the three arms of which are set to produce the two angles read off the sextant. The pointer is then moved around the chart until the three arms cut the three objects and the fix is at the center of the plotter. Tracing paper can also be used.

Station pointer

Sight reduction

The leap from a sextant observation to a position line is performed by using the almanac and sight reduction tables or a dedicated calculator. Declination and hour angle are both resolved by means of the tables into altitude and azimuth. The difference in nautical miles between tabular and true altitude is the intercept. This is plotted from the assumed position along the line of azimuth, towards the body if the observed altitude is greater than the tabular, and away from it if it is less. A line perpendicular to the intercept represents the position line.

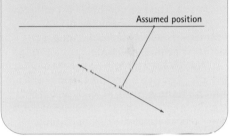

Assumed position

Noon sight

The simplest form of sight is the meridian altitude or noon sight, when the sun lies due north or south of your position. The position line at right angles to the sun's bearing thus defines a parallel of latitude, so no plotting is needed. The calculation involves finding the zenith distance, which is the altitude of the body observed minus 90°, and adding or subtracting the declination to find the latitude. The sun's declination (angle from the Equator) may be north or south, depending on the time of year. In the northern hemisphere, if the declination is north (northern summer), latitude is zenith distance plus declination; if south, declination is subtracted. To find the time (GMT) of the sun's meridian passage at your own longitude, consult the almanac for time on the prime meridian. Convert the longitude from arc into time (1° = 4 min) and add if west of Greenwich, or subtract if east.

COLLISION REGULATIONS

Every seaman should be familiar with the International Collision Regulations, which apply to all vessels on the high seas and the navigable waters connected to them. The following steering and sailing rules are of particular importance to small craft.

Risk of collision exists if the compass bearing of an approaching vessel does not appreciably alter.

Action to avoid collision should be taken in good time and be bold enough to be obvious to the other vessel.

In narrow channels, vessels should keep to the starboard side. A sailing vessel should not hinder a vessel that can navigate safely only within the channel. No vessel should anchor within a narrow channel.

Traffic lanes should not normally be crossed; if they have to be, the crossing should be made as close as possible to a right angle. A sailing vessel should not hinder a vessel under power following a traffic lane.

When there is a risk of collision between two sailing vessels, the vessel with the wind on the port side keeps clear; when both have the wind on the same side the windward vessel keeps clear; a vessel with the wind on the port side keeps clear of another if there is a doubt as to which side the other vessel has the wind.

An overtaking vessel keeps clear of the vessel being overtaken. When two power-driven vessels meet head on, each alters course to starboard. When two power-driven vessels are crossing, the vessel that has the other on her own starboard side keeps clear. The give-way vessel must take early and substantial action to keep clear. A stand-on vessel keeps her course and speed but she may take action if a collision appears unavoidable.

A power-driven vessel gives way to a sailing vessel. A sailing vessel keeps clear of a vessel not under command, restricted in her ability to maneuver, or fishing.

At night and in poor visibility, every power vessel under way must display

port, starboard, stern, and masthead lights. The legal distances from which the lights must be visible depend on the length of the boat. When entering foreign customs ports, check that your boat is equipped with the required lights for customs clearance.

Maneuvering and warning signals
Sound signals

●	I am altering course to starboard
●●	I am altering course to port
●●●	I am operating astern propulsion
▬ ▬ ●	I intend to overtake on your starboard side
▬ ▬ ● ●	I intend to overtake, port side
▬ ● ▬ ●	I agree to be overtaken
● ● ● ● ●	I do not agree to be overtaken, I doubt you will avoid a collision
▬▬▬	Warning signal and reply when approaching a bend

Shapes displayed in rigging (daymarks)

▼▼	Vessel motor–sailing
✕	Vessel engaged in fishing
▲	Fishing nets extending more than 490 ft (149 m)
◆	Vessel towing if length of two exceeds 650 ft (198 m)
●	Vessel at anchor
●●●	Vessel aground
◆●◆◆	Vessel dredging or conducting underwater operations. Pass on the side of the diamonds

Sound signals in poor visibility

▬	Power vessel making way
▬ ▬	Power vessel under way but stopped
▬ ● ●	Vessel not under command; restricted in ability to maneuver; constrained by draft; a sailing vessel; vessel towing, pushing, or fishing
▬ ● ● ●	Vessel under tow
♪♪♪♪	Vessel at anchor. If more than 328 ft (100 m) long, bell is followed by 5-sec gong

Yachts under 23 ft (7 m) must display all-round white light in time to prevent a collision.

Yachts under 39 ft (12 m) may combine stern and side lights in a tricolor masthead light.

Yachts over 39 ft (12 m) must carry stern and port and starboard lights. No masthead light.

Yachts over 39 ft (12 m) may carry an all-round red light above an all-round green.

Power-driven vessels under 23 ft (7 m) carry white, all-round masthead light above a bicolor light.

Power-driven vessels under 39 ft (12 m) display white masthead and stern- and sidelights.

Power-driven vessels under 66 ft (20 m) carry a white masthead light above a bicolor, also a sternlight.

Power-driven vessels may have a second, higher masthead light aft.

Vessels at anchor display all-round white light, visible from 2 miles (3.2 km)

When aground, two all-round red lights are shown below an all-round white light.

Vessels not under command display two all-round red lights and, if making way, side- and sternlights.

Vessels restricted in maneuverability carry a white masthead, three all-round lights, side, and sternlights.

When trawling, fishing vessels display an all-round green light above an all-round white.

When hauling nets, fishing vessels add to the trawling lights one white light over a red.

When fishing, other than trawling, vessels carry a red above a white all-round light.

When towing, vessels show two masthead lights forward, or three, if the tow exceeds 656 ft (200 m).

GPS NAVIGATION

Position fixing by satellite has perhaps produced the greatest change in navigational practice since the "discovery of longitude" (as it was termed) in the 18th century, or even the magnetic compass in the 12th century. For the first time the navigator has been able to find his position accurately in any part of the world, at any time of the day or night, and in any weather. This may be said to have made all traditional methods and instruments obsolete, but the cautious mariner must remain constantly aware that all forms of electronic navigation are entirely dependent on power. Without it not one of them will work. Although a power failure is unlikely, when it comes the navigator must be ready to revert to the established practices of navigation at sea, based on the magnetic compass and log; the paper chart with rules and dividers; and, if he is on the ocean, the sextant and almanac and reduction tables or a hand-held computer.

Navigation was one of the first practical purposes to which artificial Earth satellites were put. The US Navy's Transit system became operational in 1964 and was released for civilian use in 1967. Using five satellites orbiting above the Earth, its range was worldwide but the fixing period was intermittent and in some cases lengthy.

Currently, the most used satellite navigation system is its successor, the Navstar Global Positioning System (GPS), funded by the US Department of Defense. It gives continuous position in latitude and longitude to a determined accuracy in any part of the world. A configuration of 24 satellites is used, each of which orbits the Earth every 12 hrs at an altitude of about 12,000 miles and in six orbits each at an angle of 55° to the plane of the equator. At least four satellites are constantly visible, which means that the navigator can obtain a position fix that is updated continuously (or at the very worst every minute or so) anywhere on Earth at any time. The consequence of this is that effectively all other electronic position fixing systems, whether land- or satellite-based, have become redundant.

The GPS system is a military tool but is available for use by the public, although there is the potential that position accuracy will be slightly degraded nominally 325 ft (100 m). This scrambling of the signals to achieve a lesser accuracy is known as Selective Availability (SA). The US government "switched off" Selective Availability in 2000, though the possibility of it being switched back on remains. While SA was operating a system known as Differential GPS was developed that uses a land-based GPS receiver. The known position of the receiver is precise, to identify the fixing errors caused by the SA scrambling. These are then transmitted so that suitable sets can correct the fixes. Differential coverage is not compre-hensive, and in many parts of the world is not free. Inevitably there are political difficulties with the idea of the world's civil air and sea transport relying for

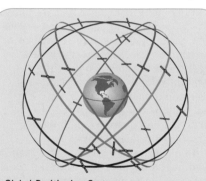

Global Positioning System

The GPS provides a global standard for measuring space and, because it measures this by comparing the time of the satellites with the receiver, time. Its great precision enables aircraft to fly closer together, with increased safety, and to follow more direct routes. Fishing fleets use the GPS to locate the best fishing areas. In-car navigation systems combine GPS technology with moving map displays, making it more difficult to "get lost." Watches with built-in GPS receivers are used by hikers and explorers. GPS tracking systems direct emergency vehicles, coordinate public transport, and dispatch taxis and delivery trucks with great efficiency. The GPS also synchronizes a range of commercial activities from financial transactions to electricity distribution.

Portable GPS receivers may have a fixed mounting.

navigation on the military system of a single nation. Therefore, plans are well advanced to develop a worldwide satellite system devoted to precise position and timing and intended for civil use. It will be sponsored by the European Commission and is to be named Galileo. The first test satellite was launched in 2005 and it is expected to be fully operational by 2008.

The simplest form of GPS receiver is the lightweight hand-held type that has a built-in antenna and operates on dry or rechargeable batteries. To reduce power consumption early sets were generally single channel and so comparatively slow, but modern sets use much less power and include facilities similar to fixed units. Many incorporate electronic charts and can be interfaced to other instruments or computers.

With all forms of electronic navigation, waypoints (reference points on the course line between the points of departure and destination) will generally be used in passage making. The coordinates and names of the waypoints can be entered in the GPS waypoint library and extracted and arranged in the correct order at a later time on another passage. The GPS set will then display the course and distance from each waypoint to the next. Cross-track error indicates how far off the direct course-line the vessel is between waypoints, and how to correct the error. If the GPS is interfaced with the autopilot this error will be adjusted automatically. Remember, however, that where circumstances permit, a shorter distance will be sailed through the water (and time

thus saved) by letting the tides so far as possible cancel each other out rather than correcting for each one in turn.

Position in terms of latitude and longitude to an accuracy that can be determined is the basic navigational information presented by GPS to the navigator. Each manufacturer's receiver, however, will carry its own dedicated computer that enables the basic position information to be used to derive a great deal more information, such as course and speed made-good, cross-track error, velocity made good to windward, speed, course, and distance to destination, expected time of arrival and so on. Further, other electronic sensors, such as the log, fluxgate compass, wind indicator, electronic chart plotter, echo sounder, radar, and so on can be interfaced with the GPS to provide the navigator with a wide range of additional navigational information, such as the measured velocity of tidal drift or current.

Like any other fix, the accuracy of a GPS fix will be determined by the geometry of the situation, or in this case the relative positions of the satellites. This is defined by what is called the horizontal dilution of precision (HDOP) and is displayed on the screen by a single number from which the accuracy of any sight can be worked out. Numbers below 5 are generally acceptable but 5 to 10 indicates a reduced accuracy.

The latitude and longitude given on charts is based on a certain figure of the Earth. This datum is usually shown on the chart somewhere near the title and with it any correction to be applied to satellite derived positions, which in the case of GPS are based on the datum WGS84. It is essential to apply such corrections to all positions transferred from GPS to the chart. However, most sets offer a range of chart datums that can be entered and, clearly, should the datum chosen correspond to that shown on the chart, no correction need be made. The navigator must, however, make sure that in all chartwork that involves GPS the two datums correspond. Failure to do so is the most frequent source of error.

The nautical chart has traditionally been printed on paper and chartwork carried out, as it has been for centuries, using parallel rules and dividers. One of the most practical and effective ways of using electronic navigation aids, such as GPS and radar, with the paper chart is the Yeoman chart plotter, a device that, controlled by a computer mouse, displays latitude and longitude on an illuminated panel with a lens that the navigator can use to plot positions manually. The instrument is referenced to the chart in use and illuminated arrows on the mouse point it to the required position or waypoint. It can be used in a wide range of circumstances, from keeping the dead reckoning to radar plotting.

The widespread introduction of electronics for practically all methods of navigation has led to an integrated navigation system with electronic charts showing the vessel's position (from the

GPS) and track in real time. There are numerous electronic chart systems in use at sea today by small craft. They fall into two main categories: raster charts, which are electronic facsimiles of paper charts; and vector charts, where each feature is coded together with its position. The main difference in operation is that one would need to use different raster charts for different levels of detail, just as with paper charts, whereas with the raster system one could use the same chart, filtering out detail as necessary. They offer virtually instantaneous chart correction, whether at sea or in harbor, by simply inserting a CD-ROM or data cartridge into the computer or downloading from the Internet. However, the electronic chart, more particularly when the system is based on a PC, offers nothing short of a complete navigation package.

Radar sets suitable for small craft are now available. This has been made possible by the use of LCD screens and more efficient electronics. It is also possible to overlay the radar image onto the electronic chart so that the location of nearby vessels in relation to navigable channels can be seen. Since most commercial shipping has been obliged to transmit Automatic Indentification Signals (AIS) giving the vessel's name, size, location, speed, direction, and rate of turn, this can also be overlaid onto the electronic chart.

Satellites and safety at sea

The use of satellites for long-range communications has made possible new Search-and-Rescue procedures based on the vessel in distress initially contacting a shore-based Rescue Coordination Center (rather than another ship) that then coordinates shipping and aircraft in the area to effect the rescue. The system, known as Digital Selective Calling (DSC) is an essential feature of the worldwide radio infrastructure known as GMDSS (Global Maritime Distress and Safety System) recently introduced to help vessels in distress. A variety of satellites

Many modern chart plotters for yachts can now incorporate radar as well as the yacht's instrument displays.

The Yeoman chart integrates electronic position fixing with conventional paper charts and is very popular.

are used for distress signals with GMDSS triggered by various emergency beacons such as the EPIRB as well as by VHF installations. New small craft VHF stations are now required to be fitted with DSC and, although large ships and coastguards will (where practicable) continue to keep a VHF watch, at least in the short term it is no longer mandatory.

Electronic systems provide much greater accuracy and security, especially in situations of poor visibility and variable water depths.

WEATHER PATTERNS

The sailor's greatest friend, and enemy, is atmospheric pressure. It not only causes daily fluctuations in wind and weather but remains the most accurate source of weather forecasts. The standard pressure at sea level is 1013.3 millibars (29.92 inches of mercury on the barometer) and it falls with altitude so that at about 20,000 ft (6,100 m) up it is approximately half that at the Earth's surface.

Variations in atmospheric pressure occur at the surface mainly because of effects in the upper air due to more air being taken out of a column (pressure falls) or being fed into a column (pressure rises). Variations in temperature of the air over any locality also have an effect. Cold air from high, polar latitudes and warm, sub-tropical air meeting in the temperate latitudes are distorted by the Earth's rotation to form high- and low-pressure circulations— anticyclones and depressions—with their associated fine and unsettled weather conditions respectively.

Warm air holds more invisible water vapor than cold air, and cooling causes moisture to condense into cloud, rain, or fog, or, if the air is very cold, into snow or hail.

When pressure falls, air expands and cools, thus increasing the amount of cloud. If the fall continues, cloud may lower and thicken enough to produce rain. When pressure rises, the air is compressed and warms, and cloud cover breaks up. If it continues to rise, becoming anticyclonic, subsidence of the air results in haze.

Wind is air moving from higher to lower pressure—or from a cooler to a warmer place. However, it does not blow directly from one to the other since it is deflected by the Earth's rotation—to the right in the northern hemisphere.

Circulation around a low is anti-clockwise, so when standing with your back to the wind, pressure will be lower to the left. In the southern hemisphere the situation is reversed, producing eastward moving fronts, and clockwise-circulating winds.

Measuring wind speed

Wind speed is measured by an anemometer, usually mounted at the masthead with the wind-direction vane. Rotating cups catch the wind and generate an electric current that is translated into wind speed on the indicator. Many systems on the market combine wind speed and direction with water speed, distance covered (log), and passage time. Most are fitted with damping circuits to eliminate variations caused by the rolling of the boat and all give the apparent wind speed, which combines the speeds of both boat and wind. A barometer, which monitors pressure changes continuously, is also essential.

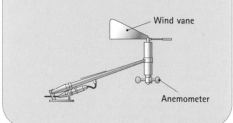

Wind vane

Anemometer

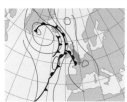

High, wispy **cirrus clouds** (shown in red above), give advance warning of low pressure moving eastwards across the Atlantic.

Cirrus clouds, the forerunner of unsettled weather, form at great heights from ice crystals. If it does not spread and thicken, the bad weather is passing to one side. Small or shapeless cirrus may accompany anticyclones, and pose no threat.

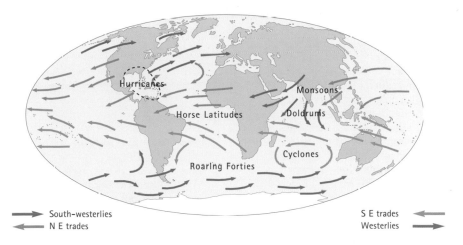

➡ South-westerlies	S E trades ⬅
⬅ N E trades	Westerlies ➡

Wind is air moving from high to low pressure. It does not blow directly from one to the other as it is deflected by the Earth's easterly rotation. The north-easterly and south-easterly trade winds blow in towards the low-pressure doldrums at the equator. High-pressure belts either side bring light, variable winds. In the past, becalmed ships offloaded their livestock cargo in these "Horse Latitudes." The poleward winds, bent by the globe's rotation, become westerlies—stronger in the southern "Roaring Forties" than in the depression laden northern Fifties. Land masses complicate wind systems and annual variations in temperature bring seasonal winds. Monsoons blow from sea to warm land in the summer and from land to warmer sea in winter. Tropical revolving storms, known as cyclones, hurricanes or typhoons, occur in the early autumn.

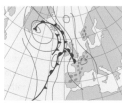

Full and fluffy "cotton-wool" cumulus clouds indicate fine weather. They spread and flatten in moist air, and thunderheads may develop if the air is particularly unstable. Forming early in the day over land, they signal the likelihood of sea breezes.

Rain and thick gray stratus (shown in red) may accompany the warm front and frequently follow cirrus formations. The following cold front brings heavy rain and heaped clouds.

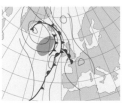

Squalls, often accompanied by local rain and hail, may occur when cumulus develop in unstable air after a cold front. The cloud grows fast, and corresponding down-drafts occur that bring down strong wind from aloft, leading to squalls and gusty winds.

Squalls and unexpectedly strong winds (shown in red above) may follow the cold front after a short period of clear sky.

INTERPRETING THE FORECAST

Use all the forecast information available: national and local radio, television, and daily newspapers. Carry a digital barometer, which has all the advantages but none of the drawbacks of a barograph, and set an alarm to catch the shipping forecasts. The times and radio frequencies of offshore forecasts vary all over the world and must be found out locally. Ask the coastguards for more precise and up-to-date actual details of weather in their own locality.

The shipping forecast may begin with a summary of gale warnings, issued if the mean wind speed is expected to rise to Force 8 (34 kn/40 mph) or if Force 9 (43 kn/50 mph) gusts are anticipated. When described as "imminent," the gale is expected to arrive within 6 hrs, "soon" means it may come within 6–12 hrs, and "later" indicates the possibility of gale force winds in more than 12 hrs. Storm cones or flags are hoisted at coastguard stations and harbors to warn of gales.

A general synopsis follows, giving details of the current position and direction of movement of High- and Low pressure systems. If the pressure is above 1020 millibars (mb) and steady, the weather should be settled for the next 24 hrs, except for sea fog. A rapid fall of 10 mb in three hours shows worsening weather with backing (anticlockwise shifting) and strengthening winds, or a gale soon; a steady fall indicates less imminent bad weather. A rapid rise brings clearing skies and a veering (clockwise shifting) wind, but often a strong short blow; a steady rise means better weather is on its way. The speed of each weather system is described as: "slowly" (0–15 kn/17 mph), "steadily" (15–25 kn/17–28 mph), "rather quickly" (25–30 kn/28–35 mph), "rapidly" (35–45 kn/35–50 mph), or "very rapidly" (over 45 kn/50 mph).

Visibility is described as: "good" (more than 5 miles, 8 km), "moderate" (2–5 miles, 3–8 km), "poor" (1,100 yds–2 miles, 1090 m–3 km), and "fog" (less than 1,100 yds, 1,097 m).

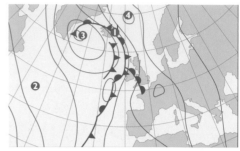

Warm front

Cold front

Occluded front

Isobars close together indicate strong winds, **1**; widely spaced over a large area they indicate slack pressure and small weather changes, **2**. After bad weather, watch for a small but vicious low forming on the trailing cold front of a large depression, **3**. A ridge of high pressure, **4**, often gives a single day (or night) of good weather between depressions. As it approaches, the wind veers and drops; there is often less cloud. When it passes, the wind backs and freshens, and high cloud appears.

Plotting a weather map
Weather centers and chandlers usually supply maps of different sea areas with a plotting form on the back. Record the shipping forecast on tape and write down every detail in shorthand on the form. Then transcribe the information on to the plotting map using symbols, shown right. Locate centers of Highs and Lows, plot reported pressures, and join lines of equal pressure (isobars). Plot reported wind, rain, and fronts and add, in another color, forecast winds and weather to show the movement of earlier systems. The symbols in one area may read:

meaning, wind south-westerly 4, becoming westerly 5 or 6, rain then showers, visibility good, 1024 (pressure) falling then rising. Note the time and date of the forecast.

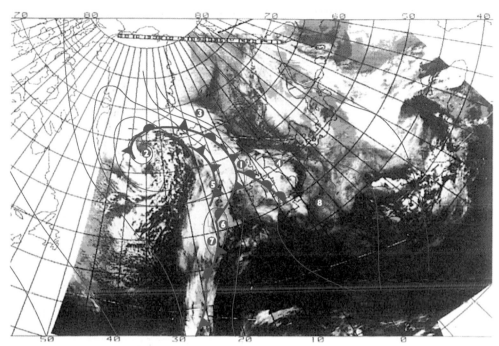

This is an old, decaying Low, 1. The cold front has caught up with the warm front and is now occluded, 2. Cloud is still thick in the north, 3, drizzle mixing with heavier rain.

As a warm front approaches, cloud steadily thickens and lowers with rain or sleet preceded by snow in winter. Here the front is weakening with the cloud breaking up, 4.

Cold fronts move faster than warm fronts, and a new, active cold front can be vicious, with heavy rain. Here a second and more active cold front, 5, has developed behind the original one, on which cloud evaporates as it weakens. Note the sharp clearance behind the following cold front, then a band of clear sky before showers or squalls develop

(likely before midday over land but at any time over the sea).

A trailing cold front may spawn a small, fierce, secondary Low, 6. This can move fast, with strong, gusty winds rapidly changing direction cyclonically, and can be dangerous if not expected. Note cloud forming. Farther south, another secondary is in

its early stages, 7, and will move around the circulation of the original low.

The high-pressure area 8, is almost free of cloud, and partly responsible for the decay of the warm front now in its influence. If a High is large and well established, approaching fronts pile up and decay. The weather stays fine though the wind may freshen.

Weather symbols

Use these symbols when taking down the radio forecast. Arrows indicate the direction and force of the wind and any expected changes. Arrows fly with the wind; a whole barb is added for two Beaufort forces; half added for one.

✓	Visibility Good		∞	Haze
—	Moderate		✳	Snow
=	Poor		△	Hail
☰	Fog		✴	Sleet
⊕	Overcast		○	Blue sky
			◐	Partly cloudy
			⌐	Drizzle

•	Rain
∴•	Heavy rain
∀	Squall
∇	Showers
⌐	Thunderstorm
<	Lightning
∀	Thundery showers

THE VISUAL CLUES

To benefit from a forecast and to check its accuracy, it is important to observe and recognize what you see in the sky. It can reveal all you need to know for the next 4–5 hrs over a distance of 30–50 miles (48–80 km). Coastal winds may differ from those generally forecast.

When there is good convective heating over the land, a sea breeze develops. When the sun comes up, warm air begins to rise and air from the sea is pulled onto the land.

Along the coast, the sea breeze is more likely to change the direction of the prevailing wind than increase its force. However, if big cumulus clouds grow over the land in the afternoon, the sea breeze may increase to as much as Force 6 or 7 in estuaries.

However, if the prevailing wind is already from seaward, it will be intensified by the sea breeze without much change in direction. If the wind is from the land, any existing cumulus will drift out over the sea. These will clear from seaward with the approach of the sea breeze. If the land wind and sea breeze converge, a line of cloud with a ragged, wispy base may form along the junction of the opposing winds. The wind often drops before the sea breeze arrives. Sea breezes occur less frequently in the late summer when the sea is warmer.

Heat thunderstorms grow mainly in the afternoon over land, but may drift out over coastal waters. If the air is hazy, towering water-filled cloud developing over the land may not be observed. The wind blowing out from the storm following the calm is often gusty and cold, bringing sudden heavy rain or hail.

If a thundery low is forecast this may produce extensive cloud of variable thickness, some thunder accompanied by squally, variable winds, and poor visibility.

When a warm front approaches, with thick cloud and drizzle, the air blowing up over cliffs will be cooled to form clouds. These often obscure the cliffs from seaward.

Fog

Fog develops more rapidly over saltwater than over freshwater. Sea fog forms when moist air moves over cold water or when cold air cools the surface of warmer water. Since the saturation or dewpoint is reached earlier in cool air than in warm, the moisture is condensed into fog.

Coastal fog may occur when sea fog is carried in by a sea breeze or when warm oceanic air blows across cold coastal water.

If you are caught in a fog, slow down, use your fog horn, radar reflector, and navigation lights. Keep a good all-round lookout and listen. Keep a close check on your position, and avoid sailing near shipping lanes.

Wind increases around prominent headlands and eddies may form on the lee side. Pass a few miles to seaward. Large coastal features will distort the strength and direction of the sea breeze.

An apparently sheltered cove may suffer from sudden powerful gusts pouring over the cliffs. At night, katabatic winds may flow down from higher ground producing usually light, coastal winds.

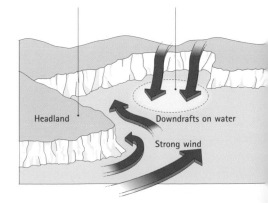

Headland

Downdrafts on water

Strong wind

If the contrail from a jet is thin and evaporates quickly, the upper air is dry and settled. If it spreads and lingers, watch for signs of change.

A large, 22° halo with red inside it, around the sun or moon, means high ice-crystal cirrus and a distant low. A visible red corona means water-droplet cloud.

Sea types

Waves are generated by gusts of wind pushing into the surface of the water, and the energy transfers from wave to wave like a ripple down a rope. Waves take time to gather momentum and their height is only partly determined by wind strength. A long swell, produced by waves formed a long way away, local wind waves, and surface ripples can cause a confused sea when they meet at different angles. When all the crests of several wave systems coincide, a "rogue" wave may result. At the coast, tides, coastal features, and water depths complicate the sea. In deep water, **1**, the energy of the waves has room to dissipate, but in shallow water, **2**, the waves are forced to rise and break. Water thus becomes turbulent over shoals and sand bars, **3**.

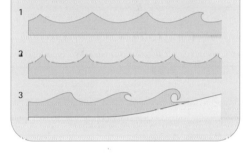

Steep cliffs may block the sea breeze, which develops around mid-morning, causing it to become intermittent or erratic.

The risk of sailing along a **steep-to lee shore** in a strong wind may be less than passing to windward of a shallow bank or shoal that causes approaching seas to heap up into steep waves.

Wind against tide creates choppy water. At a **shallow harbor entrance**, particularly with a bar, high, breaking waves are a hazard. Ensure there is adequate depth in the wave troughs.

Air always takes the easiest route and will funnel down **river valleys**. The Mistral, which blows down the Rhône valley, exemplifies the strong winds that may result.

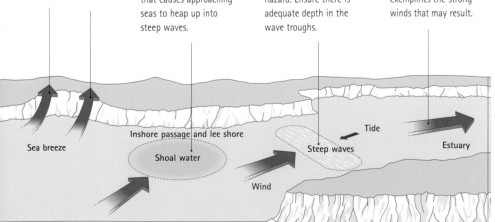

Sea breeze

Inshore passage and lee shore

Shoal water

Tide

Steep waves

Wind

Estuary

CRUISING
GROUNDS

PLANNING A PASSAGE

Half the joy of a passage is the pre-planning and the anticipation. Much of the organization depends upon the following factors.

Watches
The experience and number of crew will determine the length of the trip and the watch-keeping arrangements. On a 30 ft (9 m) boat, with two experienced sailors and two with limited-experience, it would be possible to work two watches, each with an experienced and a limited-experience sailor. However, the skipper should expect to be called at any time. Watches of 5–6 hrs can be tolerated by day, but 3–4 hrs is best at night, less if the weather is bad. See also watch systems on p. 212.

Distance
You can expect to sail 100 nm (185 km) in 24 hrs, or 60 nm (111 km) made good if sailing upwind. When planning your route, check that there are safe and convenient stop-off ports—or bolt-holes—along the way, in case of weather changes or illness aboard. GPS is now universally used for navigation, with the course broken into straight lines between waypoints. Waypoints must always be checked by the GPS to determine the course and distance between each pair of waypoints, and then checked against the chart. Plot your position on the chart at least hourly in case you have a power failure. Manual navigation can then take over from a known position.

Regulations
Acquaint yourself with the laws of the countries you intend to visit well before leaving home. In many countries notice of intended departure must be given to Customs and Immigration officials. Booklets are published annually on planning a foreign cruise, and these detail what is required for popular cruising areas.

Before you depart
Check your ship's papers are in order. If your vessel is registered in its country of origin, foreign authorities will accept the papers, but ensure your vessel is registered officially if planning a foreign cruise. If chartering carry the Charter Party document with you. Always take your VHF radio licence.

Everyone on board must carry an up-to-date passport as well as a visa for any countries you are visiting that may require one. Health regulations and vaccinations vary from country to country, so ensure everyone has the correct certificates. The skipper may be asked to produce an International Certificate of Competence (ICC) in some countries.

Most countries require a complete crew list, giving name, address, date of birth, nationality, and passport number of each crew member. It is advisable to list everybody on board as crew members, not passengers, as some countries may charge a passenger carrying vessel to enter a port.

Check that your insurance is up to date. It should cover the area you intend to cruise in, and any damage received by your boat, or caused by it. You should also have personal cover and contents insurance. If trailing a boat, check your insurance covers the boat when trailed as well as when it is in the water.

Carry the correct currency of the countries you are visiting, plus travelers' checks, and a credit card that can be used abroad. Check on any import/export restrictions that might apply.

Obtain all the information possible about your intended cruising area before sailing. More and more information is becoming available on websites. Use town names as keywords on search engines. Cruise accounts and large scale charts of harbors are often helpful. Be sure to have the relevant, updated charts and cruising guides.

Remember to take relevant tide tables, tidal stream atlases, and a list of lights, radio, and meteorological services.

Weather
Plan your passage to avoid seasonal bad weather conditions that occur worldwide at certain times of the year, and make the

Primary routes
Secondary routes

best use of fair winds. *Ocean Passages of the World*, published by the UK Hydrographic Department, has descriptions of winds, currents, and weather for all the oceans. US and British routing charts, which are published for each month of the year, give similar information. You may reach your destination faster by covering more miles with good winds than taking the more direct route where you may encounter storms and/or doldrums

The best time of year to embark on a voyage around the world depends on your point of departure and your route. A favorite route from Europe is to leave in the early autumn to take advantage of favorable trade winds across the Atlantic, and arrive in the West Indies for Christmas. Then traverse the Panama Canal in January and pick up the trade winds across the Pacific, reaching the Indian Ocean in August, which avoids the hurricane season. It is best to round the Cape of Good Hope in the southern summer.

Flags
The flags that a private yacht can normally display include its national (maritime) ensign, a yacht club burgee, a courtesy flag when in the harbor of a foreign nation, and signal or racing flags. The ensign is usually flown on a staff at the stern. When this is not possible, in gaff-rigged sailing boats it is normally worn at the peak of the sail, at the mizzen masthead in yawls and ketches, and in other rigs two-thirds up the leech of the aft sail. It is not normally worn at sea except if another vessel is approaching or land is nearby

An ensign should be worn when entering or leaving a harbor, especially a foreign one. It is bad etiquette to leave it flying overnight. It should be raised at 0800 and lowered at sunset or 2100, whichever is the earlier, or if the crew go ashore before that time.

When entering foreign waters, hoist the International Code Flag "Q" (see pp. 204–205 for international code of signals). It must be kept flying until customs formalities are completed. Always fly the national ensign of the country you are visiting, from the starboard crosstrees if possible. Some countries insist that this is done. Make sure it is not flown below any other flag other than your ensign and burgee.

Stopping off
The first port of call in any country must be a customs port, though the EU is regarded as one country. Wait to be boarded by a port official or report to the Harbor Master's office with all the necessary documents. Many yacht clubs invite visiting yachtsmen to become honorary members during their stay and some offer excellent mooring and docking facilities. For long trips, select well-spaced strategic ports to collect mail. Arrange well in advance for a bank, consulate, yacht club, post office, or business to keep it for you.

Courtesies
One of the most important courtesies when sailing is to guard against pollution. All waste should be stored and sealed in plastic sacks until it can be disposed of ashore. Discharge of oil is prohibited.

NORTHERN EUROPE

Tranquil cruising in **Scandinavia**.

Cruising grounds in the north

Holland offers varied and easy sailing, with its large expanses of land-locked water. The Friesian Islands, with their shallow, sheltered channels, and a network of inland waterways connects the western and eastern coasts of Sweden. One route takes you along a canal, about 55 miles (87 km) long, and then passes through several lakes, including Vänem and Vättern, before entering the Baltic at Mem. The waterways also lead directly to the 24,000 "Skårgard" islands, which offer some of the best sailing in the world.

You can sail north from Göteborg to Oslo and explore the picturesque south-east coast of Norway with its sheltered anchorages, before continuing up to the dramatic cruising grounds between Stavanger and Sognefjord.

From Kiel you can can sail along the German coastline to Rügen Island. The Polish coastline is unremarkable but Szczecin and Gdynia have good yacht harbors, and further east you will find the Gulf of Riga and the Estonian Islands.

If venturing on from the Swedish east coast to Finland, the Åland (Alvehanman) islands and Finland's south-west coast provide sheltered waters, well-buoyed fairways, and good fishing.

Russia's north-west inland waterways are open to foreign-flagged pleasure vessels between St. Petersburg and the White Sea.

Throughout this section the best cruising grounds appear on the charts as shaded blue areas. The position of the arrows on the wind symbols indicate the direction of the wind, while their length denotes relative frequency. The central number shows the percentage frequency of light, variable breezes.

Weather

The cruising season runs from mid-May to mid-September. The wind direction is mainly westerly during these months, although an east wind can blow for several weeks. Variable winds, changing skies, rain, and stiff breezes can be expected, but sheltered cruising areas are generally available.

Cruising grounds in the west

The west coast of Scotland, with its rugged scenery, sea lochs, and outlying islands, is one of the most unspoilt cruising grounds in western Europe. The main center for local boats is the Firth of Clyde and there are good mainland and island anchorages all the way up the west coast.

The most appealing area of Ireland for cruising lies off the south and west coasts. Friendly harbors abound between Cork and Dingle.

More crowded are the deep-water estuaries of the English West Country, though there are plenty of sheltered harbors against a cliff and river setting in Devon and Cornwall. The east coast of England has a completely different flavor. The shore is flat and the area is full of beautiful rivers.

The traditional home of English yachting is between the Chichester and Poole Harbors on the south coast, which includes the sheltered waters of the Solent.

In France, Brittany's north and west coasts are spectacular, particularly the stretch between St. Malo and L'Aber Vrac'h—sandy beaches interspersed with rocky outcrops.

The South Brittany coast has much to offer with much lighter and easier tides than the north coast. The Brest inlet includes Cameret, a much loved starting point for yachts going south. Once through the Raz de Sein, which should be taken at slack water, there are beautiful places to visit, such as Concarneau and Belle Isle. Most ports in this area now have marinas.

Canals

French Inland Waterways offer many canals through the French interior. The main access to Paris is up the River Seine from Le Havre.

Weather

Although unpredictable, the weather in this part of Europe does follow broad patterns. Britain and northern France generally enjoy prevailing westerly and south-westerly winds. In June, light winds usually accompany fine settled weather; thunderstorms are common in July; while early August brings stronger, more variable winds. The Channel Islands enjoy the most sun. The BBC issues regular shipping forecasts for the area.

British Admiralty, Imray, and Stanford charts give excellent coverage of the area, as do the *Reeds Nautical Almanac* and the *Cruising Association Handbook* (8th edition), which is a yachtsman's pilot book. The Royal Yachting Association and the French Government Tourist Office issue numerous free booklets about the area, including a list of charter companies.

THE MEDITERRANEAN

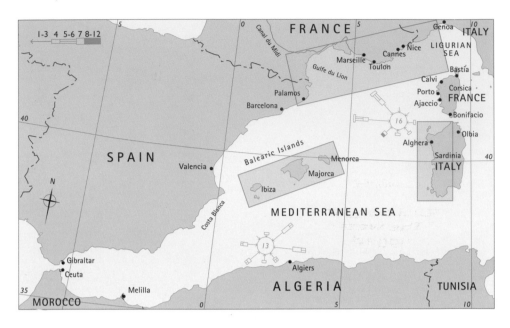

Cruising grounds in the west

Many northern European yachtsmen choose to head south through the French canals; the more hardy sail down the Spanish and Portuguese coastline and enter the Mediterranean through the Straits of Gibraltar. A compromise route is to take the Canal du Midi from Bordeaux. The whole northern coastline from Cadiz can be cruised in short sections.

There are yacht facilities in Morocco at least every 60 miles (100 km). Don't go ashore outside a recognized harbor without requesting permission, but Tunisia is certainly worth visiting. Its most southerly coastline has, unlike the rest of the western Mediterranean, a significant tidal rise and fall, and care should be taken.

The Spanish coast's Costa Blanca has some interesting harbors from which to cross to Ibiza, the most westerly of the Balearic Islands, which are among the best cruising grounds in the Mediterranean. Between Barcelona and Port Vendres there are several large marinas.

The Côte d'Azur is expensive, but St. Tropez and Monte Carlo are very glamorous and worth visiting, as are the

ports on the Italian Riviera before you reach Genoa.

Corsica has a wild coastline, and though anchorages abound, most are fair-weather ones. Sardinia, the Bonifacio Strait, and the Maddalena Islands have wonderful scenery. In the south there are good anchorages, especially Malafatano, which is a good point of departure for Tunisia.

Weather

April–October is the normal cruising season. The best sailing is in June, when the sea is warm and the weather normally stable. July and August can be very hot indeed. Close to high mountains—Corsica, for instance—the weather can be unpredictable with violent shifts of wind. Thunderstorms, common in late summer, can induce ferocious line squalls, and when the mistral blows it is better to stay in harbor.

Cruising grounds in the east

The Italian Tuscan coast with its outlying islands, among them Elba and Giglio, provide good cruising and shelter. Farther south, the Pontine (Ponziane) Islands, Ischia, Capri, and the Bay of

Naples all offer beautiful scenery, fine weather, and sheltered anchorages.

Then there is the island of Sicily. It has few marinas but many interesting old ports, including Palermo and Syracuse, and an active volcano (Etna) on its eastern side. Off northern Sicily lies the Aeolian (Lipari) Islands with another volcano, on Stromboli. Malta and the nearby island of Gozo provide many attractive anchorages, though finding a good berth in Valletta can be difficult as the main marina is for residents only. There are also the small Italian islands in the Sicilian Channel. The Italian mainland and offshore islands have some splendid marinas, but while there are many marinas in Slovenia and Croatia, the availability of spare parts and general expertise can be lacking.

Greece has everything to appeal to the yachtsman: sunshine, breathtaking scenery, and hundreds of harbors and anchorages, mostly simple but un-crowded except during July and August.

Sailing southwards down the Adriatic, Corfu and the other Ionian Islands offer delightful, easy cruising in an azure sea, with good shelter and attractive ports. On reaching Kefalonia, one can either go eastwards through the Gulfs of Patras and Corinth, and through the Corinth Canal to the Aegean, or south along the west and southern coasts of Greece to reach the southern Aegean Islands.

The Aegean is most attractive, with its islands, mountainous coastline, colorful small ports, secluded anchorages, and ancient history. Both the Greek Aegean, and the southern Turkish coast have excellent marinas, many with yard facilities, and new ones are opening every year. Friendly people, unsurpassed scenery and a myriad of coves and anchorages make it one of the best cruising grounds in the Mediterranean. From here you can sail on, either north to the Dardanelles and the Black Sea, or east to Cyprus, a popular destination for cruising yachtsmen, or to the lesser frequented Lebanon and Israel.

Weather

The weather is settled, April–October, with only local variations. The best source for weather forecasts is Navtex, which is available throughout the Mediterranean. In the Adriatic, Ionian and Aegean Seas the prevailing winds are north-west or northerly with occasional southerlies and more frequent periods of no wind at all.

THE CARIBBEAN

A pleasant anchorage in the **British Virgin Islands.**

Cruising grounds

These superb cruising grounds draw sailors to their waters like bees to a honeypot. Everywhere the water is warm and crystal clear, so much so that on calm days your boat will appear to be floating on air.

But nothing is perfect and the cruising yachtsman must be constantly aware of the weather, particularly during the hurricane season. If a hurricane is imminent don't rely on finding a safe anchorage as they are nearly always full. However, the early warning system is so good that the prudent mariner picks up his anchor and heads south well before the bad weather arrives.

Another hazard is that, apart from on the French-owned islands, navigational aids are non-existent or unreliable, so plan all trips so that you are entering an anchorage before sunset.

The best islands for cruising are the Bahamas, the Virgin Islands (British and American), and the Grenadines. Some 60 miles (100 km) east of Puerto Rico, where the warming Atlantic meets the sub-tropical Caribbean Sea, lie the incomparable Virgin Islands. Their waters are protected from the trade winds by scores of islets and cays that offer secluded anchorages. Many of the islands are uninhabited and offer a wonderful area for cruising.

The best facilities are to be found at Roadtown, on Tortola in the British Virgin Islands, and in the US Virgin Islands at Charlotte Amalie and Red Hook on St. Thomas, and Christiansted on St. Croix. If you want to stop every night, and enjoy some time ashore, 40 nm (70 km) a day is a good day's run.

To the north are the 700 Bahamian islands. They are low—the highest one is only 197 ft (60 m)—and the water is shoal, so cruising with a boat whose draft is more than 6 ft (1.83 m) is difficult. The islands offer excellent harbor facilities, particularly at Nassau. Sailing at night, however, is dangerous since there are few lighthouses.

For those already familiar with the Bahamas and Virgin Islands, the Anguilla to Antigua stretch, the Grenadines, and the north coast of South America are exotic and challenging cruising grounds. The Venezuelan coastline, especially, is still comparatively unspoilt and living is cheap, though ports with facilities are few and far between.

Cuba is being visited by yachtsmen in increasing numbers, though US nationals are discouraged from doing so by their government.

Weather

Puerto Rico, the lesser Antilles, and Venezuela and its offshore islands, are well within the trade wind belt. The

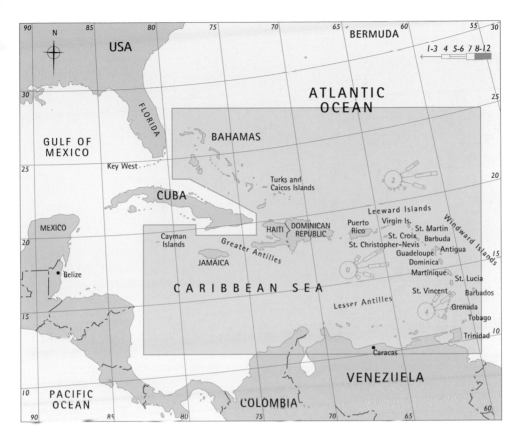

almost ever-present trade winds cool the area. Winter daytime temperatures are in the low 80s Fahrenheit (mid 20s Celsius), and drop to the upper 60s (about 20°C) at night. In the summer, as the trade winds dies out, temperatures rise to the upper 80s (low 30s C) in the day and the mid-70s (low 20s C) at night.

The Bahamas are on the northern edge of the trade wind belt. Their weather is affected by the continental land mass and from November to April there are occasional cold fronts that produce a wind shift to the north or north-west, and a drop in temperature.

Hurricanes are most frequent in the Bahamas and northern Caribbean, between June and November. Relatively few pass below St. Lucia, and they are virtually unknown in Trinidad and Venezuela. Squalls almost always approach with the wind, bringing rain and a sharp wind increase.

Chartering

Charter companies can be found throughout the Bahamas and in the eastern Caribbean from Puerto Rico to Grenada, but there is virtually no chartering out of Trinidad or Venezuela. For the less experienced, the Bahamas or the Virgin Islands, where anchorages are only hours apart, are the best. The more experienced sailor will be happy in the Grenadines.

Charts and publications

For the eastern Caribbean the waterproof Imray Iolaire charts are the most accurate. For the Bahamas the best are those privately produced by Blue Water Books, 1481 SE 17th Street, Ft. Lauderdale, FL 33316. The most popular guides for the serious cruising sailor are Don Street's five volumes on the area.

Beautiful quiet moorings abound in the sheltered waters of the East coast such as here, in Maine.

Cruising grounds

The East Coast of the USA, which stretches from Maine near the Canadian border down to the west coast of tropical Florida, has some of the best cruising grounds in North America. Maine's coastline is about 200 miles (320 km) long, and offers the cruising yachtsman a myriad of rocky inlets, bays, and channels that are unique in the United States. The Labrador Current makes the waters cold, and fog occurs all too frequently—particularly in August—when these chilly conditions combine with the warm, wet south-westerlies that often blow off the land in the summer. Despite this, Maine continues to draw the discerning yachtsman to its compara-tively uncrowded ports and Scandinavian-like scenery.

Further south is the popular sailing resort of Marblehead. Situated in Salem Sound, which is in Massachusetts Bay, Marblehead is 12 miles (20 km) north of the large and cosmopolitan city of Boston. Marblehead is a world famous base for yacht racing of all kinds but the cruising sailor will also enjoy what it and the other three historic ports in the area—Beverley, Manchester, and Salem—have to offer. Parts of Boston's harbor can accommodate yachts, but it is primarily for commercial shipping.

The Cape Cod Canal gives the quickest access to the cruising grounds of Buzzard's Bay, Nantucket Sound, and Martha's Vineyard, all of which offer plenty of natural harbors and good facilities.

Within a day's sail is Newport, Rhode Island, which, with Block Island Sound, has steady summer breezes. This and the warmer weather, and the excellent marinas and attractive ports, inevitably makes it popular for all sailors, and between June and September it is crowded. However, fog can be a problem, though it usually burns off when the sun heats the land.

Equally popular is Long Island Sound. A sheltered area of water some 90 miles (145 km) long and up to 20 miles (35 km) wide, it is situated between the mainland and Long Island. In hot weather the winds are often light and thunderstorms not infrequent, and it, too, can have fog. At the Sound's western end lies New York harbor which can be reached by the East River.

South of New York, good cruising grounds begin at Delaware Bay. The Delaware-Chesapeake Canal runs into Chesapeake Bay with its hundreds of creeks and anchorages. This large cruising area, which stretches 170 miles (275 km) from the Canal in the north to the mouth of the Bay, is best in the spring and fall as the summers tend to be hot and still. At the mouth of the Severn River lies Annapolis, a major yachting center.

The sheltered Intracoastal Waterway runs parallel to the Atlantic and Gulf coasts, from Manasquan Inlet, New Jersey, to the Mexican border. From the south end of Chesapeake Bay it takes boats 1,000 miles (1,600 km) through the Carolinas, and down to Miami, giving access to the winter cruising grounds there.

Since temperatures rarely drop, balmy days are the general rule even in mid-winter, and Florida enjoys year-round cruising. The Florida Keys, a chain of tropical islands with a coral reef, stretch south from Florida, and are an added pleasure for those escaping the harsher northern climes.

Marinas

The whole coastline is full of natural harbors and inlets, and a good port can be found about every 20 miles (35 km). Marina berths tend to be very crowded in summer, so it is worth booking in advance. However, most yacht clubs have guest moorings, anchorages, or slips for rent.

Buoyage system

IALA system B is in use throughout the coastal waters of the United States (see pp. 120–121). Buoys on the Intracoastal Waterway have some yellow markings, and lakes and inland waterways, and some other waters, use the Uniform State Waterway Marking System (USWMS). With USWMS black replaces green, and special cardinal marks are used.

Regulations

The US Coast Guard is the primary maritime law enforcement agency in the US, and it has the authority to board and inspect any vessel at any time in waters over which the United States has jurisdiction and impose a fine on those who contravene federal regulations. Also be aware that some popular cruising grounds are now designated no-discharge areas.

USA: THE WEST COAST

Sailing under the Golden Gate Bridge in **San Francisco Bay.**

Cruising grounds

Parts of this coastline offer ideal and varied cruising. In the north is a vast inland sea, entered through the Strait of Juan de Fuca. Its southern finger, Puget Sound, reaches 60 miles (100 km) past Seattle to Olympia and Tacoma, where there are secluded anchorages in quiet coves. The islands in the northern finger, the Georgia Strait, are popular cruising grounds with local sailors, as is Desolation Sound, with its spectacular fjord-like inlets. Tidal changes vary so allow for different ranges when anchoring.

The Oregon and northern Californian coastline offers the yachtsman little until San Francisco Bay is reached. This playground for thousands of sailors has over 400 sq miles (1,000 sq km) of navigable waters, 280 miles (450 km) of

varied shoreline, and a steady wind nearly every day between March and November. Early, it generally ranges between 10–12 kn (11–14 mph), increasing in some areas to 20–30 kn (23–35 mph) in the afternoon. Wherever you go you can find peaceful, isolated anchorages off sandy beaches, or marinas adjacent to busy city centers. Outside the Golden Gate, Drakes Bay and Pillar Point Harbor are ideal for a weekend cruise; for those with more time to spend, Bodega Bay and Tomales Bay are interesting to explore.

The coastline down to San Diego has many interesting ports of call. Monterey Bay has the beach resort of Santa Cruz and the historic port of Monterey, but beware of fog in July and August. Monterey is commonly the last stop before making the 24-hours' passage to Morrow Bay or, if there's a big swell, Port San Luis. The conditions may be boisterous but, if you have clear weather, the scenery is magnificent. Once past Point Conception the prevailing northerly winds moderate, and the water and weather is warmer. This allows Southern Californians to sail all year round, though they are wary of the notorious "Santa Ana" NE wind, which can blow with ferocity in autumn and winter.

After Point Conception you enter the Santa Barbara Channel, sheltered by offshore islands. You can make for Santa Barbara, California's most scenic harbor, or Ventura. Less than a day's sail away is Santa Monica Bay where the world's largest man-made yacht harbor is situated at Marina del Rey. San Pedro Bay contains within its breakwaters the commercial port of Los Angeles-Long Beach harbor. Alamitos Bay on the Bay's eastern side offers more to the cruising yachtsman. At its south-easterly end is Newport Beach, which has every conceivable facility for the visiting yachtsman and is an excellent jumping-off point for the cruising grounds around Santa Catalina Island some 25 miles (40 km) offshore.

The passage from Newport Beach to San Diego depends on whether you want to sail inshore or offshore. Those heading for Ensenada in Mexico usually sail outside the Coronado Islands, or just inside them, a course that takes them clear of commercial traffic and coastal hazards. San Diego is a large and easily accessible harbor, though fog can make the passage tricky between September and April.

Weather

With a large north-south extent, weather in the area varies considerably. The prevailing westerlies can bring severe weather at all times but good anchorages abound. South towards Mexico and north towards Canada bring much higher and lower temperature extremes respectively. (See p. 147 for US sailing regulations.)

THE GREAT LAKES

Sailing on **Lake Ontario** with Toronto as the backdrop.

Cruising grounds

The Great Lakes offer the largest expanse of freshwater, 95,000 sq miles (247,000 sq km), in the world. They extend for more than 700 miles (1,100 km) east to west, and have over 7,200 miles (11,520 km) of coastline. Though the lakes are tideless, winds can create currents that cause temporary changes of up to 8 ft (2.5 m) in the level of the water. Movement between the lakes is not always easy for yachts as the locks and canals have been built for commercial traffic.

Off the Great Lakes there are beautiful and protected inland cruising areas accessible by river and canal. The waterways are open from mid-May to mid-October, the prime sailing season, before the lakes freeze over for the winter.

The St. Lawrence Seaway and artificial canals have made the area so easily accessible that the lake ports have become, in effect, Atlantic seaports. However, the St. Lawrence Seaway, with its 2,000 miles (3,200 km) of canals, rivers, lakes, and locks is primarily a trading route and commercial traffic must take priority. For safety reasons boats under 20 ft (6 m) long or 1 ton weight may not travel through the seaway.

An alternative route to the Great Lakes from the east coast of North America is up the Hudson River to the New York State Barge Canal near Albany, then west to Buffalo on Lake Erie, or north to Oswego on Lake Ontario. This is a mast-down route, but facilities are available at each end of the canal to step and unstep the mast. It also provides accessibility to the Finger Lakes south of Lake Ontario.

The Thousand Islands, in the St. Lawrence area, is a labyrinth of twisting channels and secluded anchorages. The St. Lawrence Island National Park and marinas at Kingston and Gananoque provide excellent mooring facilities. The islands lead to the long, narrow Bay of Quinte, near Picton, Ontario—a pretty backwater with plenty of peaceful anchorages—and to Kingston harbor nearby.

The Rideau Canal connects Ottawa to Kingston on Lake Ontario, with 125 miles (200 km) of attractive scenery punctuated with 48 historic locks, and numerous dams. One of Ontario's best cruising areas, through the Rideau Lakes, begins 14 locks above Kingston City.

The Trent-Severn waterway runs from the Bay of Quinte, into Georgian Bay near Port Severn at the eastern end of Lake Huron. The waterway offers an attractive sheltered passage with excellent mooring and docking facilities, good fishing, and secluded anchorages. But be prepared for sudden squalls on Lake Simcoe and Chonchiching. Boats with a draft of more than 5 ft, 6 in (1.5 m) should contact the waterway office before setting off.

Georgian Bay, and its Thirty Thousand Islands, sandy beaches, and rocky points, has some spectacular cruising areas. But it is mainly big boat water, and smaller craft and trailer sailors will find the best cruising area lies at its eastern end, between Port Severn and Parry Sound. Off Lake Huron's northern shore is the world's largest freshwater island, Manitoulin, which has good anchorages and cruising facilities.

The northern end of Lake Michigan has archipelago islands, many of which are uninhabited. An exception is Beaver Island, which has a ferry service to the mainland and a small airport. Southern Lake Michigan is lined with towns and cities that have modern marinas, both private and municipal. Chicago offers the excitement of a major city and a canal that connects it to the Mississippi River. On the lake's north-western shore is the popular sailing area of Green Bay.

Lake Superior is over 31,700 sq miles (82,000 sq km) in size and is the largest of the lakes. It offers wilderness anchorages on its northern, Canadian side, including the Slate Islands; while its southern, American shore offers several attractive bustling ports of call. Lake of the Wood, a vast, shallow cruising area to the west of Lake Superior, is accessible from Thunder Bay.

Buoyage system
The Great Lakes buoyage system is identical to the coastal IALA lateral B system (see pp. 120–121), with the direction from the outlet of the lake being the same as from seaward. So when approaching a lake from its outlet keep the red mark to starboard, and the green to port. The system is the same on both US and Canadian sides of the border.

Regulations
Pleasure craft may enter Canada and the USA by trailer or under their own power. Customs offices are found at federal harbors, if approaching by sea, and at highway border crossings, if trailer sailing. Some harbors and canal approaches require permits, available for a nominal sum from most marinas and lock stations. Check on a licence for your boat and find out what safety equipment has, by law, to be carried aboard. In Canada, for example, the horseshoe type lifebuoy does not fulfill Coast Guard safety requirements.

Discharge of waste overboard is forbidden and should be disposed of in port. Check the charts and regulations for boating boundaries and speed limits. Some Canadian states limit speeds to 5.4 kn (10 kph) when within 100 ft (30 m) of the shore. In any case always slow down in crowded waters.

Collision regulations (see pp. 124–125) for the inland waterways of the USA and Canada vary from those used at sea. Check them carefully before proceeding.

AUSTRALASIA

Sailing in **Sydney Harbour.**

Cruising grounds

The Great Barrier reef offers a lifetime of cruising around its 2,000 miles (3,220 km) of exotic coral strewn waters along the northern half of Australia's east coast. It has strong tidal currents, but the water is kept warm all year round, with the assistance of the south equatorial current. Between the coast and the reef lie 600 mainly uninhabited islands. As a courtesy, when approaching an uninhabited one, contact its major resort or warn its "captain" of your arrival by radio or mobile phone. You may be allowed to use the facilities for a fee.

The Whitsunday Islands form the bareboat chartering center of Australia. The 74 thickly wooded and sandy-beached islands, situated 40 miles (65 km) inland of the reef, offer excellent facilities for the cruising yachtsman. Deserted anchorages abound, as do sharks, stonefish, and sea wasps, so beware, particularly if scuba diving. Local charts indicate any unusual currents or conditions.

Further south, the north-eastern coastline down to Sydney offers interesting stop-off points, such as Coff's

Harbour and Broken Bay, and places to explore. Sydney harbor and its 186 miles (300 km) of inland coastline is full of secluded bays and beaches that creates remarkably peaceful cruising grounds. However, anchorages and marina facilities for visiting yachts are limited, and the area is one of the more crowded in the country.

Onshore sea breezes, caused by the great land mass heating up, are common all round the coastline. In the west and south the prevailing winds are south-west, and from north in the spring and south in the autumn on the eastern coast. The wind is normally moderate in strength, but in summer the Fremantle Doctor off Perth can produce stiff breezes of 23 mph (20 kn) or more, and in spring thunderstorms off the north-east coastline need careful watching. Tropical cyclones can occur in the far north between December and April.

New Zealand's most popular cruising grounds around its North Island are Hauraki Gulf and The Bay of Islands. The Hauraki Gulf, some 60 miles (100 km) from north to south, offers magnificent cruising amongst its numerous islands

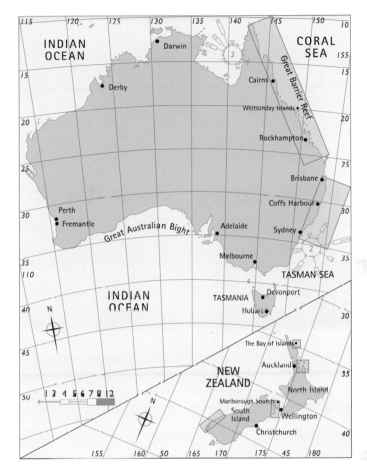

and also has the attractions and modern marina facilities of the city of Auckland. The Bay of Islands is almost 120 miles (190 km) north of Auckland on a coastline facing north-east. The main harbor is Russell and the Bay has about 150 islands in a delightful sub-tropical setting.

South Island has colder water and less predictable weather, but magnificent scenery and cruising for the more experienced sailor. Marlborough Sounds, a beautiful area of drowned river valleys and wooded islands, lies at the eastern end of Cook Strait and is a favored sailing area for the New Zealanders.

On the south-west side of South Island lies the Fjordland National Park with its numerous inlets and rugged coastline. Though caution is required, as the cruising yachtsman is exposed to the Roaring Forties and to katabatic winds that blow down from the snow-capped mountains, it is a unique area for exploration. Dusky Sound, a huge archipelago of islets, includes Pickersgill Harbour, where Captain Cook first landed in 1773.

Regulations

Cruising boats are required to follow regulations in both countries and the usual formalities when arriving or departing either country. Cruising boats do not need to be registered, but standard safety equipment has to be carried aboard. Yachts are welcome to stay as "visitors," although extending your time over 12 months may result in import duties being payable.

SAFETY AT SEA

EQUIPPING FOR SAFETY

Safety equipment on any yacht must be specified according to where it sails, its size, maximum number of crew, and the likelihood of being out in bad weather. It is rare for a new boat to come with much safety equipment and even a second-hand boat, supposedly fully equipped, may in fact be fitted with time-expired or outdated safety gear.

The first thing an owner must do is assess where he or she thinks the dangers lie, and to remember that as skipper they are responsible for the safety of the crew. Spend a day delving into the interior of the boat, checking the fuel, water, gas, and electrical systems so you are fully familiar with them.

When planning your list of essentials, start with the headings: Personal, Group/Crew, and Boat; and the attitude that once at sea you should be totally self-sufficient, with adequate training and knowledge to cope with most emergencies. This leaves the real accident, medical emergency, or situation caused by gear failure, grounding, hull damage, or inextinguishable fire for outside assistance.

Each member of the crew should develop an awareness of the types of emergency that can occur, knowledge of where all safety equipment is stowed, and how it works. Personal equipment includes appropriate clothing to combat heat and cold, safety harness to prevent falling overboard, and a personal flotation device (PFD). If the crew act responsibly, aware that a thoughtless action may endanger others, an effective safety culture is established.

As with all safety precautions, prevention is better than cure, and a regular checking and maintenance schedule of properly installed systems will help to prevent accidents.

Safety requirements

Minimum safety requirements for coastal cruising boats (A) and ocean-going yachts (B) are:

	A	B
PERSONAL (for each crew member)		
1 Warm clothing, oilskins, seaboots, PFD, safety harness	*	*
GROUP/CREW		
1 Liferaft for all crew		*
2 Horseshoe lifebelt, drogue, self-igniting light	1	2
3 Buoyant heaving line	*	*
4 Dan buoy		*
5 VHF radio	*	*
6 EPIRB		*
BOAT		
Means of propulsion		
1 Storm trysail or reefed mainsail and storm jib	*	*
2 Independent battery or hand start for engine	*	*
Anchors		
1 With appropriate chain	1	2
2 Strong mooring point on foredeck	*	*
Bailing and bilge pumping		
1 Buckets with lanyard	2	2
2 Bilge pumps (one electric, B)	2	2
Detection		
1 Radar reflector, fixed navigation lights, foghorn, powerful torch/lamp	*	*
Flares		
1 Hand-held: four red, four white	*	*
2 Hand-held smoke signals: two orange	*	
3 Buoyant smoke signals: two orange		*
4 Red parachute rockets	2	4
Fire-fighting equipment		
1 Fire blanket	*	*
2 3.5 lb dry powder extinguishers	2	2
Radio		
1 For shipping forecasts	*	*
Navigational equipment		
1 Adequate charts, tide tables, almanac, pilots, etc.	*	*
2 Steering compass, hand-bearing compass	*	*
3 Drawing instruments, barometer, depth sounder (or lead and line), watch or clock	*	*
4 GPS		*

Two horseshoe lifebelts, **1**, should be stowed in quick-release holders on the guard rails within easy reach of the helmsman. House the top and bottom parts of the **Dan buoy pole** in two short lengths of tube lashed to the backstay, **2**, fitted to the pushpit, or in a tube glassed into the stern of the boat.

A **stern boarding ladder**, **3**, makes it easier to recover anyone who may fall overboard (so long as they are kept clear of the propeller).

Stow the liferaft in the open cockpit, on deck, just abaft the mast, **4**, or in a cockpit locker where it is accessible in an emergency. Liferafts are packed either in rigid canisters with quick-release straps or in soft, easily-carried bags. The painter triggers the inflation device, so secure it to a strong point before activating.

For stability, **freshwater tanks**, **5**, should be located low down. Clean them often and check for contamination. Ensure that sea cocks to galley, heads, and engine, **6**, are always shut after use or when leaving the boat. Attach a soft wood plug of the correct size to each sea cock in case of failure.

A wet, slippery deck is dangerous when doing deck work. All surfaces that will be stepped on should have some sort of **non-slip finish**, **7**. **Netting** attached to the lifelines, **8**, will stop a foresail or even a child from going over the side.

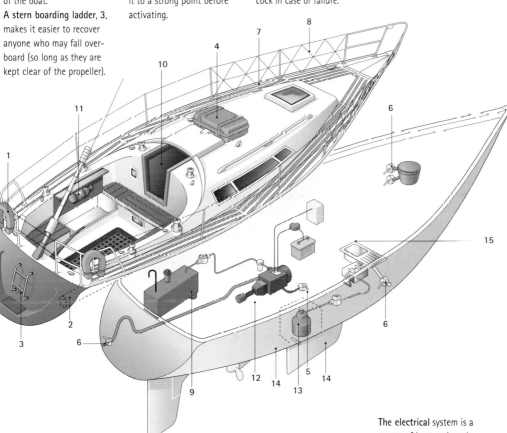

All fuels are fire hazards, so site the **fuel tank**, **9**, as far as possible from the engine and hot exhaust pipe. Keep fire extinguishers handy: one just inside the forward hatch, another by the main hatch, **10**, or in a cockpit locker, **11**.

Engine spaces, **12**, must be clean and well vented. All fuel pipes should be copper, and drip-trays large and deep enough not to overflow when heeling.

Secure the gas bottle inside a cockpit locker, **13**, with a drain directly through the topside. Turn off the gas at the bottle as well as at the cooker. A gas detector in the bilges, **14**, will give added security.

The **electrical** system is a source of heat and sparks that could cause an explosion, so cables must be adequate for the load, and fuses, insulation, and earthing efficient. Batteries should be sited close to the engine starter motor in an easy-to-reach, vented box, with an acid-proof tray beneath them, **15**.

SIGNALING FOR HELP

All the seamanship and safety equipment you can buy will not make your boat 100 percent safe. The sea is unpredictable and sometimes boats and their crew will be caught out and need help. Also, illness onboard might require a medical evacuation if a long way from port.

VHF radio is still a vital item of equipment but it is not the only way of summoning help now. GMDSS (Global Maritime Distress and Safety System), introduced in the 1990s, means that a boat fitted with a special type of VHF with Digital Selective Calling (DSC) linked to a GPS can transmit its identity, position, and the nature of the distress at the touch of a button. Once communication has been made, contact is maintained on channel 16.

However, VHF will only work over a distance of 15–30 miles (24–48 km), so if sailing further afield an MF radio with DSC and a range 150–250 miles (240–400 km), or an EPIRB (Emergency Position Indicating Radio Beacon) will be needed. A VHF and 406MHz EPIRB are now standard items. EPIRBs send a distress message, with position and identity of the vessel, which is picked up by satellites and transmitted back to an Earth station where it can be acted upon by search and rescue organizations.

EPIRBs can be activated manually but should be mounted so that they will float free of a sinking vessel if there isn't time for a member of the crew to hit the switch.

SARTs (Search and Rescue Transponders) are another development that, in an emergency, transmit a signal that radar can pick up. This allows nearby shipping, but particularly search and rescue craft, to pinpoint your position.

Both EPIRBs and SARTs are portable and can be taken into a liferaft if needed.

Despite all these electronic devices, skippers and their crew must know how to make a Mayday call manually by radio or satellite communication.

Making a Mayday call

Switch on the radio and select channel 16 on high power.

Press the transmit button and send the following message:

"MAYDAY" x 3

"YACHT NAME" x 3

"MY POSITION IS"

read off latitude and longitude from the GPS or Decca or as a bearing from a charted object, such as a lighthouse or headland.

NATURE OF DISTRESS

sinking, on fire, aground in a hazardous situation, etc.

IMMEDIATE ASSISTANCE REQUIRED

ADDITIONAL INFORMATION

number of people on board—whether you are about to abandon to a liferaft

"OVER"

now release transmit button to request response

Wait one minute and if no reply is received, check that the radio is properly switched on and that channel 16 has been selected on high power and repeat.

If there is still no reply try another channel— perhaps the working channel of the nearest port or harbor.

Print out a prompt sheet for your boat and stick it up on a bulkhead next to the VHF so that even the most inexperienced crew will be able to make a Mayday call.

Use the emergency signal PAN PAN (instead of Mayday) when the safety of the boat or a person is a priority but no immediate aid is needed. In a medical emergency PAN PAN MEDICO, but ask to be switched to a working channel away from channel 16.

It is worth noting that with the coming of GMDSS there will be no legal requirement for channel 16 to be monitored by emergency services.

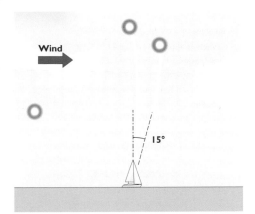

Rockets turn into the wind, so aim them vertically, or 15° downwind in strong winds. Hold handflares downwind to avoid dropping burning particles on clothing or on to a liferaft.

Beware loss of night vision when using a **white collision flare**; shield the eyes while it is burning. When using short-burning flares, fire two with an interval of about 1 min.

In low cloud fire rockets at a 45° angle downwind, so that the flare is visible under the cloud. In poor visibility do not fire all your flares at once; keep some until conditions improve.

Flares have a life of three years if well stored. **Inspect them twice a year** for signs of deterioration and replace any that are suspect. Replace all flares by the expiry date on the label.

Flares have two functions: to draw attention to the boat and to pinpoint its position. The flares you should carry depend on your cruising ground. Minimum **inshore requirements** are two red handflares and two hand-held orange smoke signals—use in bright daylight and light wind. **Coastal requirements** are two red parachute rockets, two red handflares, and two hand-held orange smoke signals. **Offshore requirements** are four red parachute rockets, four red handflares, and two buoyant orange smoke signals. All boats at sea at night should carry four white handflares for collision warning.

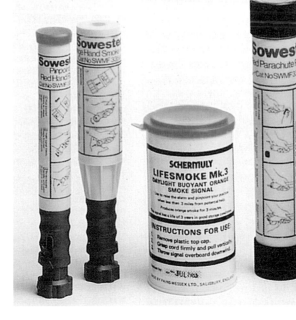

Red handflares burn for 1 min; use in poor visibility and high wind. Hand-held orange smoke signals burn for 40 secs.

Buoyant orange smoke signals burn for 3 mins; use to signal to aircraft. White handflares burn for 50 secs.

The parachute rocket projects a bright red flare to a height over 1,000 ft (305 m) that burns for over 40 secs.

RECOVERING A MAN OVERBOARD

"Man overboard" is a cry all sailors dread. Experienced sailors have been known to go into neutral with the result that vital, fast action isn't taken.

Man overboard (MOB) recovery has been written about so often that it is in danger of falling into the category of, "I know that bit so I'll move on to the next chapter." But before you do—are you quite sure that, as the skipper of your yacht, you have equipped your boat and trained your crew sufficiently well for them to pick you up at night in freshening conditions of Force 4 (15–20 mph), gusting 5 (20–25 mph)?

When any person falls into the water they are visibly immediately reduced to the size of a football, say 14 in (35 cm) high, and none of us, even the most experienced of skippers, can guarantee to find, let alone pick up, a person who has gone overboard in poor conditions. Go overboard, even in a moderate breeze, and you run the risk of not being picked up.

Established, safe working routines go a long way towards keeping the crew where they belong—on the boat. Safety harnesses used in conjunction with deck-mounted jackstays are the surest safety devices. Personal flotation devices (PFDs), also called life jackets, worn whenever there is the likelihood of being swept overboard, ensure that a person will stay afloat. A PFD must have at least 150 Newtons (approximately 35 lb) of buoyancy. Non-swimmers should use those with 275N. The type with permanent buoyancy is bulky and most people prefer the type inflated by an inbuilt CO_2 cylinder.

In the water, an insulated PFD will help to retain body heat, especially if the MOB adopts the heat escape lessening posture, or HELP. Holding the arms tight against the sides of the chest and pressing the thighs together and raising them to close off the groin area will significantly reduce heat loss from these critical areas.

Retrieval technique

IMMEDIATE action when someone falls overboard is essential. Here is one technique for retrieval:

1 Whoever sees the incident shouts "man overboard" and points to them. One crew member becomes the spotter, keeping the MOB in sight at all times.
2 The person nearest the Dan buoy and life belt throws them over, shouting "Dan buoy clear"; if the boat has a GPS with a MOB button, and most of them do, press it to store the position.
3 Immediately bring the boat head-to-wind to slow progress.
4 Start the engine, but keep it in neutral throughout, unless needed for the final approach.
5 Let the sail back, further slow the boat.
6 Turn with the headsail backed until the wind is behind the beam.

A life, or Seattle, sling makes recovery of a MOB by a single person much easier. This piece of equipment is used in conjunction with the Quick-stop method. The life sling can also be used as a hoist, when a block and tackle is attached to the main halyard and the loop passing through the D-rings on the sling. The MOB can then be hoisted aboard with the cockpit winch. A number of other retrieval systems are also on the market that each have their merits and are worth considering.

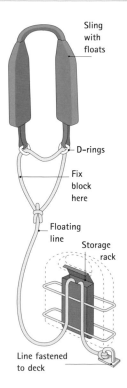

Sling with floats

D-rings

Fix block here

Floating line

Storage rack

Line fastened to deck

7 Maintain a course on the beam-to broad reach for two to three lengths before turning downwind.

8 Lower the headsails whilst keeping the mainsail centered.

9 Keep the downward course until the MOB is behind the beam.

10 Gybe the boat.

11 Approach the MOB 45°-60° off the wind.

12 Make contact with the MOB with a heaving line and effect the rescue on the windward side. Use a ladder to haul the person aboard. If he/she is wearing a PFD, life sling, or harness, a winch may be used.

Practice this maneuver again and again so that when it is needed it will be second nature to you.

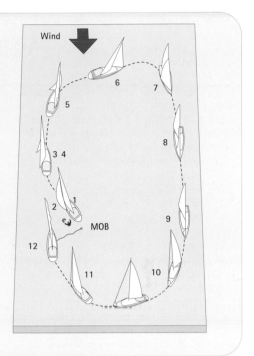

When a person goes overboard, time is of the essence. This technique, a variation on the Quick-stop method, involves an immediate reduction in speed and slow maneuvers close to the MOB.

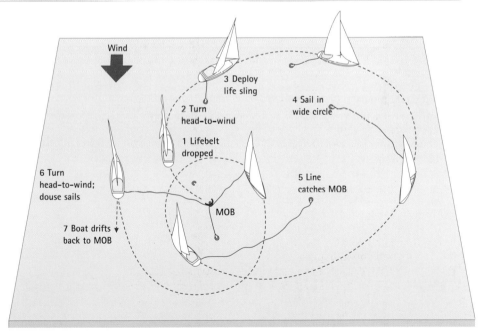

Using the Quick-stop method, the boat immediately turns head-to-wind and the life sling is deployed. The boat's movement extends the floating line and its circling motion draws the line and sling inwards to the MOB, who puts it over his head and under his arms.

STEERING FAILURES

Inability to steer may well endanger the boat and threaten the safety of all on board. It is essential, therefore, to plan ahead so that in the event of loss or damage to the steering gear, you have on board the wherewithal to make up some form of emergency rig.

On most modern designs, the fin and skeg or spade-rudder configuration results in increased windward ability, but if the steering fails the boat is very difficult to stabilize. It is almost impossible to repair or replace a spade-rudder while at sea, but it is not too difficult on most boats to fit an outboard rudder on the transom, and you might consider carrying one on this type of boat. The traditional long-keeled yacht with a transom-hung rudder is in a much better position.

If the rudder becomes jammed and cannot be freed immediately, it is essential to stop the boat making way by lowering sail or stopping the engine and heaving to. If the rudder is free it is usually possible to steer a small boat temporarily with an oar. When it is not possible to make any progress under sail, try the engine alone, using the emergency steering rig to counteract the turning movement of the propeller.

Tillers rarely break, but if they do it may be difficult to find a substitute and there is the added problem that most tillers are attached to the rudder stock with a special metal fitting. If about 1 ft (30 cm) remains it may be possible to lash the broken piece to it and to steer with rope taken to winches, but you might want to consider carrying a spare tiller and rudder-head fittings.

There is no substitute for thinking ahead, so be prepared with some plan for emergency steering and test it out beforehand.

Emergency steering
When the rudder post breaks below deck level, but the rudder is still in place and moves freely, a keel-hung rudder, 1, can be operated by ropes attached from the after end and led to the cockpit. A spade-rudder, 2, is much more difficult to rig this way, since the ropes must be brought quite far forward through blocks on the gunwales and back to the cockpit. Prepare for this by having a hole drilled in the rudder The diagram shows the spade-rudder pulled up and on its side.

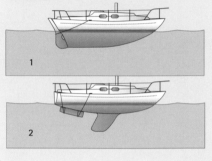

Wheel steering
With wheel steering you need a quickly rigged emergency tiller. The wheel drives a sprocket, which moves a chain inside the pedestal, 1. The wires, 2, are attached to the chain and thence to the quadrant, 3, via a number of pulleys, 4. If the wire is too slack and slips off a pulley it can jam. In this event, fit the emergency tiller, release the wires, remove the pulley and extract the wire to refit.

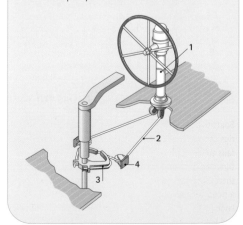

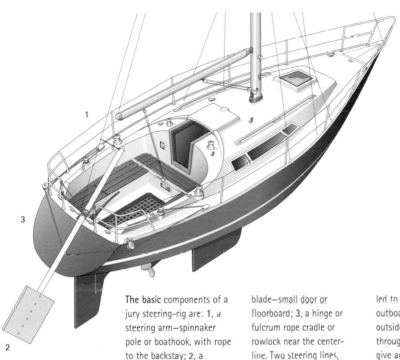

The basic components of a jury steering-rig are: **1**, a steering arm—spinnaker pole or boathook, with rope to the backstay; **2**, a blade—small door or floorboard; **3**, a hinge or fulcrum rope cradle or rowlock near the center-line. Two steering lines, led to winches from the outboard end of the pole, outside the rails and through snatch blocks, give adequate purchase.

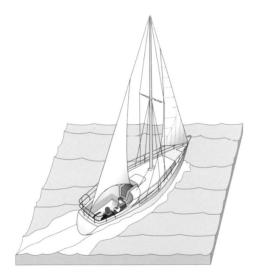

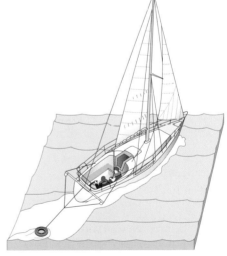

Boats that have divided rigs can be steered with sails alone simply by trimming or slackening sheets. The best rig for a sloop consists of a large jib to supply power and hold the bows off and a large riding sail set on the backstay as a steering sail. Trimming the sheet of the riding sail will cause the boat to luff, and slackening it will let her fall off.

Some steering control is obtained, at the expense of boat speed, by towing a small tire that can be shifted from side to side by using a steering bridle, attached to the tow line with rolling hitches. The farther sideways the drag can be moved, the more effective it is. Lead each end of the bridle through blocks at the ends of a spar, lashed across the stern, which extends outboard on each side.

RIGGING FAILURES

Standing rigging is carefully designed to support the mast from the minimum number of directions; once a single part of it fails, the mast is in danger of breaking or falling down.

Inspect the rigging frequently; look for worn threads on screw fittings, missing or worn clevis pins, and frayed wires, and replace or repair the part as soon as a weakness is spotted. If you notice a weakness when under sail, put the boat on the point of sailing which minimizes the stress on that area until repairs can be made.

Broken shrouds and stays can often be replaced by spare halyards, if the mast is intact, and it is a good idea to carry a spare flexible 7 x 19 or 7 x 7 wire for the longest stay, which can be cut to any required length.

No two masts break in the same way; the only general advice, therefore, is to rescue as much of the rig as possible: halyards, shrouds, sails, and pieces of the mast. If you are lucky enough to have a break above the lower shrouds you have the basis for a workable jury rig.

Masts that bend or break should be secured to the deck quickly. Retrieving the mainsail is often the principal problem because, if it runs in a groove, it will be securely held at the break or bend. Try to open up the ends of the track with a hammer and screwdriver so that the sail can be edged through and lowered. If it is attached with slides you may have to cut them off the sail.

When the mast goes over the side, it is usually to leeward and the first priority must be to avert further damage by ramming padding between the spar and the hull. You can then decide how to cope with the tangled mass of wire, rope, and submerged sails, and how to haul the mast out of the water and secure it to the toe rail, while working out a satisfactory jury rig to get you home.

Jury rigs

If you have material for spars on board, you can jury rig the boat and get it sailing again. Where the lower part of the mast is intact you can gain height by using the gunter rig, used to good effect by the Mirror dinghy. Use the spinnaker pole, boom, or top section of the mast to form the gaff and lash the top part of the mainsail to it. The sprit rig (bottom) also increases the sail area, but uses the lower part of the mainsail. Stitch a loop to the leech of the sail to take the top of the sprit; you may be able to use the cringle of the top reef. The bottom end of the sprit should be adjustable so you can tension it.

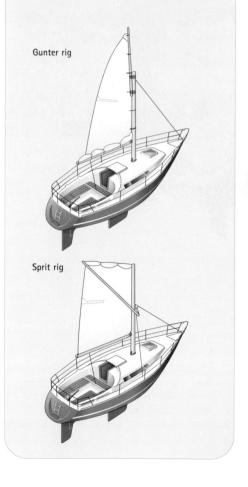

Gunter rig

Sprit rig

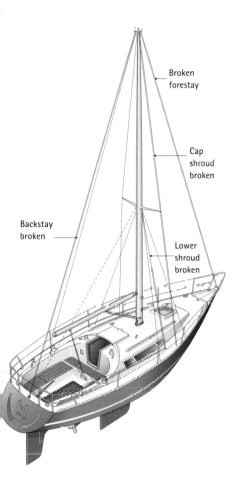

Broken
forestay

Cap
shroud
broken

Backstay
broken

Lower
shroud
broken

If the forestay snaps, the whole rig will sag back and the boat will feel "dead." Release mainsheet tension as you bear away on to a broad reach or run. Spare jib and spinnaker halyards can be rigged to the forestay anchorage, bow cleats, or samson post to provide emergency support.

If the backstay breaks, you may lose the whole rig over the front of the boat. Come on to a close reach and tighten the mainsheet. This enables the boat to fit nicely into the waves without causing the rig to sway about. Rig the topping lift or a spare halyard to a stern cleat or backstay.

The shrouds prevent the mast bending sideways. If any of them breaks under load it is most likely that the mast will also break. If it does not, tack at once so that the wind blows on the other side. When a cap shroud (upper shroud) breaks, the mast usually snaps off just above the attachment point for the lower shrouds. If one of these breaks, release all tension in the rig—kicking strap, halyards—as soon as the boat has turned on to the other tack. Rig a sheet to duplicate the broken wire, leading it to a winch via a deck-edge snatch block.

Attaching rope tails

A broken wire can be utilized by attaching a rope tail to it. Make a loop in the wire using bulldog clips and a thimble and attach the rope with a bowline or tuck splice, using a hollow fid as shown below. A blood knot (see p. 39) can also be useful in these circumstances.

Checklist for dismasting

1 Do NOT start the engine. Stray ropes could foul the propeller.
2 Do NOT rush around on deck. You run the risk of tripping overboard.
3 Get some sort of padding between the mast and the hull. Fenders or cockpit/bulk cushions are ideal.
4 Get the mast alongside.
5 Get the sails off the mast to prevent tearing; they will be needed.
6 Cut only those wires and halyards that restrict the mast's retrieval.
7 Haul the mast up out of the water.
8 Lash the mast along the deck.

FIRE HAZARDS

Fires and explosions are the principal causes of damage to pleasure craft and of personal injury. Most sailors are aware of the hazards and emergencies associated with the sea, and their boat's equipment reflects this knowledge: shelters from rain and spray, large efficient bilge pumps, and reliable diesel engines. Most owners are, however, lamentably ignorant of fire prevention and fire-fighting methods and equipment, especially of how to fight different types of fire.

The main danger areas are the cooker and its fuel system, the engine and its fuel system, batteries, and smokers—whether of pipes or cigarettes.

Cooker fuels include alcohol, paraffin/kerosene, and bottled gas. All but bottled gas should be stored in leak-proof containers whose contents must be poured into the small tank on the cooker via a funnel. Bottled gas must be stored outside the cabin space and connected to the cooker by seamless copper and flexible piping. Installations and repairs to gas piping and appliances in boats may be required by law to be carried out by a qualified installer. Being heavier than air, any gas that leaks will lie in the bilges, pervading the whole boat; if exposed to a naked flame it will ignite, and the resulting explosion will demolish the boat. Always ensure that the boat is left well-ventilated and hand-pump or bail the bilges as soon as you come on board.

More common and less disastrous is a fire in the galley, which should be smothered with an asbestos fire blanket (kept handy to the cooker and reusable) or even a wet bunk blanket, or by using a dry powder extinguisher. Never use water on burning fuel or oil, it will only spread the flames.

Some skippers will not allow smoking below decks because of the risks involved and smokers must be exceptionally careful. Ashtrays must be emptied often—overboard to leeward—and only safety matches should be used aboard, since the other type can ignite by friction.

Engines and fuel systems

Modern diesel engines have a high safety record. The fuel is less volatile than gasoline and exhaust systems are efficiently cooled with water, but once alight it burns fiercely. Gasoline engines need much more care: they should be fitted with flame traps on the carburetor, drip trays, and vent pipe and should have at least two "on/off" taps on fuel lines and a fuel filter. The filler tube has to be connected to the fuel tank, and the tank to the engine, with an electric bonding cable to ground it, and the engine compartment vented with a flameproof fan.

Flame trap on vent pipe

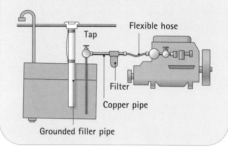

Tap — Flexible hose

Filter

Copper pipe

Grounded filler pipe

Fire extinguishers

Dry powder extinguishers, shown below left, eject chemical powder under pressure. They can be used on all types of fire and douse flames quickly. Those with a controllable discharge hold some in reserve in case the fire rekindles. The bromo-chloro-difluoro-methane (BCF), below right, is a compound liquid for killing fires in engine compartments or for fuel or engine fires in the open only, since the vapour and fumes are toxic. Alternatives are in development.

Multi-purpose dry powder   BCF

How many extinguishers do I need?

The number of fire extinguishers that should be carried varies from boat to boat.

Auxiliary craft up to 30 ft (9 m) LOA

Three extinguishers of the largest size that can be accommodated, but never less than 3 lb (1.4 kg) capacity, dry powder or BCF. Alternatives to BCF are in development.

Auxiliary craft over 30 ft (9 m) LOA

Three dry powder extinguishers, one of at least 7 lb (3 kg) capacity, and the other two of at least 3 lb (1.4 kg) capacity.

Motor cruisers with powerful engines and carrying large quantities of fuel

Two dry powder extinguishers of 7 lb (3 kg) capacity; three if more than 30 ft (9 m) LOA.

If you discover a fuel or gas leak

1 Turn off the engine, stop smoking, put out all naked flames, and switch off electrical appliances.

2 Turn off fuel and gas at source.

3 Open all hatches and portholes and air the boat thoroughly before making repairs.

If a fire occurs

1 Raise the alarm—shout "FIRE."

2 Use the fire blanket to smother the flames or to protect yourself.

3 Attack the fire with an extinguisher, aiming at the source of the flames.

Never use water on electrical, fuel, or galley fires. Only use water on wood fires or to cool down a burned area.

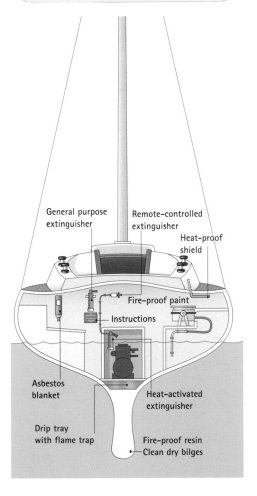

General purpose extinguisher

Remote-controlled extinguisher

Heat-proof shield

Fire-proof paint

Instructions

Asbestos blanket

Heat-activated extinguisher

Drip tray with flame trap

Fire-proof resin

Clean dry bilges

The best fire protection is given by a **fixed remote-controlled system**, backed up by portable fire extinguishers, a fire blanket and heat-proof shield in the galley, fire-proof bilge paint and a warning device.

Bottled gas and gasoline systems should be fitted with **solid state sensors** or **warning devices** of the type where an alarm is triggered by a change in air pressure, caused by the presence of a gas heavier than air on one side of a porous membrane. Another type of detector rings an alarm when a gas lighter than air (hydrogen in a battery locker) causes a platinum or palladium filament to change its electrical resistance.

Carbon dioxide extinguishers release an oxygen-smothering gas that replaces air, does no damage, and leaves no residue. CO_2 is excellent for use on inflammable liquids and on electrical fires, but should not be inhaled.

A **remote-controlled carbon dioxide installation** is particularly suitable for use in both engine and fuel tank compartments. It consists of a CO_2 gas cylinder with a lever-type piercing head, that releases the gas when operated by cable from the cockpit.

ABANDONING SHIP

Past experience has shown emphatically that unless your boat is actually sinking underneath you, the last thing you should do is abandon it. If you do have to take to your liferaft it is comforting to know that they have saved the lives of many crews and aided the survival of others, some for long periods of time.

Most liferafts are made from natural, rubber-coated nylon fabric, although recently new synthetic coatings have come into use. They normally consist of two independent buoyancy tubes, one above the other, which are automatically inflated by CO_2 and/or nitrogen when activated by the painter/lanyard. Most manufacturers offer a double floor that gives better insulation.

Stability is provided by ballast pockets that hang down underneath, but it can still prove a problem with lightly loaded liferafts. Recent research has shown that an efficient sea anchor on a long line helps prevent capsize. Most liferafts have self-erecting canopies for protection from cold, wind, and sun. These have a variety of fastenings with which to keep the door closed; some also have a window to make it easier to keep a lookout.

All manufacturers provide survival packs with their liferafts, but the quality of items and their usefulness tends to vary. Check what is provided and make good the deficiencies in your own specially prepared grab bag. Try to ensure that as many crew members as possible have done a liferaft training course.

Finally, make sure that your liferaft is carefully looked after and goes back to the manufacturer for inspection annually.

Boarding a liferaft from the sea

Ideally you should be able to board the liferaft directly from the deck of the foundering boat, but it does not always work out in this way. Occasionally a liferaft will capsize when it is launched or will inflate upside down. The best way to right it is to get into the water, stand on the gas cylinder, and heave on the righting line or straps. This is quite a difficult job even in practice conditions, and a hard struggle in severe ones, so a practical way of getting on board from the sea is an important feature of any liferaft.

Good handholds made from heavy webbing are as essential as good lifelines on the inside of the raft. The design of the boarding ladder, too, is critical. Too short and it is difficult to get your foot up to the bottom rung—too long and your legs are swept underneath the liferaft. The right length is one that brings your waist about level with the top of the buoyancy tubes, enabling you simply to roll aboard.

Abandoning ship routine

1 Send out a final MAYDAY call. Give the boat's name, estimated position, and number of crew and state that you intend to abandon ship.
2 Crew must put on PFDs before coming into the cockpit.
3 Check the liferaft painter is secured to a strong point on the boat.
4 Launch the liferaft, make sure it is fully inflated, and bring it alongside the cockpit.
5 If there is time, bail out any water.
6 Cut lifelines so that crew can step off rather than climb over.

7 Load and secure flare pack, emergency clothing, food and water, navigation pack, radio (a waterproof hand-held VHF is ideal), waterproof GPS, any mobile phones in plastic bags, a 406EPIRB, survival bags in case of hypothermia—most of these items should be prepacked in a grab bag—and two long warps.
8 Put the strongest crew member into the raft first to hold it steady and catch other members.
9 Cut the painter only when it is no longer safe to stay attached.

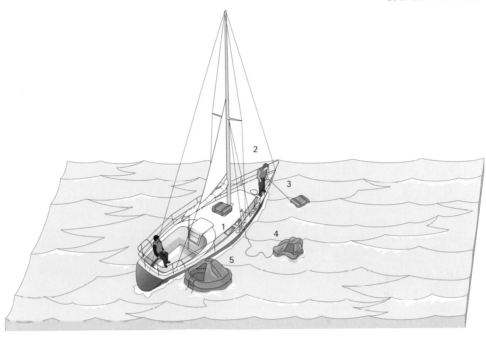

Before launching the liferaft from its place on deck, **1**, check that the painter is tied to the boat, **2**. Then release or cut the lashings and throw the liferaft over to leeward, **3**. Pull out all of the painter and jerk hard to fire the CO_2 cylinders, **4**. Allow the raft to inflate fully and vent, away from the side of the boat, **5**. If time allows, bail out the water. Load survival gear and board the raft from the cockpit. Cut the painter only when it is unsafe to stay attached to the boat.

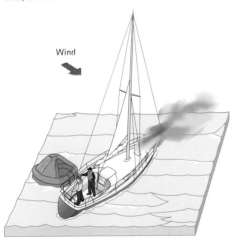

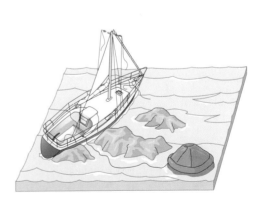

In the event of fire, launch the liferaft to windward to keep it out of smoke and flames. You may have to cut adrift before all the crew are aboard. If you do have to jump and there is burning oil on the water, shed heavy clothes, swim underwater as long as possible, then spring above the flames, take a breath, sink and swim again.

You may decide to abandon the boat if she runs aground. A liferaft should survive a trip through breakers to a sandy beach, but the crew must inflate their PFDs before entering the surf.

SURVIVAL IN THE WATER

From the moment the liferaft is cut away, the aim of each individual must be to survive. A state of shock exists, and someone must take charge to break the almost hypnotic effect of lethargy that shock induces.

No one must be permitted to sleep in the early stages of being cast adrift. Drowsiness is the first sign of capitulation and the crew must be forcibly kept awake by singing and exercising. Everybody should take a turn at being the lookout because it is a constructive action of hope, and gives a chance to breathe fresh air, which, in turn, will help, along with pills, to combat seasickness. The main threat to survival will almost certainly be from exposure and hypothermia.

It is very unlikely that many ordinary sailors will have to remain in a liferaft for long. Unless you are in the middle of the ocean, far from shipping lanes, you can expect rescue within a day or two at most. Never attempt to sail away from the area where your boat has sunk. Although wind and tide will make your liferaft drift, search and rescue craft will be aware of this and will be able to calculate your likely position.

When rescue arrives make contact if you can on VHF 16. Allow your rescuers to dictate the transfer of survivors to the rescuing craft. A big ship will probably launch a lifeboat and then transfer you to the ship's side, where you will be helped up a ladder or a scrambling net. Coastal lifeboats are purpose designed to rescue and care for survivors; once aboard you will be in good hands. Airplanes are playing an increasing part in search and rescue operations and it is quite likely you will end up being winched aboard a helicopter.

Whatever the mode of rescue, it is essential that all survivors, whatever their apparent condition, should have skilled medical attention as soon as possible to ensure that their recovery is monitored and complete.

Helicopter rescue

If your mast is still standing the winchman may tell you to jump into the sea so he can get close enough. Usually a winchman will place each survivor in the strop. If only a strop is lowered, slide the toggle up towards the wire, and place both arms up through the strop so the loop rests in the center of your back; slide the toggle down to your chest, hold your arms out wide, and signal to the winchman to haul you up.

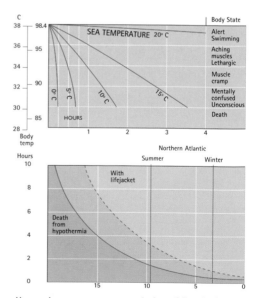

Unconsciousness occurs when the deep-body temperature falls from the normal 98.6°F to 89.6°F. At 86°F, death is caused by heart failure. In the northern summer, this takes 2–4 hrs in 40–50°F water, but survival can sometimes far exceed these times.

What to do on boarding the raft

1 Check for leaks and top up buoyancy tubes. Pay out or stream the underwater "parachute" or drogue to slow the drift of the raft.

2 Securely tie in the survival pack, grab bag, and all equipment so it will not be lost if the raft capsizes.

3 Issue anti-seasickness pills. Treat all injuries, even minor ones.

4 Post a lookout and gather any useful wreckage.

5 Make sure nothing with sharp edges—knives, shackle keys—can make holes in the raft.

6 Dry out the raft using bailers and sponges. Wring out wet clothes. Get into plastic or foil survival bags to counter hypothermia.

7 Start a routine of bailing, lookout, exercise, etc.

Special action in cold climates

1 Close the raft entrance securely.

2 Keep as warm and dry as possible. Cover yourself, including your head (an area of great heat loss), with any spare clothing.

3 Huddle together, but be careful not to upset the stability of the raft.

4 Keep moving toes, fingers, hands, and feet. Clench fists and stretch limbs to aid circulation.

5 Avoid exposure: face, ears, and hands are quickly affected by frostbite. Lookouts must wrap up well.

6 Issue sugar or glucose and frequent small snacks, if you expect early rescue. Otherwise establish a ration of food and water.

Special action in hot climates

1 Avoid all unnecessary exercise and exposure to sun. Use sunblock for protection.

2 Open the liferaft entrance fully for air. In the daytime, deflate the floor for the cooling effect of the sea underneath.

3 Keep the outside of the canopy wet with sea water to reduce the inside temperature.

4 Keep all clothing wet by day. Clothing and the raft floor must be dry by sunset; it can be cold at night.

5 Catch all rainwater or dew you can—an inflatable PFD will hold 27 lbs (12 kg) water.

If you go overboard without a PFD, either tread water, 1, to keep afloat or try "drownproofing," 2. Float restfully with the lungs full of air and face in the water. Every 10–15 secs, raise the head and breathe. Both techniques result in far more rapid body cooling than holding still with a PFD on.

Your swimming ability, amount of insulation, and water conditions will affect your decision to swim for shore. Tests show that in water of 10°C, people wearing standard life jackets (PFDs) (and light clothing can swim just over ¾ miles, 1,200 m) before being incapacitated by hypothermia.

The body cools more quickly in water than in air of the same temperature, so it helps to keep out of the water. If possible get on top of an over-turned boat or other floating wreckage. This is particularly important for children as they have a rapid rate of cooling.

Hypothermia means lowered deep-body temperature. The external tissues cool rapidly; it takes 10–15 mins for the heart and brain to cool. It is a great threat to survival: always suspect crew who are seasick, tired, clumsy, or shiver violently, or whose skin goes gray, and take action at once.

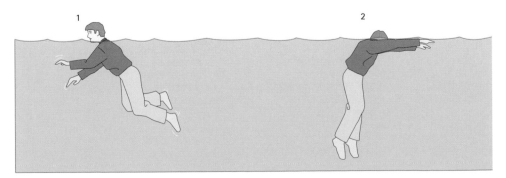

First aid afloat falls into two distinct categories: life-saving and keeping the patient comfortable until expert help can take over. As skipper, it is in your interest to have someone on board trained to administer first aid, including cardio-pulmonary-resuscitation (CPR), which combines artificial ventilation and heart massage.

A comprehensive first aid kit should contain enough items to treat most medical contingencies. Keep a modern, illustrated first aid manual on board. The information given here can only be a guide, but all crew should be aware of essential steps to take in an emergency.

If a crew member collapses after being severely injured in a fall, or after being hit by, say, the boom, follow the ABC of rescuscitation: keep the head tilted back so the AIRWAY is open; watch the chest to check for BREATHING; and check the CIRCULATION at the CAROTID pulse in the neck (left side, under the jawbone).

If the person is not breathing your first priority is to get air into the lungs at once by two breaths of artificial ventilation. If you can feel the pulse in the neck, continue, and check the pulse after 10 breaths. If there is no pulse or sign of recovery (such as return of skin color or breathing) begin CPR (see p. 174). If breathing starts place the person in the recovery position (see p. 175).

Other emergencies are burns, bleeding, and broken bones. Burned and scalded parts should be immersed in cold water for at least 15 mins. Minor burns can be left open, but major damage should be covered with a sterile dressing or even a newspaper. Elevate the burn to minimize swelling and insist that the patient drinks plenty of water. If the burned area is large, seek medical help at once.

Bleeding needs instant pressure to be applied—see opposite. Immobilize a broken limb with splints and bandages, but ensure that the flow of blood to other parts is not restricted. If the spine is damaged don't move the person—keep him warm and call for help.

First aid kit

The size and contents of the first aid box should relate to the number of crew and voyage length. The box should be waterproof, with a captive lid and a waterproof contents list and instruction sheet.

Over-the-counter medicaments

tube	antiseptic cream
tube	antihistamine cream
tube	calamine cream
1 can	cooling spray for sunburn
2 packs	antiseptic throat pastilles
packs	aspirin and Paracetamol
pack	laxative tablets
bottle	UVA & UVB skin protection
tube	UVA & UVB lip protection
pack	anti-seasickness pills
pack	antacid pills
phial	eye drops
phial	oil of cloves
sachets	electrolyte powder

On private prescription (long trips)

pack	pain killers
30	anti-diarrhea pills
sachets	Penicillin (infection)
30	anti-emetic suppositories

Bandages

2 packs	sterile suture strips
3	triangular bandages
pack	butterfly closure strips
pack	tubular or stockinette bandages
pack	non-adherent dressings
roll	gauze bandages
2 packs	variety of waterproof adhesive bandages
pack	extra large waterproof adhesive bandages
1	cold compress
1	eyepad with headband
pack	sterile eyepads
roll	adhesive waterproof strapping
2	fingerstalls
1	cold compress

Other items

pack	disposable gloves
pack	plastic face shield (for CPR)
sachets	antiseptic wipes
	scissors and tweezers
box	safety pins and clips
roll	cotton wool
	thermometer
	foil survival blankets or bags
	hot water bottles

Dealing with wounds

Wounds can so quicklly become problems that they should be attended to immediately. Any small cuts should be treated and covered to prevent infection, particularly important for anyone working in the galley.

Apply pressure

Direct pressure on one of the arterial pressure points around the body should stop almost any bleeding. Using a pad, press firmly on the point nearest the wound, on the heart side, to block off the flow of blood. As the bleeding slows down, the pressure can be slightly relaxed but not removed until a clot has formed at the site of the wound. Dress wound to prevent infection.

Stem the blood flow

Apply pressure to the site of the wound. Do not release for at least 10 mins, even to see if it is working. If possible, raise the wound above the heart level. Use a rolled bandage in a bent elbow to stem a forearm wound. Bleeding from a cut palm is stopped by gripping a roll of clean cotton.

Treat a cut

Remove obstructive clothing, clean the area with an antiseptic wipe, and apply antiseptic cream. Draw the lips of the wound together, **1**, and apply sterile suture strips, **2**, without touching their inner surface. When the bleeding stops, bandage firmly from below up. If injury is to a limb, raise it. If the wound swells, administer antibiotics.

Artificial ventilation

ABC of resuscitation

A—keep the head tilted back so the AIRWAY is open; B—watch the chest to check for BREATHING or put your ear close to the person's mouth; C—check the CAROTID pulse in the neck.

Clear the airway

Use your fingers to raise the person's jaw while pressing down on the forehead with your other hand. Make a hook of your index finger to scoop out any obstruction in the mouth. Remove any dentures.

Mouth to mouth

Pinch the person's nose with your index finger and thumb. Take a deep, full breath and seal your lips around his mouth.

Mouth to nose

Form a tight seal with your lips around the nose, open his mouth to let breath out. Blow firmly and slowly until you see his chest rise (about 2 secs). Remove your lips, wait 4 secs, then repeat. If, after four more blows the patient's skin color is not pink, the heart may have stopped. If so, deliver CPR (see p. 174).

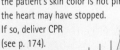

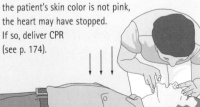

Injuries are generally easy to treat because they can be seen, but if a crew member collapses, complaining of internal pains or develops internal bleeding expert medical help is needed.

Either divert the boat to the nearest port, call PAN PAN MEDICO, or, if your communications systems are not working, indicate that you require medical assistance by flag or Morse Code or the International Code Signal W (Whiskey). If a severe accident occurs when you are two or three days from land, try to establish contact with a passing ship or yacht. It may be able to relay messages to shore stations, contact local land-based medical authorities, or reach the patient's own doctor by phone.

Symptoms requiring quick medical aid include: chest pains, with severe pains radiating to the neck or arms suggesting a heart attack; unconsciousness after a fall; abdominal pains, especially if accompanied by vomiting, clamminess, rapid pulse, and severe tenderness of the abdomen (suspect internal bleeding, especially if the patient has fallen heavily, or appendicitis if the patient has not had his appendix removed); severe pain (try to alleviate with painkillers and reassure the patient); insulin starvation, which could indicate negligence on your part if this happens to a member of your crew. You should ask everyone before you leave if they have brought adequate supplies of regular medication.

Anyone recovered from the sea risks exposure or hypothermia. Strip off his wet clothes, protect him with a blanket or sleeping bag and rush him below into a bunk, preferably warmed by someone else. In a liferaft, replace wet clothing with dry, place the casualty in a foil survival bag or large plastic bag, and surround him with other people. Watch the pulse and breathing rate.

Remember to wear disposable gloves when applying first aid to wounds. When giving artificial ventilation, you can use a plastic face shield to protect you if the person's face is bleeding or damaged.

Cardiopulmonary massage (CPR)

This procedure should be done only if artificial ventilation (see p. 173) has not worked and there is no pulse, which indicates the person's heart has stopped. Two people can work together: one to do the chest compressions, the other to give artificial ventilation. If the person has been rescued from water or has mouth injuries, give mouth-to-nose ventilation. If spine, neck, or head injuries are suspected make sure the head, neck, and trunk are supported and aligned when turning the person.

Place the person on his back, with arms by the sides. Tilt back the head so that the airway is open and begin chest compressions.

1 Place your middle finger on the point where the lowest ribs join the breastbone and place your index finger above it.
2 Place the heel of your other hand on the breastbone and slide it down to meet your index finger. Lift the first hand onto the second and interlock your fingers.
3 Leaning well over the person, with your arms straight, press downwards on the breastbone and depress it 2 in (4–5 cm). Release pressure without removing your hands. Compress 15 times during 9 secs, give two breaths of artificial ventilation, then repeat the sequence. Aim for a rate of about 100 compressions a minute.

If breathing starts, turn the person into the recovery position. Otherwise, continue CPR until help arrives.

The recovery position

This is the position in which to place someone who is unconscious and breathing. If the person is on his back, kneel beside him. Open the airway by putting one hand on the forehead and two fingers of the other hand under the chin to tilt the head well back.

Straighten the legs and arms then grab hold of the clothes furthest from you, and pull on them to turn the person toward you, resting him on your knees if he is heavy. Bend the person's leg and arm nearest you at right angles, then ease his other arm from under the body. Stay with the person until help comes. Make sure the head remains tilted and monitor breathing and pulse rate. Feel the carotid pulse by placing two fingers on the left side of the neck under the jaw.

Seasickness

Seasickness can often be prevented by avoiding excessive alcohol and strange or rich food, and by taking at least two doses of seasickness pills, at the prescribed interval, before leaving. It is worth experimenting with a variety of pills or transdermal patches until you find one that suits you. Stugeron proves effective with many people and the normal side effects of drowsiness, lethargy, and a dry mouth are minimal. Stemetil suppositories are an alternative.

Boredom and tiredness often provoke seasickness and it sometimes helps a sufferer to take the helm and fix the eye on the horizon. Anyone suffering from seasickness should be secured to the boat with a safety harness. After vomiting, stay below, keep warm and try to drink a little water with electrolyte powder to rehydrate the body. When recovering, take light, dry food, drink water every hour, and take more anti seasickness pills

Other emergencies

Removing a foreign body

To remove a foreign body from the eye, try flushing it out with tepid water. If this proves unsuccessful, pull the upper lid over the lower If all fails, soothe with eye drops, use an eye pad, and seek medical aid. If the eye is inflamed due to wind or glare, bathe frequently, use eye drops, and wear dark glasses.

If a fishhook is embedded, paint the exposed part of hook with iodine, push right through the flesh, cut off the eye, and draw the hook free. A glass or wooden splinter can be eased out with tweezers. In all cases, make the wound bleed, apply antiseptic cream, and dress with a bandage.

Violent choking

To remove an obstruction from the throat first try lying the person face down over a table with his head hanging over the edge and deliver a series of quick hard blows between the shoulder-blades. Alternatively, try the Heimlich maneuver: grasp him around the stomach, from behind, and jerk your linked fists with a sudden squeeze into the solar plexus, then release. The offending blockage should then pop out of the throat.

Fractured skull

Never treat with drugs. Lay the person down with the head raised, keep warm, and try to be reassuring. Do not try to stop bleeding from the ears unless it is excessive. Check bleeding from the bruise without putting too much pressure on the brain. Put cold cloths on the head. If the patient is unconscious, turn him carefully into the recovery position and monitor closely.

Food poisoning

Can be identified by stomach cramps, nausea, vomiting, and diarrhea. Dilute the poison by administering large quantities of water. Induce vomiting and keep the patient warm.

Appendicitis

Put the person to bed, call for medical aid, and do not give a laxative, painkiller, or food

Pulled muscles

Torn ligaments and joint pains should all be rested. Apply ice packs or cool, wet cloths and administer painkillers. Raise the affected limb

Toothache

Treat with oil of cloves, painkillers, and, if jaw is swollen, antibiotics, Fill a cavity with damp cotton wool to prevent air reaching the nerve.

Frostbite

This must never be treated with direct heat or friction. Warm the affected part gently under an armpit or in cool water, then wrap up in a blanket.

HULLS/1

Introduction

There is no such thing as a maintenance-free boat, and care and repair is more involved than you might imagine. The whole structure of a boat is in a damp and usually salt environment and much of the cabling or pipework is hidden behind linings. Boats moored or secured at a jetty are vulnerable to chafe from ropes or chain or the jetty itself, as well as damage due to collision with passing craft.

Sunlight attacks fabrics and GRP gelcoats, wind causes chafe with loose halyards or covers slapping against spars or deck fittings, while underwater growths try to eat into the hull. Below decks, if ventilation is inadequate, mold grows and rots fabrics. If there is a slight discharge from the electrical system the battery will be flat when you come aboard, and most seriously, if there is a gas leak you may blow yourself up when lighting the cooker.

All these problems are avoidable, but looking around any marina or mooring area, or listening to the flapping halyards on a windy day, it is clear that many boats need and deserve more care and attention than they get.

It is important to remember that timely maintenance, as well as being cheaper than repairs, is much more economic than a high depreciation in price before resale. In this section, the particular areas at risk are pointed out and suggestions made for maintenance and repair. The basic principle is that immediate boat maintenance leads to reliability. This is particularly true over the long term, as some components may go out of production leaving you with the problem of finding an alternative solution.

Damage

Regardless of the construction of the hull, the first priority after damage, however it is caused, is to stop the water getting through and possibly sinking the boat. The second priority is to stop water causing damage to the hull fabric, and the third is to preserve the boat's appearance.

Sudden below-water leaks

Whatever the hull structure, the action is virtually the same and must be swift. If at all possible, something must be put over the outside of the damage. Ideally, a fabric sheet should be used, but this can be very awkward to maneuver into position owing to the pressure of the water and the difficulty of moving the fabric. A berth cushion is stronger, and although it probably fits less closely to the hull, it might succeed because at least it can be placed correctly. Another solution is to carry a Subrella™, which can be pushed through the hole and opened outside. Of course, success with this relies on having access to the inside of the damage, but it is worth trying.

All boats should carry soft-wood plugs, which may not sound much good but, if nothing else can be done, a number of these hammered into a hole, side-by-side, reduces the volume of water coming in. They are very effective when a skin fitting, such as a seacock, fails.

Another idea worth considering, to restrict the flood into one compartment only, is to have panic boards, with strong backs and bolts and soft rubber gasket material on them, to place across doorways or gaps in bulkheads.

All boats should carry quick-hardening, two-part epoxy putty, which can be used to fill holes, particularly the gaps between soft-wood plugs in a split. Epoxy has better mechanical properties and lower shrinkage than polyester resin. It is easy to apply and some types will set underwater.

Assuming that the boat is saved, or that the hole is above the waterline, the next thing is to consider the actual repair.

GRP hulls—holes

The ideal procedure is to match the curve of the damaged area, either by using a piece of plastic laminate or by taking a mold off an undamaged hull of the same design. Use this as though it was part of the original mold, that is, mold-release agent, gelcoat, laminate of matt, and rovings, and lay it up over a large area of the interior.

If the job has to be done from outside it is normal to use a piece of expanded metal mesh to support the new laminate inside the hull, securing the mesh to the hull with wires around strongbacks on the outside. Once this first layer has hardened, the wire can be removed and lay-up completed from the outside. It is harder to get a fair surface from the outside by this method, but with patience and skill it can be done.

Delamination

This can happen as a result of a collision and is typified by blistering, or the sight of individual fibers or groups of fibers protruding from the main laminate. All the loose material must be chiseled away and the surrounding area sanded back to allow the new laminate patch to adhere both to the original deep material and to those areas near the surface. Build up the thickness, using successive layers of glass cloth to give a smoother surface, and sand again. Apply gelcoat, assuming that the surface is now level with the original—more glass cloth if it is not and cover with polyester film such as Melinex™, aluminum foil, or plastic laminate, both to give a surface for the gelcoat to harden against and to try to get the correct shape of the curves. Finally fill, sand, and polish until you are satisfied with the result.

If the area is below water, the color does not matter, and it is easier to replace the gelcoat with epoxy paint, which will also give the laminate better protection.

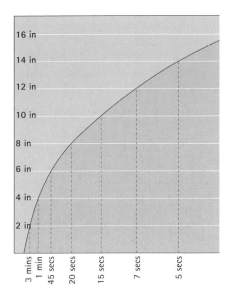

The graph above shows how long it would take a 30 ft (9 m) boat to sink if the flooding is not contained. The size of the hole (given in the vertical column in sq in) determines the rate of flow.

If, for example, the boat sustains a hole of 8 sq in, it will sink within 20 secs. With a hole as small as 2 sq in, the boat has a mere 3 mins before submerging, unless rapid action is taken.

GRP repair kit

Pre-accelerated polyester resin—3½ pints (2 liters)
Catalyst paste (safer than liquid organic peroxide)—6 tubes
Chopped strand mat—2 sq yds (1.6 sq m)
Resin putty with hardener—2 lbs (0.9 kg)
Measure for resin—small polyethylene bucket
Paper cups (not polystyrene)—10 and stirrers (popsicle sticks)

Resin brushes (Strand Glass)—10 or cheap paint brushes—1 in (2.5 cm)
Masking tape, plastic bags, clean rags (wet and dry), hand creams, rubber gloves
Acetone in metal container—0.88 pint (½ liter)
Pre-accelerated gelcoat resin, topsides color, or marine filler
1 tube water-curing polysulphide caulking compound
"Wet and dry" or glasspaper

Curing time

A boat cannot be taken to sea immediately after repair. The laminate needs time to cure; how long will depend partly on the weather conditions and the temperature in which the job is done and partly on whether any accelerator has been put into the material. Basically, the longer the job is left the better, and this will depend very much on the size of the hole. However, assuming the latter is about the size of your hand, it should be quite safe to move in two or three days in normal weather.

Splits, cracks, or scrapes

These must be opened out enough to take putty, annoying though it is to make a small blemish bigger. A router or chisel is the best tool to use, and the putty should be a mixture of gelcoat and filler, pressed firmly with a putty knife. Cover the area in the same way as before, and then polish once the gel has hardened.

Scuffs

Some of these will clean up with GRP cleaner, and more difficult ones with car cellulose rubbing-compound. If this fails then the damage must be serious enough to justify applying gelcoat.

Do not delay this sort of apparently trivial task: any opportunity for water to get through the protective gelcoat and soak into the laminate can be the beginning of real trouble and high repair bills.

Osmosis

This word, dreaded among GRP boat owners, refers to the seepage of water through the gelcoat into the laminate. It then produces bubbles in the gel, which may burst as blisters or may be pricked to reveal liquid spreading thinly down to the hull bottom. It is more prevalent in fresh-water than salt, and in warm water than cold. Some early GRP boats were particularly prone. Quite often bubbles will appear in anti-fouling, possibly due to reaction between the primer and gelcoat, so ensure this is not the simple cause before assuming the worst. Even if you can prick the bubbles and produce the ominous dampness and smell of styrene, your boat is not doomed: many boat owners are blissfully unaware of the problem.

A professional surveyor will check and give sound advice, which may well be to leave the dreaded "pox" until it has finished emerging. If only a small area has appeared there is probably more to come and an immediate repair may need further treatment in due course. Osmosis repairs are just possible for the keen owner, but are much better undertaken by professionals, under a surveyor's supervision if necessary. Nowadays, however, it is possible to avoid this expensive situation altogether. A two-part epoxy paint is the most waterproof barrier for boats yet discovered and it is becoming commonplace to paint the gelcoat with this when the boat is new. It should also be satisfactory to paint a used boat. A less drastic (and less effective) precaution is to allow the boat to dry out thoroughly for several months each year, although of course this denies you the use of your boat.

Wooden boats

Holes and splits should be repaired by replacing damaged planks, using a template to shape the wood. Each case is different. Short-term repairs—crucial to ensure that water does not penetrate into the grain—can be carried out with epoxy putty or by mixing epoxy glue with filler. However, this is unlikely to provide a satisfactory permanent repair because of subsequent movement in the surrounding timber and eventually a proper repair will become necessary.

Rot

This is generally caused by neglect or poor ventilation, either of which allow the wood to become damp. Neglect in this case means that the film of protective paint, varnish, deck-sealing compound, or caulking is broken, and water is being allowed to get in. Luckily, owners of wooden boats, or boats with wooden decks, fittings, or cabin tops, usually appreciate that a large part of the attraction of their craft is a well-maintained and gleaming appearance.

Metal hulls
These dent quite severely before actually splitting. Once again the "get-you-home" technique is epoxy putty in the split, with the surplus material adhering to a patch placed inside the hull. Once ashore, it may be possible to repair a split by straightforward welding, possibly with a patch fixed on the inside. Alternatively, a piece must be cut out and a new plate rolled and welded into place. Before doing any sort of repair to a split, it is worth drilling a hole at each end of it, thus reducing tension in the metal and also the risk of the split spreading.

Ferroconcrete
The essential thing here is that the water must not be allowed to get to the reinforcing metal mesh, or hull weakness will result when it rusts, thus reducing support to the concrete. Again, therefore, use epoxy putty for quick remedial action.

If severe damp occurs, so that the mesh is exposed, it must be cut back where it is bent or broken, the concrete cleaned off, and replacement pieces of mesh attached. This forms the basis for new cement applied, ideally on the inside against a piece of plastic laminate clamped outside. Once the material has cured (and the surface must be kept damp during this time), the outside surface can be faired, using a belt sander.

When choosing an adhesive, make sure that any to be used on the hull are waterproof. Consider the materials of the two surfaces, the setting time of the glue, and its resistance to moisture, heat, stress, and mold. Always read the manufacturers' instructions before opening the tube.

Adhesives

Epoxy resin (eg., Araldite™)
A strong, versatile and durable glue, it is excellent for general repairs. It is a two-part compound that has to be mixed before use. It is resistant to damp, mold, and heat and takes between 20 mins and 24 hrs to set depending on type and temperature.

Plastic padding™ and similar fillers
Suitable for mending rusted holes and gaps in any material.

Plastic aluminum
Good for repairing sumps, pipes, tanks, and casings. It sets hard and can be drilled.

Resorcinol and formaldehyde (eg., Cascamite™)
Excellent for bonding wood to wood. Resorcinol types are highly water resistant and durable and popular for boat building. Both types need mixing and need to be clamped for 3–10 hrs while setting.

PVA adhesives (Resin W)
A universal bonding agent that is particularly good for wood repairs below decks. Always remove all trace of the old glue before re-bonding. Although strong, it is very stress or weather resistant.

Mastic-type adhesives
Ideal for caulking, bedding door frames, and roof lights.

Polyurethane adhesives
Single part water resistant adhesive for bonding wood to wood. Sets by reacting with moisture. Foams during setting so good for filling gaps.

Contact adhesives (e.g., Evostick)
Good for general purpose use above the waterline on interiors and on laminated plastics. It requires no mixing and is cheaper and more convenient than epoxy.

Polystyrene foam cement
Good for fitting tiles to bulk- and deckheads.

SEACOCKS AND SKIN FITTINGS

Although they are out of sight and difficult to get at, seacock and skin fittings need careful routine checking, say, every three months. On many, such as engine-cooling inlets and sink or cockpit drains, which are sometimes left open for long periods, the spindle may jam in the open position. Others, such as the heads' pipes, which are often closed when not in use to prevent siphoning, quickly reveal any tendency to stick and sometimes leak. Finally, it is essential to inspect the bolts, withdrawing one from each cock every year, to ensure they are in good condition. Seacock manufacturers provide special grease to lubricate valve spindles: a much more efficient aid to water tightness than over-tightening the spindle nut. The spindle is usually tapered, so too much tension on the nut can seize the whole unit.

Hose clamps

Normally hoses from seacocks are flexible plastic, and the hose is held on to the seacock with some type of screw clip. This should always be of stainless steel since nothing else will resist corrosion as effectively. It is important, also, that there are two clamps, so that if one works loose there is less danger of springing a leak. Also check periodically that these hose clamps are tight because loose clips are the most likely cause of an accident.

Pumps

Always carry spares for all pumps, whether bilge or domestic. A basic racing rule, and one that makes excellent sense for cruisers, is to have two manual bilge pumps, one of which can be operated from below decks, and one operated from on deck, with all hatches shut, including the cockpit locker lids.

Modern bilge pumps accept and pass all types of rubbish, but the wise owner still has an accessible strum box filter on the pipe inlet.

An automatic electric bilge pump is useful, both for normal use and when the boat is left unattended on the moorings, but float switches often stick and you could return aboard to find a burnt-out pump, due to lack of water, and a flat battery.

Engine-driven bilge pumps are good in a crisis, but extra pipe work is required, to provide a bypass system when there is no bilge to clear, or some sort of easy connection to bring the pump into use when you do require it. However, the pump can also be used to provide a useful deck or anchor washing facility.

Keels

If a keel is externally bolted on, check its security. The first sign of trouble may be the breaking away of the stopping between the flange and the hull. Apart from simply checking that the bolts are tight, it is also possible to have them X-rayed. This is particularly suitable for the traditional type of keel where the ballast is the lower part of a wood or GRP fin, and the bolts are long and difficult to remove.

Rudder

Like keels, rudders tend to be neglected until something goes wrong. The most common problems with a transom-hung rudder are the pintles or gudgeons pulling out or breaking. With a through-hull rudder stock/post, the problems can include the tiller or steering quadrant working loose on the stick, the stock fastenings working loose in the rudder, and wear or stiffness in the bearings. The final disaster—the rudder blade breaking off—is normally a problem confined to spade or transom-hung rudders.

Periodical checking of gudgeon and pintle forgings, nuts and bolts, and backing pieces will ensure that they are in good order, while any slackness between rudder stock/post and tiller should become obvious by feel and inspection. The stock may have tongues protruding into the body of the rudder, which, if necessary, can be opened up for securing by bolts or epoxy cement.

The tiller should have at least a keyway and, ideally, a tapered square on which a nut can tighten the tiller head. If the stock bearings feel loose it should be possible to replace the gland packing and to retighten the securing nuts; if the steering is stiff the packing and bearing require grease. The stock is best mounted in a tube until well above the waterline and a stuffing box gland used at the lower bearing. However, the tube, being full of water, will attract marine growths and the rudder should be removed annually for cleaning. If the rudder is hung on a skeg this will involve the removal of a bottom bearing, preferably during the winter when the boat is out of the water.

Electrolysis and galvanic protection

Saltwater allows electric current to flow from anodic to cathodic material. Any two metals from two components, and their relative positions in the galvanic rating table, will determine which loses material (the anode) and which remains largely undisturbed (the cathode). The rate of wear is determined by the distance apart on the galvanic table of the two metals. Thus a sacrificial zinc anode is often fitted to the underwater area of a boat to attract any destructive currents away from bronze or steel propeller shafts, for example.

It is not enough to know that your boat does not suffer from electrolysis: a newcomer in the adjacent marina berth may start a too-friendly association with metal components on it. An easy place to fit an anode is on the propeller shaft, or covering the propeller nut. The anode should not be painted because this will defeat the purpose.

High corrosion

Metal	Voltage
Magnesium alloy	– 1.6
Galvanized iron	– 1.05
Zinc	– 1.03
Aluminum 3003	– 0.94
Cadmium	– 0.80
Aluminum	– 0.75
Carbon steel	– 0.61
Gray iron	– 0.61
Lead	– 0.55
Type 304 stainless steel (active)	– 0.53
Copper	– 0.36
Admiralty brass	– 0.29
Manganese bronze	– 0.27
70/30 copper-nickel	– 0.25
Copper	– 0.24
Nickel 200	– 0.20
Silicon bronze	0.10
Type 316 stainless steel (active)	– 0.18
Inconel alloy 600	– 0.17
Titanium	– 0.15
Silver	– 0.13
Type 304 stainless steel (passive)	– 0.08
Monel	– 0.00
Type 316 stainless steel (passive)	– 0.05

Low corrosion

To prevent electrolysis in seawater, the difference between the voltage of two adjacent metals should not exceed 0.20V. Zinc and carbon steel used together, for example, risk corrosion, while lead and active Type 304 stainless steel are compatible. Metals with a high voltage corrode faster and need a larger area to diffuse the electro-chemical reaction.

Bilge pumping equipment

1 Recommended for boats 18–45 ft (5.5–13.7 m): between one and three bilge pumps and a strum box to prevent the pipe becoming choked. One pump should be kept by the helmsman and if two are fitted, another below decks. Pumps and strum boxes need to be overhauled before each voyage.

2 Recommended for boats under 18 ft (5.5 m): one bilge pump. It should have a non-choke diaphragm with a pumping capacity of 10 gallons (45 liters) per min. A strum box to keep the pump clear is a recommended accessory. The best position for it is bolted down near the helmsman. A portable pump that can draw water from the sea may be a useful fire-fighting tool.

DECKS/1

Deck gear, hatches, and fittings are more likely to be properly looked after because they are in view and in use. Many of them also play a vital part in the safety of the boat.

Hatches and boards
If these are allowed to leak even slightly they cause untold gloom, as well as danger, if the leaks are serious. Leaking rubber seals on hatches can be replaced, but this is unlikely to be needed for several years, and some are adjustable at the hinge to ensure parallel matching of the hatch and frame. Sliding hatches normally open into a "garage" that covers the complete unit and prevents spray finding its way under the hatch and then below. Some hatches, fitted externally without this cover, require a substantial lip inside, plus drains to ensure that water is kept out. A hose test will quickly show whether the hatch should be removed and the lip increased in height.

Hatch tracks also need drains. The vertical face of a hatchway is usually secured with two or three hatchboards, slotted in behind wooden or metal strips. Hatchways on European boats usually taper so that they are wider at the top than the bottom, which simplifies removing the boards; those on American boats normally have parallel sides.

Hatchboards
At least two hatchboards (or washboards) are needed, with the lower one able to be left in place to keep spray or rain out of the hatchway. Clear or tinted plastic boards give maximum light below deck. Boards provide a convenient location for a fixed and drip-proof ventilator. This can be easily made by fitting plastic panels inside and outside of a hole cut through the board, with the outer panel covering slightly more than the top half of the hole, and the inner piece slightly more than the bottom half.

Making hatchway safe
It must be possible to bolt each board in place, and to open it from either inside or out. The usual arrangement is to fit sliding bolts to each board except the top one, which is fitted with a lanyard led through it from inside to a clam cleat outside. If the inboard end of the line is also led from a clam cleat below the hatchway, either can be freed.

Another solution is to fit a bolt with its actuating lever running through the hatchboard, allowing it to be worked from inside or out. The same applies to the sliding hatch. Indeed, in this case, it is more important because a closed hatch should hold the uppermost board in place and so must be opened first.

Each hatchboard should be loosely attached to a strong point on the boat with a lanyard in case they are dislodged in heavy weather during a knockdown, for example.

Vents
Air flows through the boat via the main hatch and the forehatch or ventilators. Each compartment in the boat requires a fixed vent that operates continuously unless it is deliberately shut off. Forward, it is usual to fit low ventilators that rely on venturi action, which creates a vacuum, to pull air and smells out of the boat. Further aft, some sort of dorade vent—named after the yacht in which the idea was first tried out in 1933—will allow in-or-out air movement. An offset draining trap stops water getting into the boat, so allowing the vent to face forward into wind and spray or rain, and driving volumes of air below, but no water.

The only maintenance required for a ventilator is periodic removal and resealing with silicone sealer. If it has corroded in the salt air the ventilator grid will need replacing.

Sheet tracks
Sheet tracks are a frequent cause of deck leaks, normally due to poor design or bad initial installation. Each hole for a securing bolt is a potential leak and a difficult one to deal with once cabin head-lining has been fitted. If you suspect a problem, remove the linings and take the boat on a good, hard-pressed punching sail to windward, making sure that there is

plenty of water running down the deck. A thorough hosing in harbor somehow does not show up defects in the same way.

To cure this leak, first remove the old fitting and, to ensure a tight fit through the deck for the new one, fill the hole with an epoxy filler. Then redrill the hole to fit the bolt exactly, so that it can be tapped or screwed through the deck. A piece of backing timber will spread the load and take up any irregular under-deck shape (with the aid of bedding compound) and a large penny washer will help to spread the load of the securing nut across the wood. As a final precaution, apply silicone sealer to the bolt before tapping it home and tightening up the nut below.

Pulpit, pushpit, and stanchion bases

These present a similar problem to the sheet tracks because the base must be bolted through. There should be no sandwich construction here, close to the deck edge, and the deck must be well reinforced because accidental heavy loads on the structure or stanchion will put severe twisting loads on bolts in the deck. A full-size metal plate under the deck provides extra support, but if it is not possible to use one, put extra-thick, penny washers below the pad piece. Stanchions may be secured to their bases by split pins, so make sure that these are well protected to prevent damage to rope, sails, or fingers.

Ventilation

1 For comfort, each person needs 14 cu ft (0.4 cu m) of air every minute, which means an air speed of about 3 ft/sec (91 cm/sec) in moderate temperatures.

2 In hot climates, an air speed of 5 ft/sec (152 cm/sec) is more refreshing.

3 The engine needs approximately 2.5 cu ft (0.7 cu m) per horse power per minute of combustion.

4 Allow engine room ventilation. If the inlet is low speed and without a fan, an extra area of 1 in² (6.5 cm²) per horse power will be needed, for sufficient air flow.

Recommendations for ventilation

Ventilator diameter	Cross-sectional area
2 in (5 cm)	3 in² (19 cm²)

Comments
Too small to supply adequate air flow, especially in calm weather.

3 in (7.6 cm)	7 in² (45 cm²)

Comments
Well suited to small craft below 30 ft (9 m).

4 in (10 cm)	12.5 in² (81 cm²)

Comments
The smallest standard-sized vent for all-round ventilation.

6 in (15 cm)	28 in² (181 cm²)

Comments
The recommended size for boats over 40 ft (12.2 m).

Recommended air changes per hour

Temperate climate	Warm climate	Hot climate
8 ch/hr	16 ch/hr	24 ch/hr
1 vent for	2 vents for	3 vents for
2 people	2 people	2 people

Main cabin
Wind scoops plus hatches and larger vents are needed in hot climates.

Heads (6.5 cu ft, 0.18 cu m)

15 ch/hr	25 ch/hr	30 ch/hr

Extractor fan with a flow of 15 ft/sec (4.6 m/sec). Or an opening porthole or hatch.

Galley

30 ch/hr	36 ch/hr	40 ch/hr

Extractor fan over cooker if not close to companionway.

Engine room
Inlet area should be 1.5 times exhaust plus 1½ in² (9.7 cm²) per horse power of engine.

Deck fittings

The same technique as described on p. 183 should be used on other deck fittings where leaks are suspected. If the deck has a molded upstand on which a fitting is placed, then the hole is somewhat elevated and the risk of a leak much decreased. It is sometimes worth mounting a fitting on a pad, though the pad must be well-varnished or protected to prevent water soaking into it and making an additional task later on.

Adding extra fittings

If the deck is of GRP sandwich construction it may not take the heavy compression loads of tightly fastened bolts without severe damage. If a heavy duty fitting is to be added, the technique is to chop away some GRP inner skin and core and to replace the core with an area of plywood, larger than the bearing surface of the fitting. This can be fixed with epoxy to the underside of the deck itself and then the cutaway; inner skin of the deckhead can be glassed back into place. Bolts can then be fitted.

Cleats

These are usually fitted to coamings where through-bolting may be required. While this is straightforward, it is important to remember that there is a considerable twisting load on the bolts unless the cleat is properly positioned. This may be difficult to arrange if the cleat is needed for a number of tasks but, if possible, it should be fitted in line with the direction of greatest load. Taking a rope around the preferred winch, towards the intended position, will give you this line.

Guard rail wires

These need protection where they pass through stanchions. Where the wires are plastic covered, which gives a more pleasant feel, they should give few worries about out-of-sight deterioration, provided the holes in the stanchions are well protected so sharp edges cannot cut the plastic. However, even smooth plastic covering can chafe sheets at an alarming rate, so it is good policy to slide some additional, loose-fitting, tubing over the wire in areas where this might happen. Polythene or plastic tubing will do, but be prepared to change it each year since light makes some plastics tacky and unpleasant to touch and they will leave a dirty deposit on sails.

Guard rail ends are frequently secured with rigging screws/turnbuckles. This is satisfactory as long as the metallic connection is broken with an insulator at some point in the ring round the boat. Otherwise some navigational instruments may be affected and become inaccurate owing to induced signals in the closed loop. A frequent solution is to fit plastic ferrules around the rigging screws; and shackle pins where they secure to pulpit or pushpit.

Often a thin rope lanyard is used to tension the guard rails. This avoids the problem of mousing the shackles and screw fittings—essential for safety—and then taping them over to stop the seizing wire of the mousing tearing at hands and sails.

There is an added bonus. Should it prove useful to drop either lower or upper guard rails when recovering a man overboard, a lashing can be cut quickly—but make sure everyone realizes what you are doing or you could have more people overboard than left on board to recover them.

Jammers or stoppers

With the growth of short-handed sailing it is becoming increasingly common to lead halyards and control lines aft with the result that more stoppers and jammers are fitted on coach/cabin trunk roofs. The technique is the same as for adding other deck fittings, but remember that because greater loads can be exerted on a jammer assembly than on a single turning block, the reinforcing and bolts must be up to size. It is often necessary to fit a pad above deck as well, to give the rope an unbent, easy lead to the winch. Jammers should require little maintenance except for removing any accumulation of salt. Use freshwater, followed by WD40™ or thin oil if the jammer is plastic.

Winches

If you need to fit an additional winch the procedure is the same as for adding extra deck fittings. Normally, for reasons of economy, the technique is to add leading blocks so that an existing winch can be used for the additional task. Another possibility is to change the winch, replacing a basic single-speed model with a 2-speed or with a self-tailer. There is usually no problem with either of these tasks except that the bolt holes of the old and replacement winches may not match.

When fitting a winch, make sure that the drain hole in the side of the base is the right way for the deck or coaming camber and, if it is the self-tailing type, make sure that the load on and off the winch makes sense; the stripper arm will be on a different position on each side of the boat.

When choosing a new winch, try to avoid one that is constructed with dissimilar metals as, with the aid of saltwater, it can cause corrosion, which leads to worn, ill-fitting units and harmful deposits in bearings and gears. The best winches allow saltwater simply to run through them. The more bearings the winch has, the easier it will be to turn under load because the drum has more support. Although this will put up the price, you will benefit from the extra life of the unit.

Winch selection chart

Boat length					
	20/23 ft	24/26 ft	27/29 ft	30/33 ft	34/36 ft
	(6/7 m)	(7/8 m)	(8/9 m)	(9/10 m)	(10/11 m)
Sheets					
Genoa	8:1	8:1/16:1	16:1/28:1	28:1/40:1	40:1
Spinnaker	8:1	8:1	8:1/16:1	16:1/28:1	28:1/40:1
Main	8:1	8:1	8:1	8:1	8:1/16:1
Halyards					
Genoa	8:1	8:1	8:1	8:1/16:1	8:1/16:1
Spinnaker	8:1	8:1	8:1	8:1/16:1	16:1
Main	8:1	8:1	8:1	8:1	16:1
Secondary	8:1	8:1	8:1	8:1	16:1

The table above gives the recommended power ratio for winches for different tasks on five different sizes of boat. This ratio is calculated by dividing the radius of the winch handle by the radius of the drum and rope, then multiplying by the gear ratio. The correct size and strength of the winch, however, will vary with circumstances. If the crew is not strong or the boat is to be raced hard in heavy weather, a larger, more powerful winch will be needed. Multihulls also need a 20 percent greater power ratio than monohulls due to the higher loads generated.

Checklist for deck repairs

1 Make sure that all cleats, winches, and blocks are firmly secured to the deck.

2 Check for dried-out sealant around bolts and screws, since it will lead to leaks.

3 Once a year, open each winch, wash off the salt, and grease the ratchets with special winch grease to keep the winch turning smoothly.

4 Always carry spare springs and ratchets.

5 Examine the guard rails, lifelines, and stanchions and tighten the fastenings if they are beginning to work loose; replace lifelines at the first sign of fraying.

STANDING RIGGING

The aluminum alloy of most modern spars needs careful preservation. The anodizing that protects it from salt and galvanic action is easily scratched and chipped, and it is worth spraying any damaged areas with a compatible metal spray to keep the material in good condition.

Some scratches, such as those caused by wire halyards when changing sails in bad weather, are unavoidable. Others, such as those caused by halyards flapping in harbor, are inexcusable. At the end of each season it is also worth checking the spars to find where halyards leading from sheave boxes have caused chafe.

Small pieces of compatible metal can be secured with screws or epoxy glue, as protection. When putting screws into aluminum alloy, it is important to remember that galvanic action will start, if brass or even poor-grade stainless steel is used, and the metal will be eaten away so that the screw will fall out. Zinc chromate paste can be used to form a barrier between the two metals.

Rigging terminals
Almost all masts are kept upright by rigging and, because it is out of sight and out of reach, the terminal on the mast is often neglected. Clevis pins must fit tightly in the tang or the strength of the unit is notably reduced. If it appears that the hole is becoming elongated, the mast-maker should be consulted. The clevis pin must also be well secured, usually with a cotter pin or split ring. Although it is a natural thing to do, refrain from opening the pin wide and ensure that it cannot catch halyards or sails.

Standing rigging
Modern standing rigging has swaged, permanently pressed-on end-fittings. They provide neat, strong terminals and are very reliable. However, if the rigging can vibrate at all, it may suffer fatigue where it emerges from the terminals so this area should be regularly inspected for broken wires.

T-terminals, which are effectively hooked into the mast and supported by backing plates inside the spar, are commonly found. It is essential that the terminals lie parallel to the mast initially and then angle out the correct amount to give the wire a direct lead to the deck fitting. There is a much greater risk of failure where the wire emerges from the terminal.

Rigging screws/turnbuckles
The same attention must be given to the rigging screw end-fittings. They must make a good fit on the clevis pin; a toggle, fitted between the lower part of the screw and the chain plate, allows for any difference in angle between the two.

Rigging screws should be 1½ times as strong as the shroud they are connected to. The correct screw should be bought to fit the rigging terminal, chain plate, toggle, etc., to which it will be linked. Rigging screws work loose remarkably easily, and it is essential to stop this happening. The easiest solution with an open screw is to pass seizing wire several times through the hole in the end of each screw thread and around one side of the frame.

Closed rigging screws have locking nuts on the end but these are less satisfactory, particularly since it is difficult to know how much of the screw thread is inside the closed barrel. The safest solution is to replace such screws with the open type.

When tension rigging, the screw may become strained by using large levers to force it tighter. If the thread is damaged in this way the screw is weakened and may well break, particularly when heavy sailing loads are carried by the rig.

Setting up the rig
Assuming that the rig was properly adjusted at the beginning of the season, or the last time the mast was stepped,

it is important to check periodically that all is still in order. The technique is broadly the same as for the initial setting up.

First check that the mast looks straight in harbor. To do this, hang a winch handle on the end of the main halyard. If the day is not too windy the handle should hang vertically, in line with the mast and about a foot abaft it.

To check it, adjust the main halyard so that its outboard end just touches the cap shroud chain plate when it is pulled tight. Now take the halyard end to the corresponding plate on the other side of the boat. Any discrepancy will show up and cap shroud adjustment will correct it. Having done this, adjust the lowers, if necessary, to get the whole mast straight. Check that corresponding stays each side of the mast are equally tight—pushing them to and fro simultaneously at shoulder height to get a feel of the approximate tension—then take the boat for a windy sail.

Once at sea, get the boat sailing well on a close reach and inspect the mast again, looking for rake fore and aft. Then, by squinting up the luff track, check for sideways error.

Getting the fore-and-aft curve right is straightforward on a cruising boat, but if excessive tension is required to get a slight bend aft when the rig is loaded, it is advisable to get a backstay tensioner, which can be released after each sail.

Sideways errors are more difficult to correct. Check for sag on each tack before making any adjustments, then check whether enough, or too much, has been achieved. On completion, secure the rigging screws/turnbuckles with seizing wire, tape over the wire and screw threads to guard against chafe, or fit plastic rigging screw bolts. Despite its tough appearance, rigging wire stretches a surprising amount, so check the mast alignment every few weeks or whenever there is enough wind to show any stretch.

Breaking strength of typical wire rope (lb)

7 x 7 construction

Diam. in (mm)	1/16(1.59)	3/32(2.38)	1/8(3.17)	5/32(3.96)	3/16(4.76)	7/32(5.55)	1/4(6.35)	9/32(7.14)	5/16(7.93)	3/8(9.52)	7/16(11.11)
Galv. plow steel	−	−	−	−	−	−	4,200	5,300	6,570	9,270	12,400
Stainless steel	135	780	1,150	2,000	2,750	4,000	4,800	6,100	7,500	10,600	14,200

7 x 19 construction

Diam. in (mm)	1/8(3.17)	5/32(3.97)	3/16(4.76)	7/32(5.55)	1/4(6.35)	9/32(7.14)	7/16(11.11)
Galv. plow steel	−	−	−	−	4,390	5,400	12,800
Stainless steel	−1,280	2,000	2,900	3,950	5,090	6,700	14,700

1 x 19 or 19-wire strand construction

Diam. in (mm)	1/16(1.59)	3/32(2.38)	1/8(3.17)	3/32(4.76)	7/32(5.55)	1/4(6.35)	9/32(7.14)
Stainless steel	500	1,100	2,100	3,200	6,100	8,000	10,000

RUNNING RIGGING

Running rigging

Rope makes the most convenient halyard for a cruising boat because it is pleasant to handle. If chafe develops where the loaded halyards wear on the masthead sheaves it is possible to cut off the last 2–3 ft (60–90 cm) every year or so (provided the halyard was over-long to begin with). Finally it can be turned end-to-end, once it is down to its minimum length.

Pre-stretched three-strand terylene/dacron seems the obvious choice, but it kinks when wet and hard. If this happens where the halyard runs into the base of the mast it will jam while you are standing on the foredeck trying to pull the genoa down. Double-braided ropes are also very low-stretch and, since they are less prone to kinking, are better for halyards. Stretch is not too big a problem, if halyards are led aft, because they are then easy to adjust, and indeed, adjustment is necessary as wind speed and relative wind angle change while you are sailing. High modulus polyethylene (eg., Dyneema™) stretches even less but is more expensive (see pp. 30–31 for different types of rope).

If the boat is fitted with wire halyards, or your enthusiasm for stretch-free halyards is unwavering, beware of the splice joining the rope tail to the wire, for this is the most frequent area of failure. Galvanized wire is better for halyards than stainless steel because the latter does not wear well on sheaves. To keep galvanized wire in good condition for a long time, it should be soaked in boiled oil each winter.

Sheets are best made of double-braided polyester and simply turned end-for-end when they have chafed slightly, usually owing to a poorly angled sheet carriage roller. It is simple and safe to attach sheets to the clew of a headsail with a bowline, but make sure the knot is well tightened or it will shake loose when the sail flaps.

Shackles should not be used on headsail clews. A small piece of metal, moving at high speed when the sail is released quickly, can do terrible damage to heads and eyes as well as the mast and other deck fittings. Snap shackles are employed on spinnaker gear, because of the need for quick release.

The topping lift is a special case for running rigging. If it is shackled to the end of the boom, the shaking of the slightly slack line will soon loosen it. In addition, the irritating noise of it chattering at the boom end, coupled with the desire to avoid the mainsail leech chafing, means it is common to move the topping lift aft to the pushpit. A snap shackle is needed to do this, plus some luck when refastening it to the gyrating boom before lowering the sail.

A better solution is to take up slack in the topping lift just above the boom by using a piece of shock cord to shorten it. Then, when the sail has been hoisted, ease the topping lift until the shock cord is nearly slack. When the sheet is pulled tight on the wind, the shock cord will be pulled taut, but the topping lift will lie quietly at the leech of the sail and cause little wear.

One of the side benefits of the topping lift is that it acts as a standby main halyard.

Short topping-lift strops fitted to the backstay are only useful as an extra, to stop the boom swinging and to pull it firmly to one side once the sail has been lowered. However, this type is useless when the topping lift is needed to support the boom when reefing.

Mast sheaves

These are divided between those under heavy load at the masthead, where halyards turn through 180°, and those lower down, where turns may be less than 90°. All of them should revolve on Tufnol™ or plastic bushes. It is important to check these for wear, the easiest way being to rock the sheave, making sure it cannot touch the walls of its box. If it can, the sheave is rubbing on the pin and the effort required to hoist or adjust the sail will quickly become excessive.

It can be difficult to remove the pins in masthead sheave boxes without dropping the latter inside the mast. Sometimes, it cannot be done with the mast stepped because the forestay blocks access, and even with the mast down, it pays to put a line round the sheave to ensure control of it.

Blocks

Running rigging blocks should last a long time provided they are properly treated. This means making sure that the block lines up with the load put on it by using a swivel or an extra shackle. Snap shackles themselves need to be lubricated, and the line that operates the release pin must be replaced, if it wears, or the snap can become painful and difficult to operate.

Going aloft

Hoisting a person aloft in a bosun's chair requires four people for complete safety. An easier alternative is to use a mast-climbing ladder that can be set taut. The climber takes his own weight so no winching is needed, and only one other person is required to work a safety halyard attached to the climber. This can be a boon for family-crewed boats where the strong winch-winder is probably also the best person to do the job at the masthead. The serious bluewater cruiser will have specified permanent mast climbing rungs.

Guide to rope sizes

These are the recommended sizes of rope for different tasks. Anchor warps, for example, need a much higher breaking strain than, say, a halyard.

Approximate sail area in sq m

Length of boat in meters	6–8	9	10	11
Mainsail	12	16	19	22
Genoa/jib	20	30	40	50
Spinnaker	45	56	65	90

Sheet sizes in mm diameter

Length of boat in meters	6–8	9	10	11
Main sheet	10	10	10	12
Jib sheet	10	10	12	12
Spinnaker sheet	8	10	10	10
Spinnaker guy	10	10	12	12

Halyard sizes in mm diameter

Length of boat in meters	6–8	9	10	11
Main halyard	8	10	10	10
Jib halyard	8	10	10	12
Spinnaker halyard	8	10	10	10

Mooring warps in mm diameter

Length of boat in meters	6–8	9	10	11
Approx. displacement in kg	2,000	5,000	5,000	6,500
Polyester/ nylon	8–10	12	12	14
Polypropylene	10–12	14	16	18

Kicking strap in mm diameter

Length of boat in meters	6–8	9	10	11
Kicking strap	8	10	10	10

Anchor ropes in mm diameter

Length of boat in meters	6–8	9	10	11
Nylon	12	14	16	16
Polyester	14	16	18	18
Nylon (kedge)	8	8	10	10
Bruce	5	8	10	10
Danforth & CQR	8	14	14	14
Chain	8	8	10	10

SAILS

Although these are the primary driving force of a sailing boat, people often try to skimp when buying them and begrudge maintenance costs. But passage times depend on good, well-setting sails and a failure at a dangerous moment could be disastrous. The sailing boat and her crew can also be much safer under sail in bad weather than when plunging and rolling under engine.

The first priority is to treat sails carefully on deck and, when setting them, to ensure that they are not snagged. When in use, try, with the aid of binoculars if necessary, to spot areas of chafe or fraying stitching.

Devote a section in your maintenance jobs notebook to sail repairs, and jot down the whereabouts of a problem; for example, "No. 2 genoa, leech, four seams from the head, stitching frayed on leech tape." Hoisting and lowering give opportunities to check for further defects.

When stowing, fold and flake the sails carefully to avoid damaging them. Try to vary the width of the flakes to prevent permanent creases forming (see p. 47). To remove creases, soak the sail in fresh, cool water and hang it up to dry by the luff.

Maintenance is a simple task, if tackled promptly—the next time in harbor if the task is small, or to pass time on passage if the problem is bigger or urgent. If it is left too long it will become a major, and probably expensive, repair.

If you do have to repair a tear, the main concern is to retain the proper shape in the sail, partly to ensure it sets well and partly to stop the patch being strained and so pulling off. One method is to stick carpet tape or special sail repair tape along the split, taking care to match the torn edges of the fabric neatly. The tape can then be sewn into place, using a criss-cross stitching pattern. This will certainly save a larger problem developing and keep the sail working until it can be repaired professionally.

The sail repair bag should include a variety of needles, kept in grease in a tube; stranded sewing thread that can be reduced to the number of strands required for the size of the job and the needle in use; beeswax to lubricate the needles and thread; and a sailmaker's palm for pushing the needle through the sail. Pliers will also be required to pull the needle through, and an upholsterer's needle, which is bent through a 90° curve, can be useful for many jobs.

If you find some area of a sail that is particularly prone to damage, such as the genoa leech where it may rub the spreader end, it is important to eradicate the problem. In this instance, protect the spreader end with a boot and also reinforce the sail. Pulpits, too, can cause bad chafing of the stitching of a low-cut genoa.

Mainsail luff slides should be supplied laced or taped on, not shackled, by the sailmaker. They should not have to be removed from the track when the sail is slab-reefed. If they are in the wrong place it will be impossible to get luff reef cringles on to the hooks at the gooseneck. It is worth correcting this fault, since replacing the slides in the track after shaking out a reef can be difficult. While the eventual solution is to move the eyelets holding the slides, for the rest of the season it should be possible to arrange for all slides below a reef line to be secured and tensioned with one lanyard and to use a different colored one for the next group of slides, and so on.

It is important, when gathering up the folds of sail resulting from putting in a reef, that the line securing the reef points does not pull any tension wrinkles from the eyelets or they may easily tear. Ideally, the reef points should be secured with light shock cord, for this will stretch and even out the tension.

Washing sails

1 Sails must be washed at least once a year, since salt, dirt, and stains weaken the cloth.

2 It is often easiest to wash sails in the bath. Use a mild soap and hot water.

3 Scrub any persistent stains with soap and a nail brush, but be careful not to catch the stitching.

4 Rinse several times in clean water and hang up by the luff to dry.

5 When dry, repair any damage immediately. Fold carefully to avoid creasing the leech and stow in a cool, dry place.

6 Do not put sails in the tumble drier or iron them, since the heat may cause shrinkage.

Removing stains

1 Oil and grease stains can be removed by rubbing Swarfega™ right into the weave, then washing in the normal way. Stubborn oil stains may have to be treated with white spirit before washing.

2 Tar may also be treated in this way, although you may need to resort to trichloroethylene. If so, do not smoke and work in a well-ventilated place.

3 If traces of paint or varnish find their way on to a sail, act immediately. Use white spirit, followed by Swarfega™ and wash in neat liquid detergent. If all else fails, try trichloroethylene, then an equal mixture of amyl acetate and acetone, then wash out.

4 Treat rust with 1 oz (28.35 g) of oxalic crystals dissolved in a pint (½ liter) of hot water. Wear rubber gloves.

5 Mildew will wash out, but air the sail thoroughly.

6 Household bleach will remove blood.

7 Treat bad stains as soon as possible and before washing the sail. First try the mildest cleaning agents and only experiment with stronger chemicals if all else fails. Always rinse out salt thoroughly.

Suggested sailcloth weights for a 30 ft (9 m) cruiser

oz/sq yd (US)	oz/sq yd (UK)	gm/sq m
Mainsail:		
6.5	8.2	278
No. 1 light genoa (up to 12-knot apparent wind):		
3.7	4.7	159
No. 1 heavy genoa (up to 20-knot apparent wind):		
5.5	7	230
No. 2 genoa:		
6	7.6	257
Jib:		
6.5	8.2	278
Storm jib:		
8	10.1	342
Spinnaker/cruising chute:		
1	1.3	43

Sail repair kit

Needles—No.s 16–19, plus some domestic.
Hand-seaming twine—No. 3, or 2–3 kg (4–6 lbs).
Machine thread—general purpose Terylene™/Dacron™.
Sailmaker's palm.
Several pre-cut patches of suitable sail cloth with heat-sealed edges. A few colored squares for the spinnaker.
Spinnaker repair tape. (White is suitable for quick repairs on main and staysails.)
Lump of beeswax or candle.
Stitch-ripper or similar tool.
Insulating tape—plastic, not linen. Waterproof sail tape.
2 yds (1.8 m) of Terylene™/Dacron™ woven webbing ½–1½ in (13–39 mm) wide.
Tubes of Clear Bostik™ or similar.
Sharp knife, scissors, fid (wedge).
Double-sided adhesive tape.
Leather (raw hide, or chrome hide, from sailmaker).
Pre-waxed whipping twine.
Selection of sail battens (long—cut to length as required), piston hanks, slides, plus the necessary tape or twine.
Bosun's bag, measuring tape.
Sail shackles.

Mylar™ sails

These need particular care if the Mylar™ film is not to be damaged. Avoid sharp creases and if cleaning, consult the sailmaker for advice if in any doubt.

ENGINES

Care of a boat engine is remarkably similar to that of an auto engine. Before starting up, check that there is sufficient fuel and that the oil is at the correct level on the dipstick. Ensure that fuel filters are clear and that the water-inlet strainer is clear of weed. Once the engine is running, check that water is coming out of the outlet and that the engine sounds right for the revolutions you are obtaining.

If petrol/gasoline engines refuse to start they are likely to be suffering from electrical problems due to salt air and damp. Diesel engines, however, need only fuel, compression, and heat to get them to start. If a diesel will not start, check that the fuel is passing right through the system to the injectors. If you have checked that the water strainer is clear, but there is no water coming out with the exhaust when the engine is running, there is the possibility that the engine suction has pulled a piece of a floating plastic bag on to the water-cooling inlet. When the engine is stopped, the plastic will probably fall away and there will be every sign that the inlet is clear. One way to check is to remove the strainer and turn on the seacock in the hull a little to ensure the water does actually come in at that stage. Polythene may also foul a propeller, in which case it may not break clear and considerable power loss can result.

Check periodically that the alternator and waterpump belts are both in good condition, and always carry a spare water pump impeller. Ensure that the alternator will not suffer from damp or saltwater being sprayed on it by a belt, if the bilge is deep. If necessary fit it with some sort of spray guard.

Propeller shafts

It is important that the stern gland (stuffing box) through which the propeller shaft leaves the boat is well lubricated to safeguard against heating of either the shaft or the gland, also to stop water getting in. This is done by a grease gun connected to a copper pipe, which forces grease around the shaft inside the gland. However, overgreasing the gland is almost as serious as not greasing it enough, so it is important that the grease gun is only turned enough to take up the slack in the thread, and not forced farther once back pressure is felt. It is probably best to do this after the first hour and then just occasionally when the engine is running.

It is good practice, on arriving in harbor, to check that there are no drips of water coming through the stern gland because they will slowly fill up the boat. If the packing around the gland is in good condition, and the grease gun has not been wound too far, there should be no grease coming out of the gland into the boat. If the gland packing becomes worn, when the boat is next out of the water the gland nuts can be undone on the inboard side, slid back up the propeller shaft, and a replacement piece of packing fitted.

The outboard end of most modern propeller shafts is water-lubricated through a rubber or neoprene bearing.

It is important to make sure that the propeller is kept clear of weeds and free from damage by passing debris. Should the propeller hit the bottom, put the boat where it will dry out, and check the propeller for dents or bending. File the blade tips, if necessary, to remove any small blemishes. A chipped propeller will prove surprisingly inefficient.

Sail drives

It is important to ensure that the neoprene gasket around the sail drive remains in good condition, or a leak will develop which could cost you your boat. It is also important that water and grit do not get inside the leg of the sail drive, otherwise the gears at the bottom will be damaged and may prove expensive to repair.

Overcoming engine failures

Gasoline engine

When the starter will not turn the engine over, first look at the electrics and check and tighten all connections in the starting circuit.

1 Begin by pulling the HT lead out of the distributor. Hold it an inch or two away from the engine block and turn the engine on. If a blue spark jumps the gap, battery ignition switch, points, condenser, and coil are in working order.

2 Check the spark plugs by removing a lead and replacing the plug with a new one. Rest the new plug on the engine and if a blue spark leaps out when you turn on the engine, the plugs are fine.

3 If there is no spark, the distributor may be at fault. If traces of deposit are visible, scrape it away to prevent it shorting the system.

4 Another reason may be pitted points, which can be filed down. Reset the gap to the manufacturer's specifications.

5 If the ignition switch is at fault, use a length of wire to bypass the switch. Connect the + battery terminal to the + coil connection. Remove it to stop the engine.

6 If the battery is flat, power can be made up by using other batteries on board. Connect the second battery to the old leads and switch on. If necessary, turn the engine over by hand.

7 A blockage in the carburetor can be cleared by blocking the air inlet with a rag and turning on the engine. If it still will not run, check the filter; it may be dirty.

8 Finally, check the fuel lift pump. Disconnect the downstream connection and hand-turn the engine. If no fuel escapes, check the pump diaphragm for dirt or a leak.

Diesel engine

Diesel engines are more prone to fuel problems than ignition defects. Ignition is effected by compression, and if the batteries are not turning the engine over fast enough to make it start:

1 Use the hand start (if one exists) with the starter motor or decompress the engine to make it turn, then push the compression lever down. It is kind to the battery to make a habit of doing this, particularly in cold weather.

2 To boost the speed of engine rotation, attach two parallel batteries. Always isolate the alternator from the circuit and remove the driving belt.

3 If the fuel becomes contaminated, it must be drawn off and filtered.

4 If the fuel is contaminated with water, a few drops of methylated spirit will absorb the water and filter it through the system.

5 The majority of diesel engines will run on only one or two cylinders, if a little reluctantly. If, however, a fracture develops in one of the high-pressure fuel pipes, do not bend it back to seal it.

6 If the fuel lift pump fails, it is possible to erect a jury-tank. Use a large jerry can and filter the fuel through a fine-mesh cloth or stocking over a funnel. The tank needs to be topped up regularly, but if it runs dry, bleed the engine before re-starting to eliminate air in the pipes.

7 The injectors are often at fault. If there is excessive leakage, the nozzle nut may be loose or the nozzle face may be distorted or worn. If the nozzle is dripping the needle may be worn or jammed or it may not be correctly positioned. The nozzle spray holes may become blocked and distort the spray and the pressure. Symptoms of a faulty injector include engine knocks, black smoke, and an engine that stops and starts instead of running smoothly.

ELECTRICS

Electrical systems are used for an increasing number of functions and in any boat the system load is enlarged by the addition of extra lamps or pieces of navigation gear. It is therefore important to give consideration to battery capacity and to recharging requirements.

Battery systems

It is easy to calculate the battery capacity required, but usually the first sign of overload is an ineffective radio, malfunctioning instruments, dim lamps, or an engine that will not start. All these potentially dangerous factors are avoidable. First, there should be at least two separate battery supplies in the boat, one exclusively for the engine (a 60 amp hr battery should be adequate), and another for domestic use. The greater its capacity, the less often you will have to run the engine or use another form of charging system; 120 amp hr would be a realistic minimum. A 180 amp hr should be satisfactory, unless there is an electric refrigerator, for example, when the load for that should be calculated and separate provision made for it. To check the state of the battery, a voltmeter is required or, better still, a hydrometer, since it also provides a most accurate check on the electrolyte levels. An ammeter is also needed to monitor the charging rate. While 25–30 amps can be accepted for perhaps 10 mins, longer periods should be at lower current. The charging output control on the alternator should take care of this, but the ampmeter will allow the adjustment of engine revs to achieve the most efficient charging rate.

Charging

Although engine and domestic supplies need to be separate, they must also be jointly charged through a system that takes into account the needs of each. This can be done by automatic charging controls or by manual switching of the alternator output. As long as the wiring is correct, the normal main battery supply on/off switches can be used to determine which battery system is used.

Alternators are almost exclusively used for charging today because they produce higher output at lower revs than dynamos, but they must not be run without an electrical load on the output or damage will result. While most alternators now have protection against this, it is still best never to turn the battery selector switch to "off" when the engine is running.

Independent chargers

To keep batteries topped up while you are away from the boat, solar panels or wind generators are a considerable help, their choice depending on climatic conditions. Some wind generators can be adapted for use with a towed rotator, so that the boat speed can be used to generate electricity, usually at a much better rate than a wind charger. As a general rule, wind chargers vibrate when rotating, and those that start charging at low wind speeds have a limited output.

Cable connection, plugs, and sockets

Proper plastic connector boards are the only real solution, apart from soldering, and the plug board must be kept dry and corrosion free. The best way to ensure this is to coat it in silicone sealant.

If soldering is preferred, and you don't have access to a soldering iron, wrap the two bare ends of wire together and lay a piece of solder alongside the bared wire. Then wrap the whole thing in metallic foil twisting the ends to ensure that liquid solder cannot escape. Light two matches simultaneously and hold the burning ends under the foil. When it has cooled, peel away the foil and wrap the joint in insulating tape.

Power requirements of electrical fittings

No.	Equipment	Watts
1	Masthead tricolor light	25
1	Bicolor pulpit light	25
1	Stern light	10
1	Masthead/steaming light	25
1	Floodlight at spreaders	20
4	20-W cabin lights	80
4	10-W cabin lights	40
1	Compass light	2
1	Vent fan	24
1	Radio	7.2
1	Log	0.2
1	Depth sounder (ddLED type)	1.2

Electrical dos and don'ts

1 Stow the battery in an accessible place, away from any hot spot in the engine space and in a free air flow. If there is a fuel leak, check that it has not reached the battery, since it may cause corrosion, leakage, and dangerous toxic chlorine gas.

2 Keep the surface of the battery clean and dry; condensation on the top may lead to a flat battery.

3 Always identify a lead to its correct terminal when connecting and disconnecting.

4 Always stop the engine and turn off all switches before disconnecting any lead.

5 Always check that the voltage and polarity are correct before connecting a battery into the system.

6 Never run an alternator with the battery disconnected.

7 All wiring should be firmly secured at regular intervals or carried in a cable tray or trunking.

8 Fuses or circuit breakers should be used to protect the circuit at source.

Maximum circuit lengths for PVC insulated cables for 0.25 volt-drop(meters)

Cable size	Current (amps)			
	1	3	5	10
14/.25	9.2	3.0	1.8	*
14/.3	13.3	4.4	2.6	*
21/.3	20.0	6.6	4.0	2.0
28/.3	26.0	8.8	5.4	2.7
35/.3	33.0	11.0	6.6	3.3
44/.3	41.0	13.9	8.3	4.2
65/.3	62.0	21.0	12.5	6.3
84/.3	80.0	26.0	16.0	8.0
97/.3	92.0	31.0	18.4	9.2
120/.3	110.0	38.0	23.0	11.4
80/.4	135.0	45.0	27.0	13.7
37/.75	225.0	75.0	45.0	22.7
266/.3	250.0	85.0	50.0	25.0

* Do not use this size cable for this or higher current values

To determine the correct size of cable for a circuit, first divide the total number of watts by the voltage to give the total current. Consult the table above and select the current that is the same or slightly larger than the circuit current. Follow the column down until you reach a figure equal to or above the length of the circuit in meters. The corresponding cable size is given at the left hand side.

Power consumption over 24 hrs

Equipment	Watts	Hours	Total (Watt hrs)
Ventilator fan	24	$1/2$	12
Radio	7.2	3	21.6
Navigation units, compass, instrument lights	3	7	21
Navigation lights (tricolor masthead)	25	7	175
Cabin lights	2 x 20	4	160
Cabin lights	3 x 10	1	30

Total power consumption for one day: 419.6 Watt hrs or 35 amp hrs for a 12V system.

TOOLS

A good set of tools increases the incentive to attempt do-it-yourself repairs and maintenance, and so avoid high boatyard repair bills. The quantity of tools you can carry is inevitably limited by the size and storage capacity of your boat, the rigors you expect to impose upon it, and your bank balance.

Tools must be kept rust free. One of the best ways of keeping them is in a plastic tool box, with trays, which is light and easy to move around the boat. It will ensure that the tools stay rust free to a large extent, and also that the box itself does not make rust marks and scratches on the boat. It is a good policy to coat tools with petroleum jelly to keep the damp out, and also to spray them from time to time with WD40™ although this does make them messier to use.

Most of the tools needed on a boat are obvious (wrenches, screwdrivers, and so on), but there are some special items which are particularly useful (for example, epoxy 2-part glue, drills, wheel brace, a vise grip, or any other sort of self-gripping wrench, Allen keys, and wrenches that will fit every nut or bolt on the engine). A socket set is invaluable because it enables you to reach around corners and get at inaccessible bolts.

An "American" screwdriver is also very useful. It is a screwdriver on the end of a cranked arm, with a conventional blade at one end, and a cross-head type at the other. Again, for getting screws into difficult places, it is a good idea to have a retaining screwdriver with a little spring-clip on the end, which holds the screw in place while you are tightening it up. The same gadget can be used for bolts. A battery powered screwdriver is good for dealing with long machine screws, especially where there is little room to turn your hand.

Drill a small hole in the handle of each of your hand tools and attach lanyards to them to help you hold on to them when you are working up the mast or over the side.

Finally, a mirror on a stalk, the angle of which can be adjusted, is excellent for working on things that are out of sight, usually on the engine. Failing this, any type of mirror is useful, if it can be supported in the position where you require it.

For more difficult repairs, power tools are helpful and will save a great deal of time. While it is possible to run them from a marina berth, it is preferable to obtain a small engine-driven generator that will give an output of 12V or 24V to charge batteries, as well as 240V to run your shore power tools. 12V power tools are an alternative, but need to be recharged.

Remember to take all power tools home in the winter when the boat is laid up and will be damp. At the end of each sailing season, it is also worth while to clear out the toolbox and lockers containing spare parts. Clean up any rusty tools and discard all broken fittings and corroded bolts, screws, and wire.

The older any equipment is, the greater will be the need for spare parts. Parts for older engines can be difficult to obtain, so it is worth ordering a stock of ignition parts, starters, and generators from the manufacturers when you can get them, to ensure that your engine will continue to function.

It is better to be well equipped with the right spares in the case of failure, than to risk wasting precious days of a cruise searching for a part. The engine manufacturer will normally supply a list of recommended spare parts and give the names of stockists.

Remember to keep the instruction manual for each piece of equipment on board, since it is possible to make a number of repairs simply with the aid of some common sense and good instructions.

General tools

A power drill that can be run from the boat's electrical system or a 240V generator
Hacksaw with 4 spare blades
Knife with multi-purpose blades
Small wood saw
Small screwdriver set (hard plastic handle) with a range of accessories
Counter sink and drills for steel ($\frac{1}{2}$ in/12 mm size) and shank to fit hand drill, to be used for wood or soft metal
Socket set 0.25–0.75 ins
Chisel ($\frac{1}{2}$ in /13 mm size)
Pliers (single joint, side-cutting type)
Claw hammer
Meter rule (extending tape type that shows millimeters and inches)
Adjustable wrench to open up to $1\frac{1}{2}$in (4 cm)

Electrical and plumbing tools

Tube cutter
Pipe wrenches
Wirecutters
Soldering iron
Crimping tool
Test meter and light

Rigging and sail-repair tools

Rigging knife
Marlin spike
Hollow fids for splicing
Splicing vise
Serving wire
Serving mallet
Wire cutters for largest size of rigging
Sail twine, plain, and waxed
Sailmaker's palm
Needles in various sizes
Grommet tool

Engine and mechanical tools

Oil can
Hand pump for engine oil
Set of engine tools
Tappet, ignition, fuel line, carburetor wrenches
Feeler gauge
Wire brush
Bottle gas torch
Vise grip pliers
Slip joint pliers
Punch
Adjustable open-end wrench
Files (rat-tail and flat)

Spare parts

Hulls

For GRP: glass mat, cloth, polyester resin, activator, expanded metal sheet, epoxy resin, epoxy resin putty
For wood: sheet plywood, sheet lead, fastenings, bedding, caulking compound
For metal: quick-drying cement, epoxy, underwater epoxy, primer paint

Rigging

Rope for halyards and sheets
Wire, length of the longest stay
Blocks, shackles
Cotter and clevis pins
Rigging screws/turnbuckles and toggles
Monel seizing wire, plastic adhesive tape
Winch repair kit and grease, pawls and springs

Electrical

Wire and fuses
Electrical tape
Starter motor and brushes
Generator or alternator
Distilled water
Hydrometer
Battery lugs, cable
Sealant
Bulbs

Sail repair

Sailcloth in a variety of weights
Chafe protection
Sail twine, serving wire, sail tie tape
Jib hanks and sail slides
Battens

Plumbing

Repair kit for heads
Pumps
Hose
Pipe fittings

Mechanical

For petrol/gasoline engine:
Gasket set
Points
Condenser
Coil
Distributor cap
Ignition leads
Plugs
Waterpump and belts
Filters
Engine oil
Hydraulic fluid
Grease
For diesel engine:
Filters
Belts
Injectors and injector lines
Waterpump impellers
Engine oil
Hydraulic fluid

PAINT

Painted boats

Repair scuffs as soon as they occur. Any blemishes left will flake back and water will get underneath the paint, causing it to lift off. If it is necessary to repaint using undercoat before a top coat, the latter must be applied as soon as the makers direct, otherwise damp will get in to the undercoat. This may sound like a chore, but it is probably easier than maintaining small areas of the hull of a GRP boat. Modern paint strippers of various types make the task of removing paint easy, and they are relatively clean to use, so there is no excuse for not having a smart-looking boat.

Varnish

Brightwork on a boat shows up neglect more than anything else. To maintain varnish, wash it off with freshwater as often as possible. Salt is very hard on varnish and if any blisters or damage occur during the season, catch the problem immediately. Keep a thinned-down pot of varnish that is three parts varnish to one of thinner on board all the time for instant repairs. If black weathering marks appear, the varnish and wood must be rubbed back until the wood looks natural, before the thinned-down varnish can be applied. After each coat of varnish, always rub down lightly to get a smooth, matt surface so that the next coat will adhere to it.

It is advisable to prepare for varnishing in the autumn because if two coats of varnish are applied then there is much less work involved the following year in getting the boat ready for the season. When the spring comes it should only be necessary to rub down lightly and apply two more coats of varnish.

Two-pot varnishes produce a harder surface and seal the wood very effectively. However, more care is needed when applying it and it is important to follow the manufacturer's instructions.

Anti-fouling

If you are buying a second-hand boat, check what anti-fouling has already been applied because it is important that what you put on top is compatible. There are barrier-type undercoats that must be applied if you are uncertain of the paint's compatibility. Some anti-foulings act better in different areas. At the end of the season, if the boat is taken out of the water, it pays to clean off all the weed and slime immediately. This is easy to do while it is wet, and means that the hull is clean and can dry out thoroughly during the winter. At the beginning of the season the hard work starts with getting the bottom as smooth as possible: equally important for both cruising and racing boats. Normally, two coats of anti-fouling are recommended.

Polish

It is a good plan to polish a GRP hull, and the smooth parts of a GRP deck, at least once a year. An ideal opportunity is at laying-up time, or in the autumn. The effect of polishing the hull is to make it more difficult for marine growths to flourish on the GRP, particularly in the area close to the waterline. Polishing also provides an opportunity to inspect the hull closely for small scrapes that need to be repaired. It should also delay the time when the hull eventually has to be painted.

Painting GRP hulls

Painting a GRP hull becomes necessary when either the gelcoat color has faded too much to be restored by polishing or when, in the case of a white hull, the dirt from near the surface of the water has changed the color. These problems can be delayed by careful cleaning with the use of GRP cleaner, and waxing with a recommended GRP polish. Eventually, though, something more serious will have to be done. The usual solution is to repaint with two-pot polyurethane paint to match the existing color of the boat; there are professional organizations that will do the work for you, but with a little care this can be done yourself.

To get a good surface the boat usually needs to be sprayed, although some professional painters always use a brush or a Scandinavian-type foam roller. When using a brush, dried paint tends to collect in the heel of the brush and work its way down the bristles to the surface being painted. As soon as this happens, clean or change the brush. To ensure an even coating, hold the brush handle at right angles to the surface with the bristles at 45°. The paint should be well stirred until any sediment is thoroughly mixed in before you start painting.

If you employ a professional, the job should be first-class, but you will also be able to see more blemishes in the hull afterwards because the restored gloss will highlight them. However, once the boat is in the water, the reflection of the surface is cast down again, and the movement of the water breaks up any imperfections. Certainly, the painting of a GRP hull can considerably improve its watertightness.

Mixing colors

1 Only mix shades of the same product.

2 Do not mix more than two colors together or the effect may be muddy.

3 Make a test mix of the desired shade and make a note of the proportions.

4 Many colors are already a mixture of hues and may produce surprising results when mixed!

5 Having established the proportions, mix the entire quantity in one go.

6 When tinting white, use small quantities, since strong shades may "drown" the white altogether.

7 Mixed shades may not retain their color as well as single colors. pale shades, for example, may fade.

8 Keep the surplus for later touch-up.

The amount of paint you will need

The following formulae can be used as a general guide to estimate the area to be covered. The covering capacities quoted on tins allow for the amount of paint normally wasted. Take measurements in meters.

Below the waterline

Medium-draft sailing cruisers with rounded bows: 0.75 x Waterline length x (Beam + Draft) = area in sq yds
Full-bodied boats such as long-keeled yachts, shallow draft yachts and motor sailers. Waterline length x (Beam + Draft) = area in sq yds.

Topsides

(Length overall + Beam) x twice average freeboard = area in sq yds.

Decks

(Length overall x Beam) x 0.75 = area in sq yds.

Covering ability of paint

	sq m/ltrs	sq yds/gal
Primers		
Metallic primer	11	60
Glass fiber primer	18.5	100
Undercoats and enamels		
Undercoating	10	55
Enamel	10	55
Two-pot polyurethane	11	60
Underwater paint		
Anti-fouling–normal	10	55
Anti-fouling–heavy	7	35
Miscellaneous		
Non-slip deck paint	7.2	38
Ordinary deck paint	8.2	44
Marine varnish	13	70

BELOW DECKS

The galley

The first essential with the galley is to keep it clean! As soon as it starts to get dirty, it will smell, which is unhygienic and does not help people who are prone to seasickness.

It must be possible to remove the cooker so that the area around it can be cleaned, since it is very easy to spill food at sea. Dirt also tends to collect in corners around the sink and it is worth keeping a tube of rubber sealant to fill up these gaps as soon as they appear. Dish washing is best done in a bowl because back pressure from the sea can force out the plug in the sink and you will lose all your hot water. The sink is very useful as a drainer to keep crockery under control while it is being dried.

Freshwater

Whatever type of tanks the boat is fitted with, freshwater will start to taste stale after a while. A frequent cause of trouble is the inlet pipe, and all plastic tubing in the system must be of good quality.

Various liquids and tablets are available for keeping the water tank clean, and if you have trouble it is worth persevering with them, particularly if there is a convenient water supply that enables you to keep flushing out the tank as directed.

At the end of the season it is important to clean the tank through with a domestic-type bleach cleanser, to rinse it out again, and then leave it empty during the winter. In cold weather water may freeze and any left in the pipe runs can cause consider-able damage that is only apparent the following spring. Most boat piping is thoroughly inaccessible, so it is worth trying to blow the piping system clear of water to ensure that you have an untroubled start to the next season.

Gas systems

If you suspect a leak in the pipe one way to check it quickly, without any elaborate equipment, is to coat the area with dish-washing liquid to see if you can raise a bubble, in very much the same way as you would check for a puncture in a bicycle tire.

The head

As with the galley, it is important to keep this equipment clean, and to make sure that everyone knows how to operate it properly. As soon as it starts to get dirty, and smells develop, it becomes another cause of seasickness and gloom throughout the boat.

The whole area around it also needs to be cleaned regularly with disinfectant. Cleaners suggested by the toilet manufac-turers should be used. Many domestic cleaners are too harsh for the surface of a marine toilet and can damage the valves in the system.

Always carry spares for the pumps and valves so that you are not caught out when at sea. When you leave the boat after a cruise or a weekend, make sure that the heads have been flushed through and that the valves are shut off. Check that they are working well at the end of each season when the boat is out of the water; also check the quality and security of the pipe clips at each end of the pipe. It is a good policy to turn off the seacocks when the toilet is not in use when sailing because they will sometimes tend to siphon back when the boat is heeled, and can flood it.

Bilges

The important thing with the bilge is to try to keep it clean. Avoid brushing dirt and crumbs into it—collect them with a dustpan instead. Make sure that limber holes through bulkheads are clear and also that water can get down from the highest point of the bilge to the bottom where the pump suction is. Rubbish collects very quickly in the bilge and easily causes a smell. It is possible to clean it out by putting dish-washing liquid into the high areas, washing it down to the lower end and then pumping it out.

Ensure that there is a proper trap (storm box) on the end of the bilge suction so that rubbish cannot be drawn into the pump. Bilges can only be thoroughly flushed out when the boat is ashore as oily water cannot be pumped into the sea.

Ventilation

This is essential for keeping the boat both clean and mildew- and mold-free for a pleasant life on board. But it is equally important during winter, if you have a cover on the boat, to ensure that air can get through underneath it. When you are away from the boat, leave all the locker doors propped open so that they cannot swing and become damaged or chip the varnish. Prop up all seat cushions and allow the air to circulate thoroughly. A dehumidifier is a worthwhile option.

Cushions and upholstery

Ideally, all cushions should have loose covers that can be washed easily. Modern polypropylene fabrics are very good in that they resist dirt and water, but they must still be removable to allow cleaning. One of the best ways to keep upholstery mildew-free during the winter, apart from taking it home, is to use electric heating in the boat.

Lighting

Maintaining lighting is a case of maintaining switches and contacts. In the event of failure, it is easy to assume that a lamp has blown until checking reveals that salt and corrosion have eaten away the switch. Some switches are difficult to work on and have to be replaced, while others can be taken to pieces—WD40™ is very useful in either instance.

Leaving lights on by mistake will flatten the battery. When going ashore, always remember to check, first, that the gas is turned off, second, that the main battery switch is off and, third, that all the seacocks are shut.

Marine housework

1 Always clean up any spillages and retrieve dropped food immediately to prevent smells developing.

2 Leave any wet items to dry in the cockpit if possible rather than in the cabin where dampness may penetrate the bunks. Leave wet towels and clothes to air frequently.

3 To clean glass windows, wash with a vinegar and water solution. Plastic windows should be washed very gently with freshwater and a soft cloth or sponge. Do not rub hard!

4 Wash the ice box or refrigerator regularly with soda, ammonia or bleach. When it is not being used, keep it wide open to allow any smells to escape. Always keep food wrapped or in containers, never loose.

5 Treat oil spots with trichloroethylene.

6 Avoid cleaners that produce a lot of suds, since they waste water. Detergents work better than soap in salt water. Keep two large sponges handy; one for work tops and the other for grimier tasks.

7 Keep the bilge clean by scrubbing it with bilge cleanser or solvent and add a few drops of pine essence to improve the odor.

8 To whiten enamel sinks or heads, fill with water and add a little bleach. The stain should soak off in a few hours.

9 To clean the cabin, use a tank-type vacuum cleaner in harbor. If the bilge is dry, vacuum up any loose dirt. Use a broom handle with a stuffed sock on the end to reach the corners, behind the cooker, etc.

10 Check cushions, curtains, and carpet for stains once a year. Most fabrics used on modern cruisers respond well to a soap and water wash.

11 Use only metal polish produced for boat work, rather than household or industrial types.

12 Leave drawers, lockers, and hatchways open as often as possible to prevent mildew and rot.

BOATS AND THE LAW

The legal problems that occasionally confront a boat owner are often more easily avoided than cured. The following points cannot cover the extensive subject of Maritime Law comprehensively, but are intended to provide some practical guidance to small-boat sailors.

Buying and selling

Although there are few legal constraints in buying or selling a yacht, the position varies from country to country, so current requirements should be verified before entering into such an agreement.

Be particularly wary when buying a boat since, unlike most forms of property, boats can carry debts with them. Claims against a boat for salvage remuneration, collision damage, and other debts may survive the sale and be enforced against the new owner. If a boat is registered there may also be registered encumbrances, such as mortgages, which remain binding until cleared off the register.

When buying or selling a second-hand boat it is advisable to record the deal in a written document. It is preferable to seek independent professional advice although standard forms of agreement, such as that sponsored by the Association of Brokers and Yacht Agents in Britain, are available. While a broker will normally assist a purchaser, he is usually the seller's agent.

Boats are invariably sold "as-is, where-is" and, since most contracts automatically free the seller of any liability for defects in the vessel, a survey is crucial. Buyers should note, however, that some contracts restrict the purchaser's right to withdraw for defects found on survey. The choice of surveyor is also important. If possible select a member of a recognized professional organization; this indicates that he is qualified and carries insurance against professional negligence.

When buying a new boat, either commissioned or from stock, you may be expected to enter into an agreement on the supplier's standard terms. If so, study the contract carefully before signature, paying particular attention to the provisions relating to payment, delays in delivery and the supplier's liability for defects after delivery, but remember that any guarantee is of limited value if the supplier ceases trading after delivery. In the case of a commissioned boat, avoid paying any part of the purchase price unless it is fully secured. Most reputable suppliers will provide a bank guarantee to secure any deposit and stage payments made prior to delivery.

Berthing and mooring

Most boat owners enter into an agreement with a yard or marina for berthing or mooring facilities. The agreement is likely to be in a standard form, but you should check carefully the extent to which the yard's liability is restricted or excluded by the agreement. Check also restrictions imposed on the owner or outside contractors working on the boat, and whether a commission is levied on boats sold from the marina.

Chartering

A written charter agreement should set out plainly the obligations and the responsibilities of both parties. Before taking out a boat on charter, take note of the extent to which you may become personally liable for damage to the boat or third parties and the penalties imposed for late return. You are liable for the consequences of your own negligence, and generally that of the crew, so insurance is essential.

As an owner wishing to let/rent your boat on charter, consult your insurance brokers and legal advisers. Existing insurance should be extended to cover the boat while on charter and the potential liability of charterers. Ensure that there is an insurance cover against misappropriation by the charterer, and against losses arising from any breach of the charter agreement by him.

Insurance

Adequate insurance is essential both for protection against damage to your own craft and against claims by third parties. Most yacht owners arrange their boat insurance through a broker who should be in a position to advise on the range of policies available and to suggest the most suitable cover.

When completing a proposal form for marine insurance, you are obliged to answer all the questions truthfully and to disclose any factors that may influence an underwriter in fixing the premium, or deciding whether to accept the risk. Any non-disclosure or misrepresentation will jeopardize the policy.

It is worth shopping around for insurance. The terms differ widely and should be examined before acceptance. Policies vary on details such as the extent to which damage by fire is covered. Damage to engines and electrical equipment caused by flooding is often restricted and many policies do not cover theft of outboard motors, unless secured by an independent locking device, or of dinghies, unless permanently marked with the name of the parent vessel.

Losses caused by wear and tear are often not covered and it is the owner's responsibility to keep his boat in seaworthy condition. You will not be covered against any loss when navigating outside the permitted cruising limits, or if using the boat during her laid-up period. All warranties must be strictly observed.

Should a claim arise, give full details to the insurers as promptly as possible. If a decision needs to be made urgently and the insurers are not available, an owner is obliged to act prudently, as if he was protecting his own interests. Any claim will generally be processed through a broker who will usually deal with the insurers for the owner.

Salvage and collision

If you have the misfortune to be involved in a collision, make a detailed note of all the circumstances of the casualty as soon as possible after the event. Details of times, headings, course alterations, speeds, signals passed between the vessels, positions, weather, and sea conditions should all be noted and recorded in the ship's log. If possible, details of the vessels, their owners and insurers should be exchanged. No admission of liability should be made.

In some circumstances, the Owner or Master of a vessel that causes damage may limit the amount of his liability to a sum prescribed by statute that is often substantially less than the cost of repairing the damage caused. The amount to which liability may be limited and the precise circumstances in which limitation may apply varies from country to country.

The possibility that a yachtsman may not be able to recover, in full, damages caused by the negligence of another, emphasizes the importance of maintaining adequate insurance cover.

Salvage is voluntary aid to property in danger at sea. If successful, the salvor is entitled to remuneration, which is assessed by taking into account many factors including the value of the property saved and the degree of danger to both vessels.

Salvage takes many forms and any voluntary act that assists an endangered vessel to safety may give rise to a salvage award. Towage assistance is often treated as salvage and anyone who accepts a tow should establish the basis upon which aid is given.

A   B   C   D   E   F   G

H   I   J   K   L   M   N

O   P   Q   R   S   T   U

V   W   X   Y   Z   Answering pendant

1   2   3   4   5

6   7   8   9   0

1st   2nd   3rd

International code flags are usually hoisted in groups of four, one below the other, and read from top to bottom. A 6 ft (2 m) gap is left between groups when more than one is hoisted on a single halyard. Flag signaling is normally used only for code signals. The answering pendant is hoisted half way up the halyard when a signal is acknowledged in the same way. It also indicates a full stop or decimal point. There are three substitute flags, used when a letter or number recurs in a group: the first substitute stands for the first flag and so on.

The phonetic alphabet should be used for radio transmissions in plain language or in code.

A Alpha	H Hotel	O Oscar	V Victor
B Bravo	I India	P Papa	W Whiskey
C Charlie	J Juliet	Q Quebec	X X-ray
D Delta	K Kilo	R Romeo	Y Yankee
E Echo	L Lima	S Sierra	Z Zulu
F Foxtrot	M Mike	T Tango	
G Golf	N November	U Uniform	

If you need to spell out a word you should say, "I spell" after pronouncing the word and then spell it using the phonetic alphabet.

Numerals should be pronounced:

1 wun	3 tree	5 fife	7 seven	9 nin er
2 too	4 fow er	6 six	8 ait	0 zero

Transit numbers higher than 9 digit by digit.

Morse code is usually transmitted using a bright lamp or torch, but can be conveyed using flags or arm signals. Use sound signals only for single-letter code signals or in an emergency, especially in fog or crowded waters. Plain languages or code can be sent.

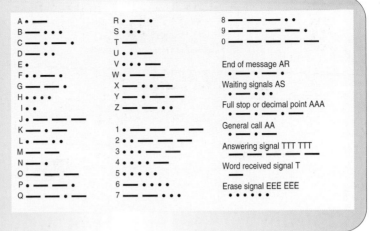

Code signals, sent by any means, are understood internationally. Each letter of the alphabet except R is a complete signal when sent individually:

A I have a diver down; keep well clear at slow speed.

B I am taking in, discharging, or carrying dangerous goods.

C Yes.

D Keep clear of me; I am maneuvering with difficulty.

E I am altering my course to starboard.

F I am disabled; communicate with me.

G I require a pilot.

H I have a pilot on board.

I I am altering my course to port.

J I am on fire and have dangerous cargo on board; keep well clear of me.

K I wish to communicate with you.

L You should stop your vessel instantly.

M My vessel is stopped and making no way through the water.

N No.

O Man overboard.

P *In harbor.* All persons should report aboard as the vessel is about to proceed to sea. *At sea.* My nets have come fast on an obstruction.

Q My vessel is healthy and I request free pratique.

R No meaning in the International Code, but used by vessels at anchor to warn of danger of collision in fog.

S I am operating astern propulsion.

T Keep clear of me; I am engaged in pair trawling.

U You are running into danger.

V I require assistance.

W I require medical assistance.

X Stop carrying out your intentions and wait for my signals.

Y I am dragging my anchor.

Z I require a tug.

Some useful two letter signals are:

AC I am abandoning my vessel.

AN I need a doctor.

RR I require a helicopter urgently.

CB I require immediate assistance.

DV I am drifting.

EF SOS/MAYDAY has been canceled.

FA Will you give me my position?

GW Man overboard. Please take action to pick him up.

JL You are running the risk of going aground.

LO I am not in my correct position: used by a light vessel.

NC I am in distress and require immediate assistance.

PD Your navigation lights are not visible.

PP Keep well clear of me.

QD I am going ahead.

QT I am going astern.

QQ I require health clearance.

QU Anchoring is prohibited.

QX I request permission to anchor.

RU Keep clear of me; I am maneuvering with difficulty.

SO You should stop your vessel instantly.

UM The harbor is closed to traffic.

UP Permission to enter harbor is urgently requested. I have an emergency.

YU I am going to communicate with your station by means of the International Code of Signals.

ZD1 Please report me to Coast Guard, New York.

ZD2 Please report me to Lloyds, London.

ZL Your signal has been received but not understood.

FACTS AND FIGURES

Feet to meters

Feet	Meters	Feet	Meters
1	0.30	26	7.92
2	0.61	27	8.23
3	0.91	28	8.84
4	1.22	29	8.84
5	1.52	30	9.14
6	1.83	31	9.45
7	2.13	32	9.75
8	2.44	33	10.06
9	2.74	34	10.36
10	3.05	35	10.67
11	3.35	36	10.97
12	3.66	37	11.28
13	3.96	38	11.58
14	4.27	39	11.89
15	4.57	40	12.19
16	4.88	41	12.50
17	5.18	42	12.80
18	5.49	43	13.11
19	5.79	44	13.41
20	6.10	45	13.72
21	6.40	46	14.02
22	6.71	47	14.33
23	7.01	48	14.63
24	7.31	49	14.94
25	7.62	50	15.24

Meters to feet

Meters	Feet	Meters	Feet
1	3.28	26	85.30
2	6.56	27	88.58
3	9.84	28	91.86
4	13.12	29	95.14
5	16.40	30	98.43
6	19.69	31	101.71
7	22.97	32	104.99
8	26.25	33	108.27
9	29.53	34	111.55
10	32.81	35	114.83
11	36.09	36	118.11
12	39.37	37	121.39
13	42.65	38	124.67
14	45.93	39	127.95
15	49.21	40	131.23
16	52.49	41	134.51
17	55.77	42	137.80
18	59.06	43	141.08
19	62.34	44	144.36
20	65.62	45	147.64
21	68.90	46	150.92
22	72.18	47	154.20
23	75.46	48	157.48
24	78.74	49	160.76
25	82.02	50	164.04

Meters to fathoms

Fathoms	Meters	Fathoms	Meters
1	1.83	26	47.55
2	3.66	27	49.38
3	5.49	28	51.21
4	7.32	29	53.04
5	9.14	30	54.86
6	10.97	31	56.69
7	12.80	32	58.52
8	14.63	33	60.35
9	16.48	34	62.18
10	18.29	35	64.00
11	20.12	36	65.84
12	21.95	37	67.67
13	23.77	38	69.49
14	25.60	39	71.32
15	27.43	40	73.15
16	29.26	41	74.98
17	31.09	42	76.81
18	32.92	43	78.64
19	34.75	44	80.47
20	36.58	45	82.30
21	38.40	46	84.12
22	40.23	47	85.95
23	42.06	48	87.78
24	43.89	49	89.61
25	45.72	50	91.44

Fathoms to meters

Meters	Fathoms	Meters	Fathoms
1	0.547	26	14.217
2	1.094	27	14.764
3	1.640	28	15.311
4	2.187	29	15.857
5	2.734	30	16.404
6	3.281	31	16.951
7	3.828	32	17.498
8	4.374	33	18.045
9	4.921	34	18.591
10	5.468	35	19.138
11	6.015	36	19.685
12	6.562	37	20.232
13	7.108	38	20.779
14	7.655	39	21.325
15	8.202	40	21.872
16	9.749	41	22.419
17	9.296	42	22.966
18	9.842	43	23.513
19	10.389	44	24.059
20	10.936	45	24.606
21	11.483	46	25.153
22	12.030	47	25.700
23	12.577	48	26.247
24	13.123	49	26.793
25	13.670	50	27.340

International nautical miles, kilometers, and statute miles

INM	Km	SM	Km	INM	SM	SM	KM	INM
1	1.852	1.15078	1	0.53996	0.62137	1	1.60934	0.86898
2	3.70	2.30	2	1.08	1.24	2	3.22	1.74
3	5.56	3.45	3	1.62	1.86	3	4.83	2.61
4	7.41	4.60	4	2.16	2.49	4	6.44	3.48
5	9.26	5.75	5	2.70	3.11	5	8.05	4.34
6	11.11	6.90	6	3.24	3.73	6	9.66	5.21
7	12.96	8.06	7	3.78	4.35	7	11.27	6.08
8	14.82	9.21	8	4.32	4.97	8	12.87	6.95
9	16.67	10.36	9	4.86	5.59	9	14.48	7.82
10	18.52	11.51	10	5.40	6.21	10	16.09	8.69
11	20.37	12.66	11	5.94	6.84	11	17.70	9.56
12	22.22	13.81	12	6.48	7.46	12	19.31	10.43
13	24.08	14.96	13	7.02	8.08	13	20.92	11.30
14	25.93	16.11	14	7.56	8.70	14	22.53	12.17
15	27.78	17.26	15	8.10	9.32	15	23.14	13.03
16	29.63	18.41	16	8.64	9.94	16	25.75	13.90
17	31.48	19.56	17	9.18	10.56	17	27.36	14.77
18	33.34	20.71	18	9.72	11.18	18	28.97	15.64
19	35.19	21.86	19	10.26	11.81	19	30.58	16.51
20	37.04	23.02	20	10.00	12.43	20	32.19	17.38
21	38.99	24.17	21	11.34	13.05	21	33.80	18.25
22	40.74	25.32	22	11.88	13.67	22	35.41	19.12
23	42.60	26.47	23	12.42	14.29	23	37.01	19.99
24	44.45	27.62	24	12.96	14.91	24	38.62	20.86
25	46.30	20.77	25	13.50	15.53	25	40.23	21.72
26	48.15	29.92	26	14.04	16.16	26	41.84	22.59
27	50.00	31.07	27	14.58	16.78	27	43.45	23.46
28	51.86	32.22	28	15.12	17.40	28	45.06	24.33
29	53.71	33.37	29	15.66	18.02	29	46.67	25.20
30	55.56	34.52	30	16.20	18.64	30	48.28	26.07
31	57.41	35.67	31	16.74	19.26	31	49.89	26.94
32	59.26	36.82	32	17.28	19.88	32	51.50	27.81
33	61.12	37.98	33	17.82	20.51	33	53.11	28.68
34	62.97	39.13	34	18.36	21.13	34	54.72	29.55
35	64.82	40.28	35	18.90	21.75	35	56.33	30.41
36	66.67	41.43	36	19.44	22.37	36	57.94	31.28
37	68.52	42.58	37	19.98	22.99	37	59.55	32.15
38	70.38	43.73	38	20.52	23.61	38	61.15	33.02
39	72.23	44.88	39	21.06	24.23	39	62.76	33.89
40	74.08	46.03	40	21.60	24.85	40	64.37	34.76
45	83.34	51.79	45	24.30	27.96	45	72.42	39.10
50	92.60	57.54	50	27.00	31.07	50	80.47	43.45
55	101.86	63.29	55	29.70	34.18	55	88.51	47.79
60	111.12	69.05	60	32.40	37.28	60	96.56	52.14
65	120.38	74.80	65	35.10	40.39	65	104.61	56.48
70	129.64	80.55	70	37.80	43.50	70	112.65	60.83
75	138.90	86.31	75	40.50	46.60	75	120.70	65.17
80	148.16	92.06	80	43.20	49.71	80	128.75	69.52
85	157.42	97.82	85	45.90	52.82	85	136.79	73.86
90	166.68	103.57	90	48.60	55.92	90	144.84	78.21
95	715.94	109.32	95	51.30	59.03	95	152.89	82.55
100	185.20	115.08	100	54.00	62.14	100	160.93	86.90

FACTS AND FIGURES

Mariner's measure

The old nautical mile (6,080 ft) has been replaced by the international nautical mile (6,076 ft). The difference, however, is too small to be of any consequence for the yachtsman.

1 fathom = 6 ft
1 fathom = 1.8288 m
1 cable = 100 fathoms approximately
1 nautical mile = 10 cables
1 nautical mile = 1,852 m (6,076.12 ft)
1 nautical mile = 1,852 km
1 nautical mile = 1.15 miles
1 knot = 1 nautical mile per hour
1 kilometer = 0.539957 nautical miles
1 mile = 0.868976 nautical miles

Electricity

Watts = Volts x Amperes $Amperes = \dfrac{Ohms}{Volts}$

Estimating speed

A rough idea of a boat's speed can be gained by noting the time it takes to travel its own length by reference to an object in the water.

$$Speed\ in\ knots = \dfrac{length\ in\ meters \times 1.94}{time\ in\ seconds}$$

$$Speed\ in\ knots = \dfrac{length\ in\ feet \times 0.59}{time\ in\ seconds}$$

Frequency/wavelength

Frequencies and wavelengths are reciprocal. In other words. 300kHz = 1000 m and 1000kHz = 300 m. The formulae for converting them are:

$Meters = \dfrac{300\ 000}{kHz}$ $kHzs = \dfrac{300\ 000}{m}$

1 MHz = 1000 kHz

Barometric pressure

The following conversion factors are calculated at 32°F (0°C) and standard gravity of 980.665 cm/sec^2
1 millibar = 0.02953 in 1 inch = 33.86387mb

Estimating speed

Knots	m/sec	MPH
1.944	1	2.237
3.9	2	4.5
5.8	3	6.7
7.8	4	8.9
9.7	5	11.2
11.7	6	13.4
13.6	7	15.7
15.6	8	17.9
17.5	9	20.1
19.4	10	22.4
21.4	11	24.6
23.3	12	26.8
25.3	13	29.1
27.2	14	31.3
29.2	15	33.6
31.1	16	35.8
33.0	17	38.0
35.0	18	40.3
36.9	19	42.5
38.9	20	44.7
48.6	25	55.9
58.3	30	67.1
68.0	35	78.3

Conversion table (Fahrenheit to Celsius)

°F	°C	°F	°C	°F	°C	°F	°C	°F	°C	°F	°C
00	-18	24	-4	48	9	72	22	96	36	121	49
01	-17	25	-4	49	9	73	23	97	36	122	50
02	-17	26	-3	50	10	74	23	98	37	123	51
03	-16	27	-3	51	11	75	24	100	38	124	51
04	-16	28	-2	52	11	76	24	101	38	125	52
05	-15	29	-2	53	12	77	25	102	39	126	52
06	-14	30	-1	54	12	78	26	103	39	127	53
07	-14	31	-1	55	13	79	26	104	40	128	53
08	-13	32	0	56	13	80	27	105	41	129	54
09	-13	33	1	57	14	81	27	106	41	130	54
10	-12	34	1	58	14	82	28	107	42	131	55
11	-12	35	2	59	15	83	28	108	42	132	56
12	-11	36	2	60	16	84	29	109	43	133	56
13	-11	37	3	61	16	85	29	110	43	134	57
14	-10	38	3	62	17	86	30	111	44	135	57
15	-10	39	4	63	17	87	31	112	44	136	58
16	0	40	4	64	18	88	31	113	45	137	58
17	-8	41	5	65	18	89	32	114	46	138	50
18	-8	42	6	66	19	90	32	115	46	139	59
19	-7	43	6	67	19	91	33	116	47	140	60
20	-7	44	7	68	20	92	33	117	47	141	61
21	-6	45	7	69	21	93	34	118	48	142	61
22	-6	46	8	70	21	94	34	119	48	143	62
23	-5	47	8	71	22	95	35	120	49	144	62

Freshwater measurements

1 liter weighs 1 kg
1 gallon weighs 10 lbs
1 cubic meter weighs 1,000 kg
1 cubic foot weighs 62.32 lbs
1 cubic meter is 1,000 liters
1 cubic foot is 6.25 gallons
1 ton occupies 35.96 cubic feet
1 ton is 224 gallons (Imperial)

Conversion tables

Multiply	By	To obtain
Pints (Imp)	1.201	Pints (US)
Gallons (Imp)	4.546	Liters
Liters	0.22	Gallons (Imp)
Gallons (Imp)	1.201	Gallons (US)
Gallons (US)	0.8327	Gallons (Imp)
Liters/sec	13.20	Gallons/min

Multiply	By	To obtain
Liters/min	3.666×10^3	Gallons/sec
Fluid oz (Imp)	28.41	Cubic cm
Fluid oz (US)	1.041	Fluid oz (Imp)
Minutes (angles)	0.01667	Degrees (angle)
Square yards	0.8361	Square meters
Square meters	1.196	Square yards
Horsepower	1.014	Horsepower (metric)
Miles	1.609	Kilometers
Miles	0.8684	Nautical miles
Miles/hr	1.609	Kilometers/hr
Cubic cm	3.531×10^5	Cubic feet
Cubic meters	1.308	Cubic yards
Cubic meters	220.0	Gallons (Imp)
Cubic yards	0.7646	Cubic meters
Cubic yards	764.5	Liters
Fathoms	1.83	Meters
Feet	0.3048	Meters
Inches	25.40	Millimeters
Kilograms	2.205	Pounds
Kilometers	3.281×10^3	Feet
Kilometers	0.6214	Miles
Kilometers/hr	0.5396	Knots
Kilometers/hr	0.6214	Miles/hr
Knots	1.853	Kilometers/hr
Knots	1.152	Miles/hr
Pounds/sq ft	0.03591	Cm of mercury

FACTS AND FIGURES

Distance of horizon for various heights of eye

Height of eye		Horizon distance	Height of eye		Horizon distance
Meters	Feet	N miles	Meters	Feet	N miles
1	3.3	2.1	16	52.5	8.3
2	6.6	2.9	17	55.8	8.6
3	9.8	3.6	18	59.1	8.8
4	13.1	4.1	19	62.3	9.1
5	16.4	4.7	20	65.6	9.3
6	19.7	5.1	21	68.9	9.5
7	23.0	5.5	22	72.2	9.8
8	26.2	5.9	23	75.5	10.0
9	29.6	6.2	24	78.7	10.2
10	32.8	6.6	25	82.0	10.4
11	36.1	6.9	26	85.3	10.6
12	39.4	7.2	27	88.6	10.8
13	42.7	7.5	28	91.9	11.0
14	45.9	7.8	29	95.1	11.2
15	49.2	8.1	30	98.4	11.4

Lights — distance off when rising or dipping (n miles)

Height of light		Height of eye							
		Meters 1	2	3	4	5	6	7	8
Meters	Feet	Feet 3	7	10	13	16	20	23	26
10	33	8.7	9.5	10.2	10.8	11.3	11.7	12.1	12.5
14	46	9.9	10.7	11.4	12.0	12.5	12.9	13.3	13.7
18	59	10.9	11.7	12.4	13.0	13.5	13.9	14.3	14.7
20	66	11.4	12.2	12.9	13.5	14.0	14.4	14.8	15.2
24	79	12.3	13.1	13.8	14.4	14.9	15.3	15.7	16.1
28	92	13.1	13.9	14.6	15.2	15.7	16.1	16.5	16.9
30	98	13.5	14.3	15.0	15.6	16.1	16.5	16.9	17.3
34	112	14.2	15.0	15.7	16.3	16.8	17.2	17.6	18.0
38	125	14.9	15.7	16.4	17.0	17.5	17.9	18.3	18.7
40	131	15.3	16.1	16.8	17.4	17.9	18.3	18.7	19.1
44	144	15.9	16.7	17.4	18.0	18.5	18.9	19.3	19.7
48	157	16.5	17.3	18.0	18.6	19.1	19.5	19.9	20.3
50	164	16.8	17.6	18.3	18.9	19.4	19.8	20.2	20.6
55	180	17.5	18.3	19.0	19.6	20.1	20.5	20.9	21.3
60	197	18.2	19.0	19.7	20.3	20.8	21.2	21.6	22.0
65	213	18.9	19.7	20.4	21.0	21.5	21.9	22.3	22.7
70	230	19.5	20.3	21.0	21.6	22.1	22.5	22.9	23.2
75	246	20.1	20.9	21.6	22.2	22.7	23.1	23.5	23.9
80	262	20.7	21.5	22.2	22.8	23.3	23.7	24.1	24.5
85	279	21.3	22.1	22.8	23.4	23.9	24.3	24.7	25.1
90	295	21.8	22.6	23.3	23.9	24.4	24.8	25.2	25.6
95	312	22.4	23.2	23.9	24.5	25.0	25.4	25.8	26.2
100	328	23.0	23.8	24.5	25.1	25.6	26.0	26.4	26.8

Vertical sextant angles — for finding distance off

Height of object	49 ft (15 m)	66 ft (20 m)	82 ft (25 m)	98 ft (30 m)	115 ft (35 m)	131 ft (40 m)	148 ft (45 m)	164 ft (50 m)	180 ft (55 m)	197 ft (60 m)
Miles										
0.1	4°38'	6°10'	7°41'	9°13'	10°42'	12°11'	13°39'	15°07'	16°32'	17°57'
0.2	2°19'	3°05'	3°52'	4°38'	5°24'	6°10'	6°56'	7°41'	8°27'	9°12'
0.3	1°33'	2°04'	2°35'	3°05'	3°36'	4°07'	4°38'	5°09'	5°39'	6°10
0.4	1°10'	1°33'	1°56'	2°19'	2°42'	3°05'	3°29'	3°52'	4°15'	4°38
0.5	0°56'	1°14'	1°33'	1°51'	2°10'	2°28'	2°47'	3°05'	3°24'	3°42'
0.6	0°46'	1°02'	1°17'	1°33'	1°48'	2°04'	2°19'	2°35'	2°50'	3°05'
0.7	0°40'	0°53'	1°06'	1°20'	1°33'	1°46'	1°59'	2°13'	2°26'	2°39'
0.8	0°35'	0°46'	0°58'	1°10'	1°21'	1°33'	1°44'	1°56'	2°08'	2°19
0.9	0°31'	0°41'	0°52'	1°02'	1°12'	1°22'	1°33'	1°43'	1°53'	2°04
1.0	0°28'	0°37'	0°46'	0°56'	1°05'	1°14'	1°24'	1°33'	1°42'	1°51'
1.1	0°25'	0°34'	0°42'	0°51'	0°59'	1°07'	1°16'	1°24'	1°33'	1°41'
1.2	0°23'	0°31'	0°39'	0°46'	0°49'	1°02'	1°10'	1°17'	1°25'	1°33'
1.3	0°21'	0°29'	0°36'	0°43'	0°50'	0°57'	1°04'	1°11'	1°19'	1°26'
1.4	0°20'	0°27'	0°33'	0°40'	0°46'	0°53'	1°00'	1°06'	1°13'	1°20'
1.5	0°19'	0°25'	0°31'	0°37'	0°43'	0°49'	0°56'	1°02'	1°08'	1°14'
1.6	0°17'	0°23'	0°29'	0°35'	0°41'	0°46'	0°52'	0°58'	1°04'	1°10'
1.7	0°16'	0°22'	0°27'	0°33'	0°38'	0°44'	0°49'	0°55'	1°00'	1°06'
1.8	0°15'	0°21'	0°26'	0°31'	0°36'	0°41'	0°46'	0°52'	0°57'	1°02
1.9	0°15'	0°20'	0°24'	0°29'	0°34'	0°39'	0°44'	0°49'	0°54'	0°59
2.0	0°14'	0°19'	0°23'	0°28'	0°32'	0°37'	0°42'	0°46'	0°51'	0°56
2.1	0°13'	0°18'	0°22'	0°27'	0°31'	0°35'	0°40'	0°44'	0°49'	0°53'
2.2	0°13'	0°17'	0°21'	0°25'	0°30'	0°34'	0°38'	0°42'	0°46'	0°51'
2.3	0°12'	0°16'	0°20'	0°24'	0°28'	0°32'	0°36'	0°40'	0°44'	0°48
2.4	0°12'	0°15'	0°19'	0°23'	0°27'	0°31'	0°35'	0°39'	0°43'	0°46
2.5	0°11'	0°15'	0°19'	0°22'	0°26'	0°29'	0°33'	0°37'	0°41'	0°44'
2.6	0°11'	0°14'	0°18'	0°21'	0°25'	0°29'	0°32'	0°36'	0°39'	0°43'
2.7	0°10'	0°14'	0°17'	0°21'	0°24'	0°27'	0°31'	0°34'	0°38'	0°41'
2.8	0°10'	0°13'	0°17'	0°20'	0°23'	0°27'	0°30'	0°33'	0°36'	0°40
2.9	0°10'	0°13'	0°16'	0°19'	0°22'	0°26'	0°29'	0°32'	0°35'	0°38
3.0	0°09'	0°12'	0°15'	0°19'	0°22'	0°25'	0°28'	0°31'	0°34'	0°37
3.1	0°09'	0°12'	0°15'	0°18'	0°21'	0°24'	0°27'	0°30'	0°33'	0°36'
3.2	0°09'	0°12'	0°15'	0°17'	0°20'	0°23'	0°26'	0°29'	0°32'	0°35'
3.3	0°08'	0°11'	0°14'	0°17'	0°20'	0°22'	0°25'	0°28'	0°31'	0°34
3.4	0°08'	0°11'	0°14'	0°16'	0°19'	0°22'	0°25'	0°27'	0°30'	0°33
3.5	0°08'	0°11'	0°13'	0°16'	0°19'	0°21'	0°24'	0°27'	0°29'	0°32

FACTS AND FIGURES

Beaufort wind scale

Force	Knots		Description	Open sea—probable wave height in meters
0	Less than 1		Glassy sea; smoke rises vertically	
1	1–3		Small ripples	
2	4–6		Light breeze; wavelets	0.15
3	7–10		Gentle breeze; crests of large wavelets break occasionally	0.60
4	11–16		Moderate breeze; small waves, with breaking crests	1
5	17–21		Fresh breeze; long waves, spray from breaking crests	1.80
6	22–27		Strong breeze; large waves with extensive foamy crests	3
7	28–33		Near gale; sea heaps up, white foam from crests blows in streaks downwind	4
8	34–40		Gale; longer, higher waves, spindrift off crests, streaky foam	5.50
9	41–47		Strong gale; high waves, crests topple	7
10	48–55		Storm; very high waves, long curved crests, sea white from large foam patches	9
11	56–63		Violent storm; huge waves, poor visibility	11.30
12	64+		Hurricane; air full of foam and spray	13.70

Watch systems

	MN		4		8		12		16	18	20		MN		4		8
A	D						D			D		D				D	
B			D					D			D			D			

	MN		4		8		12		16		20		MN		4		8
Sk	D	D	D	D								D	D	D	D	D	D
Al			D	D			D	D		D				D	D		D
Ac			D	D		D	D		D		D			D	D		
Bl	D		D	D			D		D	D				D	D		
Bc	D	D		D	D			D		D	D				D	D	

	MN	3	6	9	12	15	18	21	MN	3	6	9	12	15	18	21	MN
Sk		D			D		D			D			D		D		
			D			D		D			D			D		D	
	D			D			D		D			D			D		

Two-watch systems (A and B) for crews of 2, 5, and 3 where D = duties, Sk = skipper, MN = midnight
AL = watch leader, AC = watch crew, BL = watch leader, BC = watch crew

Port entry signals (international)

Light	Type	Main Message
● ● ●	Flashing at least 60 flashes per minute	Serious emergency—all vessels stop or divert according to instructions
● ● ●	Fixed or slow occulting	Vessels shall not proceed
○ ○ ●		Vessels may proceed—one-way traffic
○ ○ ○		Vessels may proceed—two-way traffic
○ ○ ○		Vessels may proceed only when they have received specific orders to do so

Exemption signals and messages

	Type	Message
● ● ● ○ ○ ○	Fixed or slow occulting	Vessels shall not proceed, except that vessels that navigate outside the main channel need not comply with the main message. A vessel may proceed only when it has received specific orders to do so, except that vessels that navigate outside the main channel need not comply with the main message.

Abbreviations for harbor facilities

AB	Alongside berth		LB	Lifeboat
Anch	Anchorage		M	Mud, sea miles
Bar	Licenced bar		ME	Marine Engineering repairs
BY	Boatyard		MRCC	Marine Rescue Coordination Center
C (x Ton)	Crane (x Ton)			
CG	Coastguard		MRSC	Marine Rescue Sub-Center
CH	Chandlery		P	Petrol/gasoline
D	Diesel		PO	Post Office
Dr	Doctor		R	Restaurant
EC	Early closing		Rds	Roads, roadstead
EI	Electrical repairs		SC	Sailing Club
FW	Freshwater		Sh	Shipwright, hull repairs
HMC	Her Majesty's Customs		Subm	Submerged
HW	High water		V	Victuals, food stores
Hr Mr	Harbormaster		YC	Yacht Club
L	Landing place			

GLOSSARY

Terms that are referred to in the text without a full explanation are included in the glossary. Some other terms that are clearly defined in the book are not included.

A

aback: describes a sail when the wind strikes it on its lee side.

abaft: towards the boat's stern.

abeam: at right angles to the *centerline* of the boat.

aft: at or near the stern.

a-hull: to ride out a storm with no sails set and the helm lashed to *leeward.*

amidships: the center of the boat, *athwartships* and fore-and-aft.

anti-fouling: a poisonous paint compound used to protect the underwater part of a hull from marine growths.

apparent wind: the direction and speed of the wind felt by the crew. It is a combination of *true wind* and that created by the movement of the boat.

astern: behind the boat; to go astern is to drive the boat in reverse.

athwartships: at right angles to the fore-and-aft line of the boat.

azimuth: angular distance measured on a horizon circle in a clockwise direction, usually between an observer and a heavenly body.

B

back: when a wind backs, it shifts anticlockwise.

back a sail: to sheet it to *windward* so that the wind fills it on the side that is normally to *leeward.*

backstay: a stay that supports the mast from aft and prevents its forward movement.

baggywrinkle: rope, teased out, plaited together, and wound around *stays, shrouds,* etc., to prevent chafing.

ballast: extra weight, usually lead or iron, placed low in the boat or externally on the keel to provide stability.

ballast keel: a mass of ballast bolted to the keel to increase stability and prevent a keel boat from capsizing.

batten: a light, flexible strip, fed into a batten pocket at the *leech* of the sail to support the roach.

beam: 1, the maximum breadth of a boat; 2, a transverse *member* that supports the deck; 3, on the beam means that an object is at right angles to the *centerline.*

beam ends: a boat on its beam ends is heeled over so far that the deck beams are almost vertical.

bear away: to steer the boat away from the wind.

bearing: the direction of an object from an observer, measured in degrees true or magnetic.

beat: to sail a zigzag *course* towards the wind, *close-hauled* on alternate *tacks.*

belay: to make fast a rope around a *cleat,* usually with a figure-of-eight knot.

bend: 1, to secure a sail to a *spar* before hoisting; 2, to connect two ropes with a knot.

berth: 1, a place occupied by a boat in harbor; 2, to moor a boat; 3, a sleeping place on board.

bight: a *bend* or loop in a rope.

bilge: the lower, round part inside the hull where water collects.

block: a pulley in a wooden or plastic case, consisting of a *sheave* around which a rope runs. It is used to change the direction of pull.

boot-topping: a narrow colored stripe painted between the bottom paint and the *topside* enamel.

bottlescrew: see *rigging screw.*

broach: when a boat *running* downwind slews broadside to the wind and *heels* dangerously. It is caused by heavy following seas or helmsman's error.

broad reach: the point of sailing between a beam *reach* and a *run,* when the wind blows over the *quarter.*

bulkhead: partition wall in a boat normally fitted *athwartships.*

C

carvel: edge-to-edge wooden planking that gives a smooth hull surface.

catamaran: a sailing boat with twin hulls, connected by crossbeams, developed from Polynesian craft.

catboat: a boat with a single sail.

caulk: to make the seams between wooden planks watertight by filling with cotton, oakum, or a compound.

cavitation: the formation of a vacuum around a propeller, causing loss in efficiency.

centerboard: a board lowered through a slot in the *keel* to reduce *leeway.*

centerline: center of the boat in a fore-and-aft line.

center of effort (COE): the point at which all the forces acting on the sails are concentrated.

center of lateral resistance (CLR): the underwater center of pressure about which a boat pivots when changing *course.*

chain pawl: a short lug that drops into a toothed rack to prevent the anchor chain running back.

chain plate: a metal plate bolted to the boat's side to which the *shrouds* or *backstays* are attached.

chart datum: reference level on a chart below which the tide is unlikely to fall. Soundings are given below chart datum. The datum level varies according to country and area.

chine: the line where the bottom of the hull meets the side at an angle.

claw ring: a fitting, which slips over the boom like a claw, to which the main *sheet* is attached after *reefing* the mainsail.

cleat: a wooden, metal, or plastic fitting around which a rope is secured.

clevis pin: a locking pin through which a split ring is passed to prevent accidental withdrawal.

clew: the after, lower corner of a sail where the foot and *leech* meet.

clinker-built: a construction method in which adjacent wooden planks overlap each other.

close-hauled: *the point of sailing* closest to the wind; see also *beat.*

close reach: *the point of sailing* between *close-hauled* and a beam *reach*, when the wind blows forward of the *beam*

close-winded: describes a boat able to sail very close to the wind.

coamings: the raised structure surrounding a *hatch*, cockpit, etc., which prevents water entering.

contrail: a trail of condensation left behind a jet aircraft, giving weather clues.

cotter pin: soft, metal pin folded back on itself to form an eye.

course: the direction in which a vessel is steered, usually given in degrees. true, magnetic, or compass.

cringle: 1, a rope loop, found at either end of a line of reef points; 2, an eye in a sail.

D

dead run: running with the wind blowing exactly *aft*, in line with the *centerline.*

deviation: the difference between the direction indicated by the compass needle and the magnetic *meridian*; caused by metal objects aboard.

displacement: 1, the weight of water displaced by a boat is equal to the weight of the boat; 2, a displacement hull is one that displaces its own weight in water and is only supported by buoyancy, as opposed to a planing hull, which can exceed its hull, or displacement, speed.

downhaul: a rope fitted to pull down a sail or *spar.*

draft: the vertical distance from the *waterline* to the lowest point of the *keel.*

drag: 1, an anchor drags when it fails to hold; 2, the force of wind on the sails, or water on the hull, which impedes the boat's progress.

drift: 1, to float with the current or wind; 2, US: the speed of a current (rate in UK); 3, UK: the distance a boat is carried by a current in a given time.

drogue: a sea anchor put over the stern of a boat or liferaft to retard *drift.*

drop keel: a retractable keel that can be drawn into the hull, when entering shallow waters and recovering on to a trailer.

E

eye of the wind: direction from which the *true wind* blows.

F

fair: a well-faired line or surface is smooth with no bumps, hollows or abrupt changes in direction.

fairlead: a fitting through which a line is run to alter the direction of the lead of the line.

fathom: the measurement used for depths of water and lengths of rope. 1 fathom – 6 ft – 1.83 m.

fid: a tapered tool used for *splicing* heavy rope and for sail-making, often hollow.

fiddle: a raised border for a cabin table, chart table etc., to prevent objects falling off when the boat *heels.*

fix: the position of the vessel as plotted from two or more *position lines.*

forestay: the foremost *stay*, running from the masthead to the stemhead, to which the headsail is hanked.

freeboard: vertical distance between the *waterline* and the top of the deck.

G

genoa: a large headsail, in various sizes, that overlaps the mainsail and is hoisted in light to fresh winds on all *points of sailing.*

gimbals: two concentric rings, pivoted at right angles which keep objects horizontal despite the boat's motion, eg., compass and cooker.

go about: to turn the boat through the *eye of the wind* to change *tack.*

gooseneck: the fitting attaching the boom to the mast, allowing it to move in all directions.

goosewing: to boom-out the headsail to *windward* on a *run* by using a *whisker pole* to hold the sail on the opposite side to the mainsail.

GLOSSARY

ground tackle: general term used for anchoring gear.

guard rail: a metal rail fitted around the boat to prevent the crew falling overboard.

gudgeon: a rudder fitting. It is the eye into which the *pintle* fits.

guy: a steadying rope for a *spar*; a spinnaker guy controls the fore-and-aft position of the spinnaker pole; the foreguy holds the spinnaker pole forward and down.

gybe: to change from one *tack* to another by turning the stern through the wind.

H

halyard: rope used to hoist and lower sails.

hank: fitting used to attach the *luff* of a sail to a *stay*.

hatch: an opening in the deck giving access to the interior.

hawse pipe: see *navel pipe*.

head-to-wind: when the bows are pointing right into the wind.

headfoil: a streamlined surround to a *forestay*, with a groove into which a headsail *luff* slides.

head: the toilet.

headway: the forward movement of a boat through the water.

heave to: to *back* the jib and lash the tiller to *leeward*; used in heavy weather to encourage the boat to lie quietly and to reduce *headway*.

heaving line: a light line suitable for throwing ashore.

heel: to lean over to one side.

I

isobars: lines on a weather map joining places of equal atmospheric pressure.

J

jackstay: a line running fore-and-aft, on both sides of the boat, to which safety harnesses are clipped.

jibe: see *gybe*.

jury: a temporary device to replace lost or damaged gear.

K

kedge: a small, light second anchor.

keel: the main backbone of the boat to which a *ballast keel* is bolted or through which the *centerboard* passes.

ketch: a two-masted sailing vessel with a *mizzen* mast slightly smaller than the main and stepped forward of the rudder stock/post.

kicking strap: a line used to pull the boom down, to keep it horizontal, particularly on a *reach* or *run*.

L

lanyard: a short line attached to one object, such as a knife, with which it is secured to another.

lapstrake see *clinker-built*.

leech: 1, the after edge of a triangular sail; 2, both side edges of a square sail.

lee helm: the tendency of a boat to *bear away* from the wind.

lee shore: a shore on to which the wind is blowing.

leeward: away from the wind; the direction to which the wind blows.

leeway: the sideways movement of a boat off its *course* as a result of the wind blowing on one side of the sails.

let fly: to let a *sheet* go instantly, spilling the wind from the sails.

lifeline: a wire or rope rigged around the deck to prevent the crew falling overboard.

limber holes: gaps left at the lower end of frames above the keel to allow water to drain to the lowest point of the *bilges*.

list: a boat's more or less permanent lean to one side, owing to the improper distribution of weight, eg., *ballast* or water.

log: 1, an instrument for measuring a boat's speed and distance traveled through the water; 2, to record in a book the details of a voyage, usually distances covered and weather.

luff: the forward edge of a sail. To luff up is to turn the boat's head right into the wind.

luff groove: a groove in a wooden or metal *spar* into which the *luff* of the headsail is fed.

lurch: the sudden rolling of a boat.

M

marinized engine: an auto engine that has been specially adapted for use in boats.

marlin spike: a pointed steel or wooden spike used to open up the strands of rope or wire when *splicing*.

mast step: the socket in the *keel* in which the base of the mast is located.

measured mile: a distance of one nautical mile measured between buoys or *transits/ranges* ashore, and marked on the chart.

member: a part of the skeleton of the hull, such as a wooden frame or *stringer* laminated into a fibreglass hull to strengthen it.

meridian: an imaginary line encircling the Earth that passes through the poles and cuts at right angles through the Equator. All lines of longitude are meridians.

mizzen: 1, the shorter, after-mast on a *ketch* or *yawl*; 2, the fore-and-aft sail set on this mast.

mouse: to bind thin line around a hook to prevent it jerking loose.

molded plywood: a form of construction whereby a hull is built up by bonding a number of thin skins of wood together over a framework.

N

navel pipe: a metal pipe in the foredeck through which the anchor chain passes to the locker below.

no go area: the area into which a boat cannot sail without *tacking*.

noon sight: a vessel's latitude can be found, using a sextant, when a heavenly body on the observer's *meridian* is at its greatest altitude. The sight of the sun at noon is the one most frequently taken.

O

off the wind: with the *sheets* slacked off, not *close-hauled*.

on the wind: *close-hauled*.

outhaul: a rope used to pull out the foot of a sail.

overall length (LOA): the boat's extreme length, measured from the foremost part of the bow to the aftermost part of the stern, excluding bowsprit, self-steering gear, etc.

P

painter: the bow line by which a dinghy, or *tender*, is towed or made fast.

pay out: to let a rope out gradually.

pintle: a rudder fitting with a long pin that slips into the *gudgeon* to form a hinged pivot for the rudder.

pitch: 1, the up and down motion of the bows of a boat plunging over the waves; 2, the angle of the propeller blades.

point of sailing: the different angles from the wind on which a boat may sail; the boat's *course* relative to the direction of the wind.

port: the left-hand side of a boat, looking forward (opposite of *starboard*).

port tack: a boat is on a port tack when the wind strikes the port side first and the mainsail is out to *starboard*. A boat on the port tack gives way to a boat on a *starboard tack*.

position line/line of position: a line drawn on a chart, as a result of taking a *bearing*, along which the boat's position must lie. Two position lines give a fix.

pulpit: a metal *guard rail* fitted at the bows of a boat to provide safety for the crew.

pushpit: a metal guard rail fitted at the stern.

Q

quarter: the portion of the boat midway between the stern and the beam; on the quarter means about 45° *abaft* the beam.

R

rake: the fore-and-aft deviation from the perpendicular of a mast or other feature of a boat.

range: 1, see *transit*; 2, of tides, the difference between the high- and low-water levels of a *tide*; 3, the distance at which a light can be seen.

rating: a method of measuring certain dimensions of a yacht to enable it to take part in handicap races.

reach: to sail with the wind approximately on the beam; all sailing points between *running* and *close-hauled*.

reef: to reduce the sail area by folding or rolling surplus material on the boom or *forestay*.

reefing pennant: strong line with which the *luff* or *leech cringle* is pulled down to the boom when *reefing*.

rhumb line: a line cutting all *meridians* at the same angle; the *course* followed by a boat sailing in a fixed direction.

riding light or **anchor light**: an all-round white light, usually hoisted on the *forestay*, to show that a boat under 50 ft (15 m) is at anchor. It must be visible for 2 miles (3 km).

riding sail: a small sail hoisted to enable a boat to maintain *steerage way* during a storm.

rigging screw: a deck fitting with which the tension of *standing rigging*, eg., *stays, shrouds*, is adjusted.

righting moment: the point beyond which the boat will no longer right itself when *heeling*, but capsizes.

roach: the curved part of the *leech* of a sail that extends beyond the direct line from head to clew.

run: to sail with the wind *aft* and with the *sheets* eased well out.

running rigging: all the moving lines, such as *sheets* and *halyards*, used in the setting and *trimming* of sails.

GLOSSARY

S

sailmaker's palm: a strong leather protective loop that fits across the palm of the hand. It has a hole for the thumb and metal reinforced plate on the palm to accept the eye of a needle, and is worn when mending sails or *splicing* ropes.

schooner: a boat with two or more masts, with the mainmast aftermost.

scope: the length of rope or cable paid out when mooring or anchoring.

scuppers: holes in the toe rail that allow water to drain off the deck.

seacock: a valve that shuts off an underwater inlet or outlet passing through the hull.

sea room: room in which a boat can maneuver, clear of land or dangers.

seize: to bind two ropes together, or a rope to a *spar*, with a light line.

serve: to cover and protect a *splice* or part of a rope with twine bound tightly against the lay.

serving mallet: tool with a grooved head, used when serving a rope to keep the twine at a constant and high tension.

set: 1, to hoist a sail; **2,** the way in which the sails fit; **3,** the direction of a tidal current or stream.

shackle: a metal link with a removable bolt across the open end: of various shapes; D, U.

sheave: a grooved wheel in a *block* or *spar* for a rope to run on.

sheet: the rope attached to the clew of a sail or to the boom, enabling it to be controlled or *trimmed*.

shrouds: ropes or wires, usually in pairs, led from the mast to *chain plates* at deck level to prevent the mast falling sideways; part of the *standing rigging*.

skin fitting: a through-hull fitting where there is a hole in the skin, through which air or water passes. A seacock is fitted to close the hole when not in use.

sloop: a single-masted sailing boat with a mainsail and one headsail.

spar: a general term for any wood or metal pole, eg., mast or boom, used to carry or give shape to sails.

spindrift: spray blown along the surface of the sea.

spinnaker: a large, light, balloon-shaped sail set when *reaching* or *running*.

splice: to join ropes or wires by unlaying the strands and interweaving them.

split pin: see *cotter pin*.

spreaders: horizontal struts attached to the mast, which extend to the *shrouds* and help to support the mast.

stall: a sail stalls when the airflow over it breaks up, causing the boat to lose way.

stanchion: upright metal post bolted to the deck to support *guard rails* or *lifelines*.

standing part: the part of a line not used when making a knot; the part of a rope that is made fast, or around which the knot is tied.

standing rigging: the *shrouds* and *stays* that are permanently set up and support the masts.

starboard: right-hand side of a boat looking forward (opposite of *port*).

starboard tack: a boat is on the starboard tack when the wind strikes the starboard side first and the boom is out to *port*.

stay: wire or rope that supports the mast in a fore-and-aft direction; part of the standing *rigging*.

steerage way: a boat has steerage way when it has sufficient speed to allow it to be steered, or to answer the helm.

stem: the timber at the bow, from the *keel* upwards, to which the planking is attached.

sternway: the backward, stern-first movement of a boat.

stringer: a fore-and-aft *member*, fitted to strengthen the frames.

strop: a loop of wire or rope used to attach a *block* to a spar or to make a sling.

strum box: a filter fitted round the suction end of a *bilge-pump* hose to prevent the pump becoming blocked by debris.

T

tack: 1, the lower forward corner of a sail; **2,** to turn the boat through the wind so that it blows on the opposite side of the sails.

tacking: working to windward by sailing *close-hauled* on alternate *courses* so that the wind is first on one side of the boat, then on the other.

tack pennant: a length of wire with an eye in each end, used to raise the *tack* of a headsail some distance off the deck.

tackle: a purchase system comprising rope and *blocks* that is used to gain mechanical advantage.

tang: a strong metal fitting by which *standing rigging* is attached to the mast or other *spar*.

tender or dinghy: a small boat used to ferry stores and people to a yacht.

terminal fitting: fitting at the end of a wire rope by which a *shroud* or *stay* can be attached to the mast, a tang or a *rigging screw/turnbuckle*.

tide: the vertical rise and fall of the oceans, caused principally by the gravitational attraction of the moon.

toe rail: a low strip of wood or molding running around the edge of the deck.

topping lift: a line from the masthead to a *spar*, normally the boom, that is used to raise it.

topsides: the part of a boat's hull that is above the *waterline*.

track: 1, the *course* a boat has made good; **2,** a fitting on the mast or boom into which the slides on a sail fit; **3,** a fitting along which a *traveler* runs; used to alter the tension of the *sheets*.

transit: two fixed objects are in transit when seen in line; two transits give a position *fix*.

traveler: 1, a ring or hoop that can be hauled along a *spar*; 2, a fitting that slides in a *track* and is used to alter the angle of the *sheets*.

triatic stay: a *backstay* led from the head of one mast to that of another.

trim: 1, to adjust the angle of the sails, by means of *sheets*, so that they work most efficiently; 2, to adjust the boat's load, and thus the fore-and-aft angle at which it floats.

true wind: the direction and speed of the wind felt when stationary, at anchor, or on land.

turnbuckle; see *rigging screw*.

U

under way: a boat is under way when it is not made fast to the shore, at anchor or aground.

uphaul: a line used to raise something vertically, eg., the spinnaker pole.

V

veer: 1, the wind veers when it shifts in a clockwise direction; 2, to pay out anchor cable or rope in a gradual, controlled way.

W

wake: the disturbed water left astern of a boat.

waterline: the line along the hull at which a boat floats.

waterline length (WL): the length of a boat from stem to stern at the *waterline*. It governs the maximum speed of a *displacement hull* and affects a boat's *rating*.

weather helm: (opposite of *lee helm*).

weather side: the side of a boat on which the wind is blowing.

wetted surface: the area of the hull under water.

whisker pole: a light pole used to hold out the *clew* of a *headsail* when *running*.

winch: a mechanical device, consisting usually of a metal drum turned by a handle, around which a line is wound to give the crew more purchasing power when hauling taut a line, eg., a jib *sheet*.

windage: those parts of a boat that increase *drag*, eg., rigging, *spars*, crew, etc.

windlass: a *winch* with a horizontal shaft and a vertical handle, used to haul up the anchor chain.

windward: the direction from which the wind blows; towards the wind (opposite of *leeward*).

Y

yawl: a two-masted boat with the *mizzen* stepped *aft* of the rudder stock/post.

INDEX

ACKNOWLEDGMENTS

The publishers received invaluable help from the following:
Jazz Wilson, who researched Cruising Grounds; Alison
Tomlinson; Sonya Larkin; Candy Lee; Jan Storr; Wally
Buchanan, master rigger; David Johnston of Ingledew, Brown,
Bennison and Garret; Roy Flooks; John Hutchinson; Ted Spears;
Brookes and Gatehouse Ltd; Conyer Marine Ltd; Force Four
Chandlery; International Association of Lighthouse Authorities;
International Paint; Keen International Marine Electronics;
Kemp Masts Ltd; Lewmar Marine Ltd; Lucas Marine; Marlow
Ropes Ltd; Royal Cork Yacht Club; Royal Ocean Racing Club;
Royal Thames Yacht Club; Royal Yachting Association;
Schermaly Ltd; Simpson Lawrence Ltd; Sowester; Stowe
Equipment Ltd; Thomas Foulkes; Volvo Penta; Westerley
Marine Construction Ltd; Yachting Magazine (for help with US
charter companies). The revised 2006 edition owes much to
the help of Mike Senior.

Picture credits

b=bottom; c=center; l=left; r=right; t=top

p.7	©Panoramic Images/Getty Images
p.8/9	©Photographer's Choice/Getty
p.11	©Popperfoto
p.12/13 t	©Mary Evans Picture Library
p.12/13 b	©Museum of the City of New York/Robert Harding Picture Library
p.14/15	©Photonica/Getty Images
p.21	©Philipp Mohr/Alamy
p.23	©Ingrid Abery/Actionplus
p.25	©Paul A. Souders/Corbis
p.29	©Ingrid Abery/Actionplus
p.30	©Marlow Ropes Ltd
p.32	©Daniel Forster/Time Life Pictures/Getty Images
p.40/41	©Neil Rabinowitz/Corbis
p.42 t	©Ingrid Abery/Actionplus
p.42 c	©Sylvia Cordaiy Photo Library Ltd/Alamy
p.42 b	©Ingrid Abery/Actionplus
p.50	©Cristel Clear
p.52	©Cristel Clear
p.57	©Photo Resource Hawaii/Alamy
p.62	©Kos Picture Source/Alamy
p.65	©Thierry Martinez/Kos Picture Source
p.66 t	©Ingrid Abery/Actionplus
p.66 b	©Christel Clear
p.74/75	©Ingrid Abery/Actionplus
p.81	©Cristel Clear
p.82/83	©Crewsaver
p.84/85	©Cristel Clear
p.86/87	©Robert Frerck/Stone/Getty Images
p.89	©Christel Clear
p.92/93	©Ingrid Abery/Actionplus
p.95	©John Watney
p.96	©BYB/Rex Features
p.98	©John Kershaw/Alamy
p.102/3	©Tony Arruza/Corbis
p.104	©Sami Sarkis/Alamy
p.112	©Raytheon Marine
p.116/17	©B&G
p.119	©Raytheon Marine
p.122	©Ingrid Abery/Actionplus
p.127 t	©Garmin
p.127 b	©Ingrid Abery/Actionplus
p.128	©Christel Clear
p.129 t	©Yeoman
p.129 b	©Doug Wilson/Alamy
p.130	©Brian SeedArt Directors Photo Library
p.131 l	©Art Directors Photo Library
p.131 r	©Ann Welch
p.133	©Meteorological Office
p.134	©Robert Harding Picture Library
p.135 t	©Walter Rawlings/Robert Harding Picture Library
p.135 b	©R. K. Pilsbury
p.136/7	©Ingrid Abery/Actionplus
p.140	©Jim Leggett/Daily Telegraph Colour Library
p.144	©Ingrid Abery/Actionplus
p.146	©Travis Rowan/Alamy
p.148	©Sebastien Baussais/Alamy
p.150	©Bill Brooks/Alamy
p.152	©Ingrid Abery/Actionplus
p.154/5	©Tom Morrison/Stone/Getty Images
p.159	©Peter Smith Studios
p.170	©A. T. Willett/Alamy

Every effort has been made to credit all photographs correctly.
Marshall Editions apologizes for any unintentional omissions
or errors and, if informed of any such cases, would be pleased
to update any future editions.